Essential Actions for Academic Writing

A Genre-Based Approach

Nigel A. Caplan
&
Ann M. Johns

University of Michigan Press
Ann Arbor

Published in the United States of America
The University of Michigan Press
Manufactured in the United States of America

♾ Printed on acid-free paper

ISBN-13: 978-0-472-03796-4 (print)
ISBN-13: 978-0-472-12973-7 (ebook)

2025 2024 2023 2022 4 3 2 1

Acknowledgments

We are deeply indebted to our many colleagues, students, and former students who have tested our materials, contributed interviews or texts to the volume, and influenced our work more generally. Nigel's University of Delaware English Language colleagues, including Scott Partridge, Scott Duarte, Kendra Bradecich, Chris Elliott, and John Millbury-Steen, piloted and responded to early drafts. Sabrina Halli and Leketi Makalela generously agreed to be interviewed and featured in the Project 1 magazine profiles. The work of John Swales, Christine Feak, and Christine Tardy guided us throughout our entire writing process. Nigel thanks the University of Delaware for his sabbatical semester, which allowed him to start writing this book. In addition, we gratefully acknowledge two anonymous reviewers and Kelly Sippell, whose guidance, support and editing are evident on every page of the book, as well as Danielle Coty-Fattal and the entire ELT team at the University of Michigan Press.

The sources of all authentic examples are listed at the end of each unit. In addition, grateful acknowledgement is given to these individuals and publishers for permission to reprint their work or previously published materials:

- The *Seattle Times* Editorial Board for "Stick with later start times that boost Seattle high schoolers' success" (December 17, 2018).
- The Society for Research in Child Development for *Social Policy Report Brief*, Volume 32, Issue 1: *Understanding and addressing the effect of digital games on cognitive development in middle childhood* (2019).
- Teresa Parodi for permission to adapt and reprint "Speaking in tongues" from *The Conversation.*
- Ellen Bialystok for permission to reprint an excerpt from her preface to *Bilingualism in development: Language, literacy, and cognition.*
- The University of Michigan for material from the Michigan Corpus of Upper-level Student Papers (MICUSP).
- Karen Muñoz for the student emails in Unit 1.
- Ziang Zhou for the persuasive essay in Unit 7.
- Francisco Garcia and Sri Shatagopam for two of the Personal Statements in Project 4.
- Christine Tardy for the extension requests in Unit 1.

Contents

Scope and Sequence

Unit	Goals	Writing Tasks	Language Focus
1: The Rhetorical Planning Wheel	▪ Understand the Rhetorical Planning Wheel ▪ Analyze, compare, and contrast texts ▪ Analyze academic writing prompts	▪ Emails to different audiences ▪ Short-answer "ID" questions	▪ Language conventions in emails
2: Everyday and Academic Genres and Their Registers	▪ Understand and apply genre ▪ Analyze everyday, professional, and academic texts from different genres ▪ Understand the connection between genre and register	▪ Report about a writing experience ▪ Genre transformation	▪ Can I use *I*? ▪ Register
3: Explain	▪ Understand definitions and glosses ▪ Use sources in definitions ▪ Analyze process explanations ▪ Analyze cause-and-effect explanations	▪ Contested definition ▪ Explanation of processes, causes, and effects ▪ Test-question answers ▪ Extended definition ▪ Language blog post	▪ Relative clauses ▪ Defining verbs ▪ Process connectors ▪ Cause-and-effect language
4: Summarize	▪ Chart texts for purpose, main ideas, and language use ▪ Understand and use relationships between a source text and a summary ▪ Organize summaries effectively	▪ Functional summary ▪ Informational summary ▪ Problem/solution summary ▪ Argument summary ▪ Academic article summary ▪ Press release	▪ Category nouns ▪ Introducing sources ▪ Direct quotation
5: Synthesize	▪ Take notes on sources ▪ Comparative/ contrastive synthesis ▪ Informational synthesis ▪ General/specific organization	▪ Contrastive synthesis ▪ Informational synthesis ▪ Integrative synthesis ▪ Literature review	▪ Comparing and contrasting connectors ▪ Framing sentences

Unit	*Goals*	*Writing Tasks*	*Language Focus*
6: Report and Interpret Data	▪ Describe data in a table, chart, or graph ▪ Interpret the data in a table, chart, or graph ▪ Hedge and boost claims about data	▪ Data commentary ▪ Policy brief	▪ Writing about numbers ▪ Verb tenses to write about data ▪ References to tables and figures ▪ Hedging interpretations
7: Argue	▪ Analyze arguments in different disciplines ▪ Analyze claims and evidence ▪ Support claims with examples and sources ▪ Counterarguments and contradictory findings	▪ Argument essay ▪ Opinion editorial (op-ed)	▪ Hedging and boosting ▪ Introducing examples ▪ Hypothetical examples ▪ Countering language
8: Respond	▪ Differentiate response from summary ▪ Write text-to-self, text-to-text, and text-to-world responses ▪ Understand critique and evaluation ▪ Understand reflection assignments	▪ Summary and response ▪ Review ▪ Reflection ▪ Discussion board post ▪ Letter to the editor	▪ Signaling responses ▪ Hedging and boosting responses ▪ Concession ▪ Evaluative language ▪ Verb tenses to describe experiences
9: Analyze	▪ Differentiate analysis, explanation, and argument ▪ Understand disciplinary frameworks ▪ Analyze arguments using a rhetorical framework (ethos, logos, pathos, kairos) ▪ Reorganize and synthesize information	▪ Rhetorical analysis ▪ Visual analysis ▪ Ad analysis	▪ Verbs for analysis ▪ Nominalization

Unit	*Goals*	*Writing Tasks*	*Language Focus*
Project 1: Transforming Texts	▪ Analyze texts about bilingualism from different genres ▪ Plan and conduct an interview	▪ Academic book blurb ▪ Blog response ▪ Magazine profile	▪ Shifting perspective between direct and indirect speech
Project 2: Problem-Solution Inquiry	▪ Analyze and research a problem in your community or coursework ▪ Identify root causes and possible solutions ▪ Evaluate solutions	▪ Problem-solution inquiry paper ▪ Literature review ▪ Reflective cover letter ▪ Public presentation	▪ Comparing solutions ▪ Signaling problems and solutions
Project 3: Research Paper	▪ Analyze the sections of an IMRaD research paper (introduction, methods, results, and discussion) ▪ Write focused research questions ▪ Collect and analyze data	▪ IMRaD paper ▪ Annotated bibliography ▪ Abstract	▪ Passive and active voice ▪ Question formation
Project 4: Personal Statement	▪ Understand the writer's role in the -personal statement ▪ Analyze the prompts, audience, purpose, and structure of personal statements	▪ Personal statement for a scholarship or university application	▪ Proofreading
Online Source Use Appendix	▪ Analyze assignments ▪ Find useful sources online and from library databases ▪ Evaluate the reliability of sources ▪ Use integral and nonintegral citation ▪ Avoid plagiarism ▪ Plan a paper with sources ▪ Understand style guides	▪ Paraphrases ▪ Quotations ▪ List of references	▪ Word families ▪ Reporting verbs

Introduction

Essential Actions for Academic Writing is a genre-based writing textbook that draws from extensive studies of the writing demands made upon novice academic students. By "novice," we mean students who may need particular academic support to succeed in the next stage of their higher education. They are novices in the sense that they have little experience with the expectations, genres, and/or language that are required in their college, university, or graduate classes. Novice students may be international students, English learners, multilingual students, or first-generation college students. They may also be students who did little writing (or little writing in English) in their prior education or who have written nothing but formulaic five-paragraph essays. They may be students who identify themselves as struggling writers or as confident writers elsewhere but not in school. We wrote *Essential Actions* for all these students: in first- and second-year writing classes, community colleges, graduate preparation and support classes, and ESL writing classes including foundation year, pathways, or bridging programs.

Because these writers, many of whom use English as a second or additional language, have yet to be initiated into their disciplines, and because large-scale studies of writing assignments indicate a wide variety of writing demands (Melzer, 2014; Nesi & Gardner, 2012), *Essential Actions* focuses on exploring and practicing the key *actions* that appear consistently and often in combination across academic assignments and genres, such as explaining, summarizing, synthesizing, and arguing.

We wrote these course materials for a very simple reason: we couldn't find a writing textbook for our classes. Though we teach very different student populations in very different contexts on opposite coasts of the U.S., the goals for our writing classes are remarkably similar: to help novice undergraduate and graduate students understand how to develop the rhetorical flexibility to write effectively across a potentially bewildering array of tasks throughout their academic and professional careers. In writing this textbook, we have combined genre theories, research into academic writing, proven pedagogical practices, and accessibility for teachers and students in order to meet a variety of novice student needs.

Guiding Principles

Essential Actions is built on these principles, which represent our core beliefs about writing:

- **There's no such thing as universally "good" writing.** As students take classes across the university or college (if they are in a liberal arts program or taking general education courses) and in their specific majors and minors, they will need to write in a wide range of ways that are effective in different disciplines or for different academic and professional audiences. No writing class can hope to prepare students for every future task, and presenting a universal form (typically the five-paragraph essay) as a panacea is inadequate, at best (Caplan & Johns, 2019). But we can teach our students to "read" their classes and assignments, understand their instructors' expectations, analyze their readings and assignments, and make effective (or, if they prefer, unconventional) choices even when facing new tasks.

- **We write in genres**, which in essence means that all writing responds to a context that encompasses the writer's identity, the reader's expectations, the purpose of the text, and the conventions that shape it (Tardy, 2019).

- **Writing is a "social action"** (Miller, 1984) or, more often, a series of actions that are combined in different ways to reach the writer's goal and respond to externally assigned tasks (Martin, 2009). These actions are more than the traditional **modes** (e.g., description, comparison, process, argument) because they rarely occur by themselves but are often combined in complex writing tasks. All student writers need to know the techniques and language needed to define, summarize, synthesize, interpret, argue, comment, analyze, and reflect. They also need to know how to combine the actions in extended writing.

- **Most academic writing tasks draw on sources**, from the textbook and lecture to the internet and library databases. Successful student writers know how to analyze prompts, identify sources, conduct independent research, evaluate the reliability of sources, paraphrase, quote, cite, summarize, and synthesize in the context of specific genres. These skills are challenging and essential.

■ Although writing, composition, and ESL departments are often aligned with the humanities, **students will write across the curriculum**. Therefore, *Essential Actions* includes models and tasks that practice writing in a variety of disciplines, including data commentaries, empirical research papers, policy briefs, and short-answer test questions.

■ **Language is at the heart of good writing instruction**, whether students use English as their first, only, second, or additional language. By embedding language instruction in the writing class, we are not suggesting that grammatical accuracy (e.g., subject-verb agreement, commas, run-on sentences, articles and the suchlike) are the sole hallmarks of good writing, although they may all be important in some contexts. Nor do we believe that "ESL grammar" should be relegated to an appendix and taught out of context. Instead, we believe that all student writers need access to what Schleppegrell (2004) has called "the language of schooling"—that is, the grammar and vocabulary resources that allow students to engage effectively in the actions of academic writing. There is no magic list of words and phrases that students can memorize and trot out just to impress the reader. Instead, all writers need to understand how their language choices construct the ideas they are expressing, the stance they are taking, and the text they are shaping. Therefore, **Language Boxes** are integrated throughout the units in contexts where students can immediately apply the grammar, vocabulary, and metadiscourse (e.g., signaling phrases, connectors) in their own writing.

■ Above all, **academic writers need to develop rhetorical flexibility** to move comfortably among disciplines, interrogate new genres, and choose linguistic resources to make their texts do what should be done.

What Is Not in This Textbook?

Essential Actions includes the elements that are essential for academic writing instruction while providing flexibility for a wide range of programs and instructors teaching in face-to-face and online classes. It deliberately differs from other writing and composition textbooks in these ways:

- ❒ Neither "the essay" nor "the research paper" are prominent, although both are included, specifically the argument essay and both library and empirical research papers. Though Melzer (2014) in his extensive study of academic writing assignments across the U.S. college curriculum found that essays and research papers are the two pedagogical genres mentioned most often by faculty, these terms have become so general that they have become meaningless and, as a result, end up limiting students rather than expanding their repertoires (Russell & Yañez, 2003). In *Essential Actions,* **we instead show students how to apply the essential actions of academic writing to a wide range of pedagogical, professional, and disciplinary genres**—such as literature reviews, press releases, discussion board responses, and magazine profiles.
- ❒ There are no long readings. The texts included here are quite short and designed as models for students to analyze as they prepare to write. **The readings students are assigned should depend on their needs, interests, and the situations in which they are studying.** Thus, readings should be selected by you, the writing instructor, and not mandated by textbook authors who are unfamiliar with the teaching and learning contexts where you are working.
- ❒ We have avoided lengthy discussions of rhetorical theory, writing studies, styles, and techniques. Our goal is not to teach rhetoric as a discipline but rather the rhetorical principles that apply to student writing. ***Essential Actions* is relatively short and economical, and most of its pages are devoted to activities and tasks.** Supporting information and additional examples appear in the teachers' manual.
- ❒ Not everything written in academic settings is an argument, and simply knowing something about *ethos, logos,* and *pathos* does not guarantee a successful student text. Therefore, there's a unit on argument, but there are units on other typical actions, too. **When learning to argue, students explore how to construct effective arguments using claims, evidence,**

sources, examples, and counterarguments. However, composition instructors will find a discussion of rhetorical appeals in Unit 9 (Analyze) as a disciplinary lens with which students can analyze different types of argument.

- Reference and citation styles vary across contexts and often take up too much textbook space, even though this information is available online or from university libraries. Instead, **we focus on the need for and rhetorical use of citation throughout, including negotiating contested definitions, responding to readings, supporting arguments, analyzing texts, interpreting data, and identifying gaps in prior research.** An Online Source Use Appendix is available on the companion website (www.press.umich.edu/elt/compsite) with instruction in finding, evaluating, citing, paraphrasing, and quoting sources.

How the Content Is Organized

Part I: Understanding Texts and Contexts

The units in Part I create the basis for the rest of the textbook by introducing students to rhetorical situation, genre, and register.

- Unit 1 introduces the framework for understanding how to approach any new writing task, the Rhetorical Planning Wheel. Through examples of emails and short-answer ("ID") questions, this unit shows students how to analyze any writing situation in terms of its rhetorical components: writer's role, audience, purpose, structure, evidence, language, and conventions.
- Unit 2 helps students understand the concept of genre by comparing and analyzing everyday, professional, and academic genres. In addition, students learn a nuanced understanding of register to write effectively in their assigned genres. This includes the language choices used to construct and connect ideas, establish stance, and create cohesion.

Part II: Exploring Essential Actions

Each of the units in this section is devoted to one of the essential actions in academic and professional writing by modeling and providing practice in the genres and the language that support the action. The units include these features:

- ❒ **goals** for students to accomplish in the unit
- ❒ clear, concise **explanations** of writing techniques
- ❒ **models** of student and professional texts, adapted for length and comprehension, that students analyze through guided questions
- ❒ **activities** to practice each goal of the unit
- ❒ **Language Boxes** with grammar, vocabulary, and metadiscourse relevant to the writing techniques presented in the unit, each with practice activities
- ❒ **writing tasks** with short assignments throughout the unit to consolidate the actions, language, and techniques
- ❒ **two major assignments** that put the action into practice: ***a pedagogical genre*** (a task assigned for the purpose of teaching a particular skill or content area such as a summary or argument essay) and a ***genre in action*** (a professional or disciplinary writing task that simulates an authentic writing situation such as a press release or op-ed column).

The actions in Part II are:

- ❒ **Explain** (Unit 3), including techniques for writing definitions, glosses, process explanations, and cause-and-effect explanations.
- ❒ **Summarize** (Unit 4), including practice in analyzing the structure of and summarizing different types of source texts for different purposes.
- ❒ **Synthesize** (Unit 5), containing three types of synthesis (comparative/contrastive, informational, and integrative), starting with synthesizing two texts and expanding to a review of the literature.
- ❒ **Report and Interpret Data** (Unit 6), building the components of a data commentary based on a table, chart, or graph.
- ❒ **Argue** (Unit 7), including analysis of argumentation in different disciplines, making and supporting claims, using sources and examples, and dealing with counterarguments and contradictory findings.
- ❒ **Respond** (Unit 8), using three strategies for response as well as critique, evaluation, and reflection.

- **Analyze** (Unit 9), applying a disciplinary framework (the rhetorical appeals of ethos, logos, pathos, and kairos) to focus, reorganize, and synthesize information, culminating in rhetorical and visual analyses.

Part III: Integrating Actions

Here students engage in the difficult work of combining the actions in different genres and contexts. These units provide ideas for longer projects that require students to write effectively in pedagogical, disciplinary, and personal genres. The projects include traditional academic assignments (e.g., an empirical research paper and a problem-solution inquiry project or term paper), as well as a project that stretches students' resources as writers (a text transformation project). In the final project, students learn how to write a personal statement for a university or scholarship application, a vital and challenging genre.

Companion Website

A companion website is available at www.press.umich.edu/elt/compsite, containing:

- **The Online Source Use Appendix**—a unit of instruction on finding, evaluating, paraphrasing, quoting, citing, and referencing online and library databases sources.
- **Charts, tables, and handouts** for exercises in the textbook that can be printed for use in class or completed digitally as classwork or homework.

How to Use This Content

Essential Actions is not designed to be taught cover to cover in a single semester! However, we recommend that all classes start with Part I, Units 1 and 2, since they lay the groundwork for everything else in the book. The Online Source Use Appendix can either be presented in its entirety near the start of a course, or in sections as the need arises (e.g., paraphrasing, quotation, and citation when teaching summary and synthesis, saving the sections on choosing and evaluating sources for teaching argument and research papers).

Here are some alternatives for working with Parts II and III:

- You might choose one or two projects from Part III as major assignments for your course and teach the actions from Part II that your students will need for success in those assignments. For example, the problem-solution inquiry project is a library research paper for which students need to explain, summarize, synthesize, and respond to sources.

- ❒ Alternatively, you could select the actions in Part II that best align with your curriculum, learning outcomes, and your students' needs. If time allows, you might end the course with the project from Part III that is most appropriate for your context, or use the writing tasks in Part II as your major assignments.
- ❒ We expect teachers to choose between the Pedagogical Genre and the Genre in Action assignments in Part II rather than attempt both, although they can certainly be taught in sequence, too. For example, after students have written a summary (a pedagogical genre), they could rewrite their paper as a press release (a professional genre) and reflect on the differences.
- ❒ Although we have provided models that demonstrate the targeted actions, writing techniques, and language, you may prefer to replace or supplement them with texts that are more relevant to your students' academic careers, educational context, or interests. Many writing teachers find it useful to adopt a theme for their course and align all the readings and assignments with that theme. You could follow the themes suggested in Project 1 (bilingualism) or Projects 2 and 3 (health and nutrition), or others such as globalization, ethics, government, community activism, and environmental protection.

In all substantial writing tasks in *Essential Actions*, we recommend a writing process that includes modeling, planning, drafting (multiple rounds), conducting peer feedback, revising, performing self-review, and editing. However, we have left the assignment directions open so that you can specify the timeframe, length, sources (if relevant), and format.

For more ideas, including options for assessment, please see the companion volume, *Genre Explained: Frequently Asked Questions and Answers about Genre-Based Instruction* by Christine Tardy, Ann Johns, and Nigel Caplan (University of Michigan Press).

References

Caplan, N. A., & Johns, A. M. (Eds.). (2019). *Changing practices for the L2 writing classroom: Moving beyond the five-paragraph essay*. University of Michigan Press.

Martin, J. R. (2009). Genre and language learning: A social semiotic perspective. *Linguistics and Education, 20*, 10–21. https://doi.org/10.1016/j.linged.2009.01.003

Melzer, D. (2014). *Assignments across the curriculum: A national study of college writing*. Utah State University Press.

Miller, C. R. (1984). Genre as social action. *Quarterly Journal of Speech, 70*, 151–167. https://doi.org/10.1080/00335638409383686

Nesi, H., & Gardner, S. (2012). *Genres across the disciplines: Student writing in higher education*. Cambridge University Press.

Russell, D. R., & Yañez, A. (2003). Big picture people rarely become historians: Genre systems and the contradictions of general education. In C. Bazerman & D. R. Russell (Eds.), *Writing selves/writing societies: Research from activity perspectives* (pp. 331–362). The WAC Clearinghouse and Mind, Culture, and Activity. http://wac.colostate.edu/books/selves_societies/

Schleppegrell, M. (2004). *The language of schooling: A functional linguistics perspective*. Lawrence Erlbaum.

Tardy, C. M. (2019). *Genre-based writing: What every ESL teacher needs to know*. University of Michigan Press.

PART 1:
TEXTS AND CONTEXTS

1 The Rhetorical Planning Wheel

Goals

- ❒ Understand the Rhetorical Planning Wheel's components that shape successful writing
- ❒ Analyze and write emails using the Rhetorical Planning Wheel
- ❒ Recognize the importance of context in writing
- ❒ Analyze academic writing prompts
- ❒ Respond to an "ID" question, a typical short writing task

What Is Successful Writing?

It is surprisingly difficult to define **good writing**. A great poem is very different from an excellent research paper, an effective email to a professor, or a social media post that your friends all like. Different types of writing can be successful or unsuccessful depending on what, where, when, why, and to whom you are writing. This unit explores the different components of successful writing by introducing a tool, the Rhetorical Planning Wheel, which you will use throughout the units to help you respond successfully to a variety of writing tasks.

Activity 1.1: Discussion

Discuss these questions with a partner or small group.

1. What types of writing have you done in and outside class?
2. What do you think makes some writing successful and other writing unsuccessful?
3. What do you consider when you are planning to write something new?

Activity 1.2: Analyzing Emails

These three emails all have the same general purpose and were all sent to a university instructor, Dr. Christine Tardy. As you read, think how you would react to each of these emails if you were the instructor. Take notes as you read to answer these questions. Then share your ideas with a partner or small group.

1. What is the purpose of these three emails?
2. In what ways are the three emails similar?
3. In what ways are the emails different?
4. Which is the most successful email? Why?

Email 1:

Dear Professor Tardy,

Is it possible to request a small extension on the Class Observation paper? I have 4 assignments due at the same time and there are literally not enough hours in the day to accomplish everything, considering the fact that I am taking a full load of classes and working 20 hours a week.

Best,

(Student's name)

Email 2:

Dear Dr. Tardy,

I hope this email finds you well. I regret to inform you that due to my poor time management, I will be unable to complete the Student Feedback Assignment by the start of class tomorrow. I humbly request an extension until midnight tonight in order to complete the assignment. I am more than willing to accept whatever penalty you impose.

Regards,

(Student's name)

Email 3:

Dear Professor Tardy,

May I please get an extension on the article annotations? I'm running out of time.

Thank you, (Student)

Some criteria for a successful request email written by a student to an instructor in the context of a university class are presented in Table 1.1. Is each email successful in meeting each criterion? Possible answers for Email 1 are provided the Table 1.1. How would you complete the chart for Emails 2 and 3?

TABLE 1.1:
Analysis of Email 1

Criteria	*Email 1*
Include an appropriate greeting and closing.	Polite greeting (Prof. is a general title for university instructors.) Best is less effective than thank you.
Prepare the reader for the request.	None—the email starts directly with the request.
Provide a specific request.	The assignment is clearly identified, but how long is a "small" extension?
Give appropriate reasons for the request.	Maybe—the writer is clearly busy, but are they giving other assignments greater priority?
Maintain a polite tone.	Yes. "Is it possible to ask?" is polite.

Using the Rhetorical Planning Wheel

Activity 1.2 showed that there are many factors to consider even when writing a short text with a simple purpose. In fact, all writing involves consideration of a similar set of factors, which we call the components of successful writing. These components form the Rhetorical Planning Wheel (Figure 1.1), a tool that appears throughout *Essential Actions* to help you think about the many dimensions of any writing situation.

You can download a document with the Rhetorical Planning Wheel from the book's companion website.

Notice that the word *genre* is at the center of the wheel. *Genre* refers to a type or category of text. The genre of the texts in Activity 1.2 is a *request email*, and more specifically request emails written by students to their professor. Other examples of academic genres include syllabi, research papers, short-answer (or "ID") questions, class presentations, and case studies. Under the word *genre* in Figure 1.1, notice *actions;* these are what writers do in writing to achieve their goals. The principal action of request emails is, of course, to *make a request*.

The components of successful writing in any genre are situated around the edge of the wheel and are explained, using the sample request emails, in Table 1.2.

FIGURE 1.1:
The Rhetorical Planning Wheel (RPW)

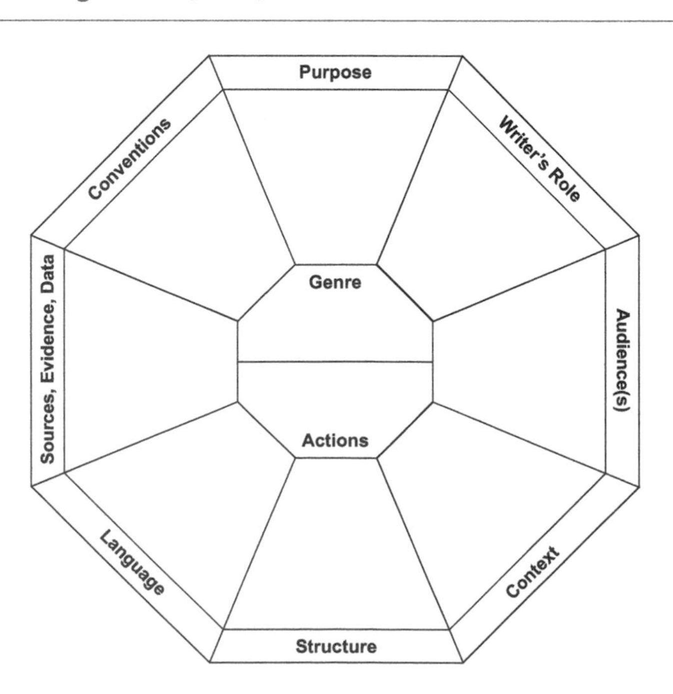

TABLE 1.2
The RPW For Request Emails

RPW Component	*Description*	*Request Email to a Professor*
Purpose	A writer may have one or several reasons for producing a text. The **purpose** is what the text can achieve. The **actions** are the ways writers attempt to achieve their purposes.	The purpose of these emails is to ask for an extension of the deadline for an assignment.
Writer's Role	The role and status of writers are central to what they write. Writers need to ask themselves: Am I an authority on the topic, or do I bring authority to the topic through use of sources or data? What role (e.g., student, applicant, opponent) am I taking in the text?	The writer's role in these cases is *student*, specifically a student who wants something from the audience, the professor.
Audience(s)	Writers need to ask themselves: What does the audience already know? What are the audience's values and expectations? How will the text be received, evaluated, and/or used by its audience(s)?	The only audience for these particular request emails is the professor. The professor presumably values assignment deadlines and expects polite emails because an extension affects their workload.
Context	The context of writing can include the place where the writing is completed or print/online platform where it is published. It is useful to ask questions like: What is going on where the writing takes place (e.g., the classroom or workplace)? Why is the text being written now? What texts came before it? What will happen next?	The context for the request email is a class that has assignments with fixed deadlines. This text is partly a response to a prior text—such as the course syllabus—that probably contains policies and rules about late submissions. Since this is a request, the writer expects the reader to reply with an email that either accepts or denies the request.
Structure	The way in which a text is organized may be determined principally by the genre (e.g., lab reports), or it may be quite varied, depending on the purposes of the writer (e.g., personal statements).	Request emails follow a predictable pattern: greeting, optional self-introduction and background, request, reasons/justifications for the request, thanks, and closing.
Language	Different genres, and different parts of a text from a genre, require different language choices. These choices involve vocabulary use, sentence structure, and grammar. Together, they are considered the **register** of the text (Unit 2).	The register of these request emails can be described as polite and somewhat formal. The reader is addressed as Dr. or Professor, not by their first name. Full sentences are expected. Features of text messaging (e.g., abbreviations, emojis) are inappropriate.
Sources, Evidence, Data	In many academic and professional tasks, written sources or data are required. Writers may cite evidence of various types from research, articles written by experts, observations, lecture notes, visual material, or other sources. The types of sources, details, and arguments depend on the genre, the discipline or profession, and the context.	There are no sources for these texts. However, the reader will probably be more persuaded by certain types of reasons for the extension, such as the difficulty of the task or individual circumstances.
Conventions	Conventions are those features that assist readers in immediately identifying a text as representing a particular genre. Conventions may be found in the use of paragraphs, headings, and terms of address. Some conventions are required by an assigned classroom task and must be followed—for example, formatting rules (e.g., margins, line spacing, etc.) or citation formats (e.g., MLA, APA).	Email conventions in this context include a clear subject line, an appropriate greeting, the use of short paragraphs, a closing (e.g., *thank you*), and signature (the writer's name).

The Rhetorical Planning Wheel demonstrates two important facts about writing:

- ❒ There are **similarities** or "family resemblances" (Swales, 1990) between texts from the same genre. For example, many request emails have a similar purpose and structure.
- ❒ There is **variation** among texts in the same genre because all writing is **situated.** This means that the situation (audience, writer's role, and context) affects all the other components of the Rhetorical Planning Wheel. For example, a request from a student to a professor might include different language choices, sources of information, and conventions than a request email from a professor to a student, or from one professor to another. There are other factors in the contexts of these emails that might affect the language, as well. For example, in a large class, students need to introduce themselves. Some instructors want to be called "Professor" or, more informally, by their first name.

Activity 1.3: Applying the Rhetorical Planning Wheel

We can use the Rhetorical Planning Wheel to analyze a genre or an individual writing situation. Read this email written by a first-year undergraduate student, Karen Muñoz. As you read, think about the ways that this text is similar to or different from the request emails to professors you have already analyzed.

To: Leticia Casares

From: Karen Muñoz

Date: April 23, 2019

Subject: Your talk, my involvement

①My name is Karen Muñoz and I am an undergraduate student at SDSU. ②I want to thank you for coming to my civic engagement class today at SDSU. ③I appreciate you taking your time to come speak to us. ④You are a very inspirational person and made my peers and I feel empowered as young citizens.

⑤I would love to become more involved with your campaign in any way I can. ⑥Please let me know if there is any way I can be of any help. ⑦You definitely deserve to win this election and you are already changing lives.

⑧ It was great meeting you. ⑨ Thank you once again.

⑩Best Regards,

Karen Muñoz

Answer these questions using components of the Rhetorical Planning Wheel.

1. Look closely at Sentences 2 and 5. What are Karen's **purposes** for writing this email to Leticia Cesares, a political candidate for a local elected office?
2. Look closely at Sentences 1 and 6. What different **roles** does Karen take as a writer?
3. What is Karen's relationship to her **audience**, Leticia Cesares? How well do they know each other? What clues are given to tell you that?
4. What is the **context** for this email? What happened before Karen sent the email? What does she hope the reader will do next?
5. What is the **structure** of this email? Which sentences are part of each function (or "move")?
    a. introducing the writer
    b. providing background for the request (thanking the speaker)
    c. making a request
    d. justifying the request (why is it important to the writer?)
    e. offering thanks and closing
6. Look again at the sentences where Karen makes her request. What **language** does she use to make the request? Why do you think she uses these phrases?
7. Does Karen follow all the usual **conventions** of the request emails to a professor?
8. Karen's email was successful. Leticia Cesares replied immediately and offered her a job on her election campaign. Why do you think her email was successful?
9. How is this email similar to and different from the request emails in Activity 1.2?

Language Box: Language Conventions in Emails

The choices of language used in different situations are known as **registers** (see Unit 2). We all use different registers as we speak or write in different contexts: to different members of our family, to our friends, to those we know well, and to those we don't know well at all, like some of our professors.

In writing an email, some aspects of register to consider include:

- The greeting: Although it sounds familiar, we often use *dear* in formal contexts, perhaps because it is a convention of traditional letter writing.
- The choice of name: In North American universities, students usually refer to their teachers as Dr. Samuels or Professor Samuels. If you are writing a formal email to someone you do not know outside the university, you can use Mr. Cortes, Ms. Cortes, or the person's full name if you prefer not to specify their gender (e.g., *Dear Leticia Cortes*). You can use first names to your friends, family, and people who have told you to use their first name. We do not usually write a title with a first name (e.g., not *Dr. Ann* or *Mr. Nigel*).
- Is it appropriate in this message to ask questions (e.g., *Is there a time I can meet with you?*), give commands (*Send me some times we can meet.*), or make exclamations (*That's great!*)?
- Will the reader expect full sentences or incomplete sentences (*OK; no problem*)?
- Do you need to use longer, more polite or formal expressions (*Thanks for seeing me; Thank you for taking the time to meet me*)? Can you use abbreviations (e.g., *Weds.* instead of *Wednesday*), features of text messages (*thx, lol*), or emojis?
- What level of formality do you need for the closing of the email (*Thanks; See you in class; Sincerely; Best regards*)?

WRITING TASK 1.1: Write a Request Email

Use your analyses of request emails in Activities 1.2 and 1.3, as well as your understanding of the Rhetorical Planning Wheel, to write your own request email.

A. Choose one of these situations.

1. You have started a paper for a class, but for personal or professional reasons, you have been unable to complete the final draft by the due date. Write an email requesting permission to turn the paper in late.
2. You have been working in a lab for a professor and would like to continue this work next semester. However, the professor can only accept a limited number of students in their lab. Write an email asking if you can continue, giving reasons why the work is important and why you should be allowed to stay in the lab.
3. You have read a news article or heard a podcast that you really enjoyed and that is relevant to a paper you are writing. In an email, tell the author why you liked their work and request an interview you can use to support your paper.

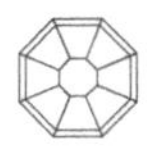

B. Plan your request email by answering these questions based on the Rhetorical Planning Wheel. You may know the answer to the questions if you are writing to a current instructor, lab professor, or the author of an article you have actually read. If not, discuss realistic answers with a partner.

1. Who is the audience for your text? What do you know about them? What are their values and expectations, particularly in terms of the request you are making? For Situation 1, what are the policies about late assignments in the syllabus?
2. What are your roles as writer?
3. What are your purposes for this email?
4. What is the context for the email? What's going on in your life or in the classroom that is relevant to your request?
5. What reasons and requests do you think the reader will accept? What information would be relevant and irrelevant?
6. What do you expect to happen if your reader accepts your request? What will you do? Or what are you asking the reader to do?

C. Draft your email after considering the questions in Part B and the Language Box.

D. Peer Review: Share your draft email with one or two partners. Read your peers' emails as if you were the audience for the email. Use these questions to give peer feedback:

   1. Is the email appropriate and effective for the audience and context?
   2. Does the email achieve its purpose(s)?
   3. Has the writer taken on an appropriate role?
   4. Is the register (language use) appropriate for the context?
   5. Does the text meet the conventions for an email in this context?
   6. Would you respond positively to this email if you received it?
   7. How else could the writer improve the email?

E. Self-Review: Revise your email using your peers' feedback. Have you done everything on this checklist?

   - ☐ My email is appropriate for the audience and context.
   - ☐ My email achieves its purposes.
   - ☐ As the writer, I have taken an appropriate role.
   - ☐ My use of language (register) is right for the occasion.
   - ☐ I have followed all the conventions of a polite request email.

What else do you need to work on? Make further revisions to your email if necessary.

Understanding the Importance of Context

The **context** for writing influences all aspects of the text you write. For example, although request emails have family resemblances, they also vary depending on the situation. This principle applies to all academic writing. Many assignments are called *essays* or *research papers,* but the requirements of each task can vary greatly depending on the level of knowledge you have as a writer, the expectations of the instructor, the type of class you are taking, the discipline (subject) of the course, and the conventions you need to follow. Therefore, you cannot simply learn a few patterns of organization and apply them to every assignment. Sometimes the same writer will produce two very different, but successful, texts in similar genres to similar audiences because of important differences in the context.

Activity 1.4: Analyzing Context

As you read the letter, think about the role of context in the Rhetorical Planning Wheel.

West Coast University
COLLEGE OF LETTERS AND SCIENCES

February 6, 2021

Dear Mr. Solis:

①Congratulations! On behalf of the faculty and staff at West Coast University, I am pleased to offer you admission to the Spanish major in the College of Letters and Science for the Fall 2022 quarter. Your selection from a pool of thousands of qualified applicants recognizes your extraordinary academic accomplishments and exceptional personal qualities.

②West Coast University has much to offer you, and we look forward to welcoming you to our vibrant educational community. We believe that our impressive academic reputation, scientific innovation and pre-professional opportunities, coupled with our spectacular campus location, will encourage you to achieve your highest dreams. At the university you will find world-renowned faculty who will challenge you to think critically and independently. As part of our community of undergraduate scholars, you will engage in educational, cultural and recreational life with the Pacific Ocean as an ideal backdrop.

③Your first step in becoming part of our university family is to reserve your space in the Fall 2022 class by submitting your Statement of Intent to Register by 5/01/22. To finalize your admission, complete the Steps to Enrollment. This site also contains a wealth of information about academic programs, resources and student services. We invite you to visit the campus in person to see for yourself all that the university has to offer.

④Again, congratulations on your admission to one of the finest institutions of higher education in the United States. West Coast University is ranked as one of the top public universities in the nation and is home to six Nobel Laureates. You and your family have every reason to be proud of your tremendous accomplishments. We sincerely hope that you will join us and make the university's vast possibilities and beautiful surroundings your own. Welcome to the WCU community!

Sincerely,

Estella Stone
Director of Admissions

1. How would you complete the analysis chart (Table 1.3)? Some of the answers are completed for you. Download a handout with the analysis chart to complete from the companion website.

TABLE 1.3:
Analysis of an Admissions Letter

Component	*Description*	*Admissions Letter*
Purpose	What are the purposes of this text?	Inform the reader that their application was successful Persuade the reader to accept the offer
Writer's Role	Who wrote the letter? What is their relationship to the reader?	
Audience(s)	Who are the audiences for this letter? What do they want to know? How might they react to this text?	
Context	What is the context for this text? What happened before it was written? What might happen next?	
Structure	How is the text organized? What types of information are included?	Greeting Paragraph 1: Announce the decision Paragraph 2: ____________ Paragraph 3: ____________ Paragraph 4: Repeat congratulations and make final appeal to accept the offer Closing
Language	What types of language are used? Does the text sound formal or informal? Why? What kind of persuasive language does the writer use? Does the writer ask questions, give commands, or make exclamations?	
Sources, Evidence, Data	What types of evidence does the writer give to show the quality and attractions of West Coast University?	
Conventions	What are the conventions of a formal letter?	

2. Compare Table 1.2 with Table 1.1. How is an admissions letter similar to and different from a request email? Consider these components of the Rhetorical Planning Wheel:
   a. Purpose
   b. Relationship between the reader and writer
   c. Structure
   d. Conventions

Activity 1.5: Variation in Context

Now read a different letter from the same university sent at the same time but to a different applicant. As you read, think about how the purposes, structure, and language of this letter are different from the letter in Activity 1.4.

West Coast University
COLLEGE OF LETTERS AND SCIENCES

February 6, 2021

Dear Ms. Robins,

①We have arrived at the end of our applications review period, and I am sorry to say that we are unable to offer you a space in this year's incoming class.

②Please understand that our decision is in no way a statement about your ability to succeed in college, nor is it any kind of judgment about you as a person. Be proud of your accomplishments and press on in your pursuit of higher education.

③This year, admission to West Coast University was more competitive than ever before. We could not accommodate an unprecedented number of outstanding candidates, including many students with outstanding academic records, remarkable talent, strong character, enriching experiences, and unique perspectives. I hope that you can find some comfort in knowing that none of us enjoys turning away exceptional students.

④Numbers do not tell the whole story, but I hope you find the context helpful: We received about 59,500 applications for admission, but we only have the capacity to enroll fewer than 3,100 students in our entering class. Of those offered admission, most achieved nearly straight-A averages and presented standardized test scores at or above the 98th percentile.

⑤Beyond grades and test scores, we considered many other factors presented in your application materials. Ours is a qualitative process, in which opinions are weighed with facts. Your application was carefully, respectfully, and thoughtfully reviewed multiple times, by many individuals.

⑥Ms. Robins, this decision was especially difficult for us given your ties to the university. Your eventual enrollment at West Coast University is of great interest to us, so I invite you to consider our Transfer Plan, which will assist you in gaining admission as a transfer student within the next two or three semesters. We have set aside time during the month of June for you to meet one-on-one with a member of our admission staff to learn how to maximize your chances of admission for a future term.

⑦If you would like to take advantage of this opportunity, please visit your applicant portal in early May to schedule an appointment. I hope you will consider this option.

⑧Thank you for considering West Coast University. We wish you all the best in your college plans.

Respectfully,

Estella Stone
Director of Admissions

In what ways are the admissions letter (Activity 1.4) and rejection letter similar and different? Discuss the letters in a small group. Consider the purpose, context, structure, supporting information, language, and conventions of the letters.

Analyzing Academic Writing Assignments

The Rhetorical Planning Wheel is a very flexible tool that can help you understand how to start any writing task, including the writing assigned in your academic courses. The purpose of academic writing is often to demonstrate understanding and knowledge of the content of the course, but it may also be to express opinions, reflect on your learning, or generate and share new knowledge. The purpose depends on your role as a writer, the audience's (instructor's) expectations, and the context. These will shape the structure, claims, evidence, language, and conventions of your writing.

To achieve the purpose of the task, you need to take certain actions in the text. These may include defining, comparing, contrasting, listing, summarizing, arguing, analyzing, and reflecting. For example, here is an in-class writing prompt from an undergraduate course in ethics; the **action words** appear in bold:

> Medical researchers, cosmetic companies, and others often perform experiments on animals. Many people feel that experimentation on animals is wrong and should be stopped immediately because animals do feel pain and there are other alternatives. **Identify** the groups that take both sides of this issue, and **list** the reasons for each side's point of view.

We can analyze the prompt using the Rhetorical Planning Wheel, as shown in Table 1.4.

TABLE 1.4:
Analysis of a Writing Prompt

Component	*Description*	*Ethics Writing Prompt*
Purpose	What is the purpose of the text to be written based on this prompt? What actions will the writer take?	To demonstrate knowledge about course content. The writer will identify two groups and list the reasons for their positions.
Writer's Role	Who is the writer? What is their relationship to the reader?	A student who is learning about animal testing for a course in ethics.
Audience(s)	Who is the reader? What do they want to know?	A course instructor, an expert in the field of ethics, who wants to see if the student has understood and can apply the course content.
Context	What is the context for this text? What happened before it was written? What will happen next?	A university course. The student has read about the topic, heard a lecture, participated in a discussion, and possibly conducted independent research.
Structure	How is the text organized? What types of information are included?	The prompt asks writers to identify the two groups taking sides and then list the reasons for and against animal testing.
Language	What types of language should be used in response to this prompt? Should the writer use every day or technical vocabulary?	The student should use some technical vocabulary from the readings and lectures as well as the specific names of groups and organizations that have taken sides on the issue.
Sources, Evidence, Data	What are appropriate sources and types of supporting information?	The arguments presented should represent the opinions of groups on both sides, not the writer's personal opinions.
Conventions	What are the conventions of the task?	The student should read the syllabus and the test directions or ask the instructor about the conventions. For example, is a list of bullet points acceptable? Does the student need to write full sentences? Are there requirements for writing, typing, or submitting the answer?

Activity 1.6. Analyzing Prompts

Read these writing prompts from university classes. As you read, think about the components of the Rhetorical Planning Wheel.

A. Define procedural knowledge and relate this term to the studies of amnesic patients. (Psychology)

B. Scholars of the 18th and 19th centuries frequently used a tripartite scheme for social evolution. Some described material culture; others defined the history of society, and some looked at family structure. List the names given to each of these groups, and connect them to museum artifacts, culture, and family organization. (Anthropology)

C. Explain why Modernism is so pessimistic. (Philosophy)

D. After reading and viewing the various sources about the Invisible Hand, discuss your position on the free market vs. government intervention. (Economics)

1. Choose one of these prompts or choose an assignment from another class you are taking now. Answer the questions based on components of the Rhetorical Planning Wheel.
   a. Purpose: What is the purpose of your writing? What actions would you take as a writer?
   b. Context: What is the context for the prompt? What do you think the class has studied? Do you think this question comes from a test or a homework assignment?
   c. Structure: How could you organize your writing? Do you need to write an introduction and conclusion? How much do you think you would need to write to answer the prompt?
   d. Sources, Evidence, Data: What are appropriate sources and types of supporting information for your answer?
   e. Language: Are there terms in the prompt or from a textbook that have to be copied because they are technical? What can be paraphrased and what must be exactly as written?
2. Compare your answers with a classmate who analyzed a different prompt. How are they similar and different?

A simpler way to prepare for a writing assignment is to complete a **do what/with what analysis** (see Figure 1.2).

FIGURE 1.2:
Do What/With What Analysis of a Writing Prompt

PROMPT: Identify the groups that take both sides of this issue [animal testing] and list their reasons for each side's point of view.	
DO what actions?	**WITH what information?**
IDENTIFY	groups on both sides
EXPLAIN	their points of view
LIST	reasons supporting each point of view

3. Make a **do what/with what** chart for the prompt you analyzed in Part A. Common actions in ID questions include *identify, explain, list, define, compare, contrast, give an example, connect,* and *apply.*

Download a **do what/with what** chart to complete from the companion website.

Responding to Short-Answer (ID) Questions

Short-answer questions, also called **ID (identification) responses**, are among the most common and important writing assignments in undergraduate classes (Melzer, 2014). ID responses usually ask you to respond in a few sentences or a paragraph by identifying, explaining, and sometimes applying a concept from your reading or lectures. Answers usually directly respond to the prompt without an introduction or conclusion. You should use your own words and not copy from the textbook or other sources, although you should also try to use the correct technical vocabulary to show you understand the content. In fact, demonstrating understanding of the course content is usually the most important purpose of an ID response.

For example:

Prompt: What are the principal differences between a university acceptance letter and a rejection letter?

Response: Acceptance and rejection letters vary in terms of structure and language use because their purposes vary. In an acceptance letter, the writer's purpose is to persuade the reader that they should enroll at the university. Rejection letters, on the other hand, need to be very audience-centered and compassionate, with an attempt to persuade the readers that they are among the many accomplished students who have been rejected despite their academic records. Thus, acceptance letters are structured to congratulate the student and praise the university; rejection letters are organized to soften the blow of rejection and then sometimes mention alternatives for future enrollment.

WRITING TASK 1.2: Answer an ID question

A. Choose one of these prompts, which refer to this unit:

1. What is the Rhetorical Planning Wheel? Why is it important to writers?
2. Name at least three purposes for writing you have studied in this unit. Explain why understanding the purpose of a text is essential for writers.
3. How is writing an email to a professor different from writing a text message to a friend? Explain your answer using components of the Rhetorical Planning Wheel.

B. Complete a **do what/with what** chart for the prompt you chose (see Figure 1.2). Download a do what/with what chart to complete from the companion website.

C. Draft your response. Write a paragraph, giving as much detail as you can. Write in your own words, quoting from this unit if necessary.

D. Peer Review: Share your draft response with one or two partners. Read your peers' responses, and use these questions to give peer feedback:

1. Does the response fully answer all parts of the prompt?
2. Does the writer give enough information?
3. Is the answer mostly in the writer's own words, quoting the chapter if necessary?
4. How could the writer improve the response?

E. Self-Review: Revise your response using your peers' feedback. Have you done everything on this checklist?

- ☐ I identified the actions in the prompt (*do what?*). My response achieves its purposes.
- ☐ I located the information from the chapter I needed (*with what?*).
- ☐ I wrote enough to fully answer the prompt.
- ☐ I wrote several sentences or a paragraph in an academic register using the conventions of an ID response.

What else do you need to work on? Make further revisions to your response if necessary.

Reflection

What was the main goal of this chapter? How can you use this goal in your writing?

References

Melzer, D. (2014). *Assignments across the curriculum: A national study of college writing*. Utah State University Press.

2 Everyday and Academic Genres and Their Registers

Goals:

- ❒ Understand and apply the concept of genre
- ❒ Analyze everyday, professional, and academic texts from different genres
- ❒ Understand the connection between genre and register
- ❒ Write a report about your previous academic writing experiences
- ❒ Transform a text from one genre into another

What Are Genres?

The term *genre* refers to a category of texts that are similar in purpose and written in response to similar contexts. Genres are typically named by people who use them. A **book review**, for example, is a category of texts published in several media to describe and critique books. On the other hand, **book blurbs,** written to sell books, appear on the back covers of published volumes and in sales brochures. So reviews and blurbs belong to two different genres because they serve two different purposes in two different contexts.

Because you have probably been reading and writing for much of your life, you can recognize and name texts from many genres. When you read the term *book review,* for example, you already have a sense of what a text from this genre does—that is, what actions authors take to achieve their purposes. With your genre knowledge of these repeated actions, you are better able to read or produce a text in this genre.

Some genres are, for the most part, "fixed." This means that texts from these genres are very similar across time and contexts. For example, **lab reports**, though varied in content, often follow a structure dictated by a lab manual from which student writers do not deviate. More frequently, though, texts from a genre vary, sometimes considerably, depending on a number of factors represented in the components of the Rhetorical Planning Wheel. For example, you probably know that movies of the same genre (romantic comedies, action movies, etc.) have some similarities but also many differences.

Activity 2.1: Brainstorming Genres

1. Choose an entertainment medium such as movies, music, or literature.
2. Make a list of all of the categories (genres) in this medium you can think of (e.g., horror films, romances, fantasies, etc.).
3. Work in groups with others who have chosen the same medium to combine your lists into one.
4. Identify one example of a genre from your list, such as comedies. Discuss how you recognize items from this category when you see or experience them. What are the shared features within each of the genre?
5. Present your findings to the class.

Contrasting Everyday and Academic Genres

This unit is about written texts from the genres with which you may be familiar. You will be asked to name genres you know from the past or present, both **everyday** genres from your life outside of school and **academic** ones which you have been assigned in classes. After you list these texts from the past and present, you will analyze them using the Rhetorical Planning Wheel and discuss why the texts vary depending on context, writer, audience, and other factors.

It is sometimes difficult to distinguish between everyday and academic genres. Rather than an either/or separation between these two broad classifications, we can think about a scale or continuum from the genres you might use daily to those that are more academic.

Activity 2.2: Everyday and Academic Genres

1. Consider this list of common written academic and everyday genres. With a partner, arrange the genres in order from the most everyday to the most academic.

   national newspaper article
   academic journal article
   university lecture
   office hour conversation
   student research paper
   text message invitation
   student newspaper article
   group discussion in class
   movie review
   class discussion board post
   textbook chapter
   email request
   university home page
   online ad
   essay exam

2. Explain your order of the genres to another pair.
3. Add other genres from your reading and writing experience to the list.

Activity 2.3: Comparing Everyday Genres

1. Choose a text (anything that involves writing) that you find in your life outside of school, not something you have read or written for a class. The text can be in English or any other language. It could be written by you or by someone else.

2. Download and complete the Rhetorical Planning Wheel analysis from the companion website.

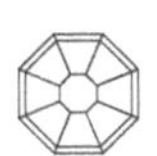

3. Now, collect a second text from the same genre. List the ways that it is similar to and different from the first. Consider the components of Rhetorical Planning Wheel: **purpose, writer's role, audience, context, structure, language, and conventions.**

WRITING TASK 2.1: Writing Texts in an Everyday Genre

Select the everyday genre that you have been studying so far in this unit. Note the "family resemblances"—that is, those features that the texts from the same genre have in common. Then, using the Rhetorical Planning Wheel, prepare your own text in that genre, retaining the "resemblances" but changing other components like the audience or context. For example, if you were working on menus, your audience might be only those who can eat gluten-free foods and the context might be a university campus.

Academic Genres

In their study of prior genre knowledge, Reiff and Bawarshi (2011) asked their first-year university students to name all of the genres in which they had written on different platforms (blog, online journal, instant messaging) and in print for classrooms. Because this is an academic writing textbook, this project will be retained but somewhat narrowed. You will be asked to name and analyze only those genres on which you were graded, either in assignments or examinations. Of course, what you wrote in secondary school or in other countries may differ dramatically from what you will be writing in the future. However, it is important to consider your academic writing history so that you can recognize and analyze genres that are new to you.

Activity 2.4: Exploring Your Academic Genre History

1. Think of all of the genres that you can remember writing in for assignments and/or assessments in previous classes/settings. Use the genre names that your instructor, textbook, or test/exam used. If you speak more than one language, list what you wrote in your other language(s) as well as English.

2. Share your genres with a partner first and then with the whole class.

Activity 2.5: Analyzing Academic Genres

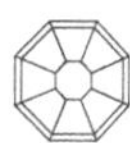

1. Select one academic genre from the master list and work with a partner or group who has picked the same genre. Together, answer these questions about two texts belonging to that genre. For example, you and your partner might both have written a book report, designed a poster, or written a persuasive essay.
   a. **Genre**: What did the teacher call this text?
   b. **Writer**: What was your role as a writer? In addition to a student, were you assigned another role, such as an expert?
   c. **Audience**: Who read and evaluated this text? What were the most important criteria for evaluation?
   d. **Purpose**: Why did you write this text? Were there reasons for writing beyond getting a grade?
   e. What **actions** did you take (e.g., explain, synthesize, argue, respond, analyze)?

f. **Context**: Where was the classroom? What else were you learning? Does this genre appear in other classroom contexts, as well?

g. **Structure**: How was this text organized? Did it have a fixed or flexible structure?

h. **Sources/data**: What types of sources or data did you use, if any? Or, what kinds of evidence and examples did you use? What referencing style (APA, MLA, etc.) were you required to use?

i. **Language**: What kinds of vocabulary and grammar did you use? What language was emphasized by the teacher or the textbook?

j. **Conventions**: What were the features of this text (e.g., figures, fonts, use of paragraphs)?

2. Compare your answers with others in the class. As a class, can you come up with some generalizations about the academic papers you have been assigned previously?

Language Box: When to Use the Pronoun *I*

One of the unfortunate myths about academic writing is that students should never use personal pronouns (*I*, *me*, *you*, *we*, etc.). Instead, many guidebooks and websites tell writers to use impersonal constructions such as *it is believed that*, *the report was completed*, or *the project ended*. However, language choices are a component of the Rhetorical Planning Wheel, so the decision to use personal or impersonal styles is connected to the context, the audience, the writer's role, and the conventions of the genre. There are no absolute rules for all academic writing such as "Don't use *I*." Instead, for each task, you need to know what is allowed, expected, and effective in this particular genre. In many research papers and ID questions, you will choose impersonal language, but in reflections, discussion board posts, personal statements, and some types of research writing, you will certainly use *I* to highlight your ideas, work, and personality. When you write about your own experiences (e.g., Writing Task 2.2), you should use personal pronouns. However, you should probably only use *we* when you are writing as a group not an individual as is often the case for students involved in laboratory or experimental projects.

The pronoun *you* is very rare in most academic genres, except when you are communicating with other people directly (e.g., emails to professor, questions after a presentation). Most academic writing is not very interactive, so addressing the reader directly can feel uncomfortable and is usually ineffective.

WRITING TASK 2.2: Academic Genre Report

Your experiences with academic writing will vary from those of other students depending on where and when you went to secondary school, college, or university. Write a short report about the written genres that were most common in one stage of your education (e.g., high school, an intensive language course, or a previous degree program). A **report** is a common academic and professional genre whose purpose is to present information to a specific audience. Reports often end with recommendations or evaluations.

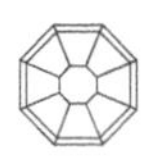

The **purpose** of this assignment is to report on the genres of writing you produced in one stage of your education. The **audience** is your current writing class and teacher, and the **context** is that you will share your report with the class. Your **role** is an expert because you know your previous schooling well. Since you are writing about yourself, you should use personal pronouns in your **language** choices and past tense verbs when you are writing about previous experiences. The **structure** of your report will use these headings:

- ☐ **Introduction**: Describe the educational setting (e.g., type of school, location, student demographics, classes you took). State the purpose of this report.
- ☐ **Findings**: Explain the most common genres in which you wrote. This section could be a list of bullet points or short paragraphs. Use concepts from this chapter such as components of the Rhetorical Planning Wheel to discuss the genres. Organize the genres logically (e.g., order of frequency, order of importance, or order of difficulty).
- ☐ **Evaluation**: You could answer some of these questions: What do you think about the genres you experienced? Do you feel well prepared for the next stage of your education? What changes would you make to the educational system described in this report?

Read this example report.

Introduction

I did my undergraduate degree in Modern Languages at a traditional British university located in the southeast of England. Admission was very competitive, and perhaps for this reason, professors assumed that we already knew how to write. There were no actual writing or composition classes, but we had to write a lot every week for our courses. Unlike students in North America, British students do not take "general education" courses in different disciplines. They only study their chosen subject. As a result, I wrote a lot about literature and linguistics. Almost all my writing was in English, although I did have to translate to and from French and German, and in my final year, I had to write an exam in French.

Findings

Most assignments in my experience were called "essays." We wrote essays every two weeks in each course, which our professor then critiqued in small-group sessions called tutorials or supervisions. Thus, our audience was always an expert plus one or more peers since we read and commented on each other's papers. However, within the broad category of essay, there were some different genres. For example, some of our literature essays were called "prac crit" (short for "practical criticism"). The source for a prac crit was a short text such as a poem, and the purpose was to analyze the content, themes, structure, and language in as much depth as possible. We also cited other sources (books about literature), but I do not remember following any particular conventions for references.

Evaluation

Although we received a lot of detailed feedback on our writing, some of it highly critical, we never revised our essays. Instead, most courses were focused on the exam at the end of the year, where we had to write three essays in three hours. I now feel that this was not especially good preparation for more advanced academic writing, which requires a great deal of rewriting and revision. I wish we had been evaluated on our coursework more than on our exams.

A. Take notes on each section of your report. Then, discuss your ideas with a partner or share them on an online discussion board. Ask and answer questions to help your classmates add more detail to their reports.

1. For your **Introduction**, think about which stage of your education you will write about, the type of school it was, and where it was. Consider the courses with writing assignments.
2. For your **Findings** section, think about the genres you wrote and about their purpose, structure, audience, and context.
3. For the **Evaluation** section, think about your feelings about the genres you wrote in—that is, did they prepare you for later stages of your education? Are there things you wish you could change about the types of writing you did?

B. Write a draft of your report using the Introduction, Findings, and Evaluation headings and any conventions for title and format that your instructor provides.

C. Peer Review: Share your draft report with one or two partners. Use these questions to give peer feedback:

1. Is the report appropriate and effective for the audience and context?
2. Do you feel you understand the academic genres that your peer wrote in their previous education? What else do you want to know?
3. Is the report clearly organized under the three headings (Introduction, Findings, Evaluation)?
4. How else could the writer improve the report?

D. Self-Review: Revise your response using your peer's feedback. Have you done everything on this checklist?

- ☐ My report contains all the necessary information and follows the conventions required by my instructor.
- ☐ I have clearly described the context for my previous academic writing.
- ☐ I have discussed one or more genres I wrote using the components of the Rhetorical Planning Wheel.
- ☐ I have evaluated my previous writing experiences.
- ☐ I have checked my language carefully, including the use of personal pronouns.

What else do you need to work on? Make further revisions to your email if necessary.

Register

Writers make different language choices in texts from a genre based on their roles as writers and based on the audience, situation, genre conventions—all the elements of the Rhetorical Planning Wheel. Together, these language choices are called the **register** of the text. You may have learned that register is "formal" or "informal" or "high" or "low." However, the term *register* is more specific than that: it refers to the ways that texts vary in response to their context. If you look back to the texts you have already studied in *Essential Actions*, you may be able to see how some language choices were affected by the context. For example, if a friend texts you and asks if you would like to meet after class for a coffee, you might reply *yesss* or *Sure, where*. However, if a professor emailed you to arrange a meeting to discuss your research paper, you would probably reply very differently, for example: "Thank you for offering to help me with my research. Should I come to your office after class?"

Activity 2.6: Comparing Registers in Different Genres

In this task, you will see how register varies in texts from different genres. In 2016, officials in Seattle, Washington, changed the start time for public schools. Elementary schools started earlier, and middle and high schools started about an hour later than before (8:45 AM instead of 7:50 AM). In 2018, researchers released a study into the effects of this change. You are going to read three texts that refer to this research. As you read them, think about genre: Where would you expect to find each text? Don't worry about unfamiliar vocabulary.

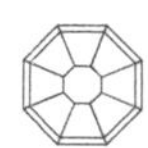

Discuss these questions from the Rhetorical Planning Wheel.

1. Where do you think each text was published?
2. What is the audience for each text? How do you know?
3. What is the purpose of each text? What roles do the writers take?
4. What were the principal actions taken by the writers?
5. How do the three texts use sources and evidence?
6. What similarities and differences in register do you notice among the three texts?
7. What do you think people who read and write each text would call it?

Text 1:

Adolescents typically have a preference to stay active until late in the evening and to wake up late in the morning. This timing of daily activity or "chronotype" is not only a consequence of a change in social life and the use of electronic devices that keep teenagers awake during the evening, but is also a result of changes in both the circadian and homeostatic regulation of sleep.

We show that a delay in the high school start times from 7:50 to 8:45 a.m. had several measurable benefits for students. The change led to a significant lengthening of daily sleep of over half an hour. We also show that the later school start time is associated with a better alignment of sleep timing with the circadian system, reduced sleepiness, and increased academic performance. Although it is highly likely that increased sleep was the cause for reduced sleepiness, it is much harder to attribute causality for 4.5% higher grades on increased sleep; nevertheless, it is certainly reasonable that students who are better rested and more alert should display better academic performance.

Text 2:

The results showed students averaged 34 minutes more sleep after start times for high schools and most middle schools changed from 7:50 to 8:45 am.

Researchers noted higher science class grades—from an [average] grade of 77.5 percent in 2016 to 82 percent in 2017—according to the study published Wednesday in the journal *Science Advances*.

The Seattle district and others in the region are moving in the right direction. Others resist the change because changing start times upsets established bus schedules, could cost districts more money, and can interfere with after-school activities. They should pay more attention to the research.

The district should continue to track high school student [data] to quantify the impact of the later start times. And the later start times should continue.

Text 3:

Not getting enough sleep is common among high school students and is associated with several health risks as well as poor academic performance. One of the reasons adolescents do not get enough sleep is early school start times. The American Academy of Pediatrics has recommended that middle and high schools start at 8:30 a.m. or later to give students the opportunity to get the amount of sleep they need, but most American adolescents start school too early.

During puberty, adolescents become sleepy later at night and need to sleep later in the morning as a result of shifts in biological rhythms. These biological changes are often combined with poor sleep habits (including irregular bedtimes and the presence of electronics in the bedroom). During the school week, school start times are the main reason students wake up when they do. The combination of late bedtimes and early school start times results in most adolescents not getting enough sleep.

Everyone can play an important role

Parents: Model and encourage habits that help promote good sleep.

School officials: Learn more about the research connecting sleep and school start times. Good sleep hygiene in combination with later school times will enable adolescents to be healthier and better academic achievers.

Academic Registers: Language in Academic Genres

Register is sometimes defined as the ways that *context* gets into *text*. In other words, a writer's language choices reflect the situation, purpose, writer's role, audience, conventions, and source use expectations of the genre in a text written for a specific situation. This is important because there is no single academic register. You will need to write (and speak) in different registers in different classes for different types of assignments or assessments.

One way to understand register is by asking three sets of questions about the language of a text (see Figure 2.1): (1) How do language choices create the **content** in the text? (2) How do they reflect the writer's **purpose**, stance, and opinions? and (3) How do they **structure** the text?

A glossary of grammatical terms is provided at the end of the book if you are not familiar with concepts such as passive voice, boosting, hedging, and verb tenses.

FIGURE 2.1:
Questions to Analyze Register

Language for Writing about Information (Content)	▪ What are the key words and phrases? ▪ How much technical language is used? ▪ Are acronyms and abbreviations used? ▪ Are contractions acceptable (e.g., *don't, isn't*)? ▪ Does the text use a lot of long noun phrases? ▪ What verb tenses are used?
Language for Taking a Stance (Purpose)	▪ Does the writer report information or take a position? ▪ Do writers show agreement or disagreement with sources? ▪ Does the writer report sources without opinion? ▪ Is the author present (by using *I*, *we*, or personal language such as *unfortunately*) or absent (impersonal structures, passive voice, objective language)? ▪ How do writers hedge (reduce the strength) and/or boost (increase the strength) of claims?
Language for Organizing (Structure and Conventions)	▪ What language is used to connect sentences and paragraphs? ▪ Does the first part of each sentence (up to and including the subject) help organize the text? ▪ How are sources cited or referenced? ▪ Do writers use headings and subheadings?

Activity 2.7: Analyzing Register

By now you should have realized that Text 1 in Activity 2.6 was from an academic journal article (Dunster et al., 2018), Text 2 was an op-ed (opinion) column in a regional news source ("Stick with later start times," 2018), and Text 3 was a webpage with official recommendations (Centers for Disease Control and Prevention, 2020). Re-read the three texts and analyze their registers using some of the questions in Figure 2.1. The first text has been analyzed for you (Figure 2.2).

What do you notice now about the similarities and differences among the three texts? How are these language choices connected to or dependent on other elements of the Rhetorical Planning Wheel (writer's role, audience, context, and purpose)?

FIGURE 2.2:
Register Analysis of Seattle Sleep Text 1

Language of Content	▪ Technical vocabulary (e.g., *chronotype, circadian, homeostatic adolescents, sleep onset/offset*) ▪ Mostly present tense verbs ▪ Verbs turned into nouns *(regulation, sleepiness, performance*) ▪ Long noun phrases ▪ Some passive voice
Language of Purpose	▪ Mostly neutral, but some evaluative language in the conclusion ▪ Some author presence but only discussing results (*we = the researchers*) ▪ Conclusions are hedged (*highly likely, point to*)
Language of Organization	▪ Connecting words show logical relationship between ideas (*although, not only . . . but also, nevertheless*) ▪ Categorizing language (*several benefits*) ▪ Numbered footnote citations (in the original; not printed in this textbook)

WRITING TASK 2.3: Genre Transformation

In 1863, in the middle of the U.S. Civil War, President Abraham Lincoln gave an important speech dedicating the battlefield at Gettysburg, Pennsylvania, as a memorial and announcing his decision to end slavery throughout the U.S. (the Emancipation Proclamation). It's one of the most famous and important speeches in American history; you can easily find the original text online. Peter Norvig (at the time, the Director of Research for Google) wrote a parody of academic presentations by imagining the presentation slides for Lincoln's Gettysburg Address (http://www.norvig.com/Gettysburg/index.htm).

A. Discuss these questions.

1. How did Norvig use the conventions of presentation software to recreate the Gettysburg address?
2. In what ways did he change or keep the language of the original?
3. What other genres or formats could you use to present these ideas?

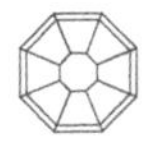

B. Now, choose a new genre to rewrite the information from the Seattle sleep study (Activity 2.6). Some examples of genres include: formal essay, discussion board post, autobiography, presentation slides, TED talk, blog, podcast, photo-essay, Twitter thread, TikTok video, or song lyrics (activity adapted from Tardy, 2016). Then answer the questions about your chosen genre using the Rhetorical Planning Wheel.

1. **Genre:** What do people call this type of text?
2. **Writer:** What is your position, role, or persona?
3. **Audience:** Who will read the text?
4. **Purpose:** Why do people read and write in this genre?
5. **Context:** In what situations is this genre used?
6. **Structure:** What patterns of organization are appropriate?
7. **Register:** Which language choices are typical of this genre?
8. **Conventions:** What other features and conventions should be included?

C. Write a first draft your genre transformation.

D. Peer Review. Share your draft with one or two partners. Use these questions to give peer feedback:

   1. What genre is the writer attempting to produce?
   2. Does the writing have the purpose, structure, register, and conventions of this genre?
   3. Does the writing contain information about the Seattle sleep study?
   4. What else could the writer do to improve their text?

E. Self-Review: Revise your response using your peers' feedback. Have you done everything on this checklist?

   - ☐ It is easy to identify the genre of my writing.
   - ☐ My writing has a clear audience, purpose, and context.
   - ☐ I have chosen an appropriate register for my text.
   - ☐ I have followed all the conventions for the genre of my text.

What else do you need to work on? Make further revisions to your response if necessary.

Reflection

Look at the examples of different genres that you studied in this unit. How would you explain in your own words the differences between academic and non-academic genres? How are they similar?

References

Centers for Disease Control and Prevention. (2020, May 29). *Schools start too early.* https://www.cdc.gov/sleep/features/schools-start-too-early.html

Dunster, G. P., Iglesia, L. de la, Ben-Hamo, M., Nave, C., Fleischer, J. G., Panda, S., & de la Iglesia, H. O. (2018). Sleepmore in Seattle: Later school start times are associated with more sleep and better performance in high school students. *Science Advances, 4*(12). https://doi.org/10.1126/sciadv.aau6200

Reiff, M.J., & A. Bawarshi (2011). Tracing discursive resources: How students use prior knowledge to negotiate new writing contexts in first-year composition. *Written Communication, 28*(3), 312–337. https://doi.org /10.1177%2F0741088311410183

Stick with later start times that boost Seattle high schoolers' success [Editorial]. (2018, December 17). *The Seattle Times.* https://www.seattletimes.com/opinion/editorials/stick-with-later-start-times-that-boost-seattle-high-schoolers-success/

Tardy, C. M. (2016). *Beyond convention: Genre innovation in academic writing.* University of Michigan Press.

PART 2:
EXPLORING ESSENTIAL ACTIONS

3 Explain

Goals

- ❒ Write one-sentence definitions and glosses to explain terms
- ❒ Use sources to write comparative and contested definitions that explain technical concepts
- ❒ Explain processes, causes, and effects
- ❒ Pedagogical Genre: Write an extended definition
- ❒ Genre in Action: Write a blog post

What Is the Action?

You will probably write lots of explanations: about processes, causes, effects, and even historical events. Many explanations are in fact **definitions:** you will need to learn the meaning of many technical and discipline-specific terms in each class you take, and often you will write definitions as the answer to a test question or as part of a longer assignment. When you go on to discuss consequences, factors, conditions, and processes, you are writing an explanation or **extended definition**, often drawing on sources.

Here are some prompts from textbooks, assignments, and assessments that require students to explain:

- ❒ Describe the role of ethics in a business environment.
- ❒ Explain what it means to be a professional of integrity.
- ❒ Define photosynthesis.
- ❒ Explain what it means to be an effective entrepreneur.

Activity 3.1: What Do You Know?

Can you find these parts in each explanation from the textbook excerpts provided? Discuss with a partner.

application	*effect*
cause	*example(s)*
condition	*process*
definition	

1. What a buyer pays for a unit of the specific good or service is called price. The total number of units that consumers would purchase at that price is called the quantity demanded. A rise in price of a good or service almost always decreases the quantity demanded of that good or service. Conversely, a fall in price will increase the quantity demanded. When the price of a gallon of gasoline increases, for example, people look for ways to reduce their consumption by combining several errands, commuting by carpool or mass transit, or taking weekend or vacation trips closer to home. Economists call this inverse relationship between price and quantity demanded the law of demand. (Greenlaw & Shapiro, 2017)

2. Primary sources are original documents we study and from which we collect information; primary sources include letters, first editions of books, legal documents, and a variety of other texts. A primary source may contain dated material that we now know is inaccurate. It may also contain personal beliefs and biases that the original writer didn't intend to publish. Readers can still gain great insight from primary sources if they understand the context from which the writer of the primary source wrote the text. (Baldwin, 2020)

3. When an individual thinks about how he or she thinks, this practice is called *metacognition*. Developmental psychiatrist John Flavell coined the term metacognition and divided the theory into three processes of planning, tracking, and assessing your own understanding. For example, you may be reading a difficult passage in a textbook on chemistry and recognize that you are not fully understanding the meaning of the section you just read or its connection to the rest of the chapter. Students use metacognition when they practice self-awareness and self-assessment. You are the best judge of how well you know a topic or a skill. In college especially, thinking about your thinking is crucial so you know what you don't know and how to fix this problem, i.e., what you need to study, how you need to organize your calendar, and so on. (Baldwin, 2020)

Sentence Definitions

A one-sentence definition can be a useful way to start a longer project, answer a test question, review a reading, or study for a quiz. The goal is to capture the essence of the term in a single sentence. Typically, this includes the term, the category, and its defining characteristics, for example:

term category defining characteristics

Primary sources are *original documents* which we study and from which we collect information.

Definitions may be introduced with the verb *be*, as in this example (primary sources *are*), a verb such as *defined as*, the conjunction *or*, and other sentences structures, as shown in Activity 3.2.

Activity 3.2: Identifying Definitions

Read these sentences from an introductory economics textbook (Greenlaw & Shapiro, 2017). The terms that are defined are printed in **bold**. Find the language that shows you where the definitions are as well as the category and/or defining characteristics in each definition.

1. Recent decades have seen **a trend** toward globalization, which is the expanding cultural, political, and economic connections between people around the world.

2. **Exports** are the goods and services that are produced domestically and sold abroad. **Imports** are the goods and services that are produced abroad and then sold domestically. **Gross domestic product (GDP)** measures the size of total production in an economy.

3. Economists use the term **demand** to refer to the amount of some good or service consumers are willing and able to purchase at each price.

4. Economists call this inverse relationship between price and quantity demanded **the law of demand.**

5. The **equilibrium price** is the only price where the plans of consumers and the plans of producers agree. The word equilibrium means "balance."

6. **Barriers to entry** are the legal, technological, or market forces that discourage or prevent potential competitors from entering a market.

7. One method for creating a barrier to entry is known as **predatory pricing**, in which a firm uses the threat of sharp price cuts to discourage competition.

Language Box: Relative Clauses

Relative clauses either extend or narrow the meaning of a noun or of another clause. They usually start with a relative pronoun: *who, that, which,* or (less commonly) *whom, whose, where,* or *when*. Two different types of relative clause are commonly used in definitions:

1. **Restrictive relative clauses** limit the meaning of a noun phrase, so they are often used for the defining characteristic that shows how the key term is a special case of the broader category. Do not use commas with restrictive relative clauses.
   - Primary sources are original documents *that historians study*.
   - Exports are the goods and services *that are produced domestically and sold abroad*.
2. **Non-restrictive relative clauses** extend the meaning of the sentence, for instance by saying what a word or sentence means. Non-restrictive clauses are separated by a comma and cannot begin with *that*.
   - Recent decades have seen a trend toward globalization, *which is the expanding cultural, political, and economic connections between people around the world*.
   - Successful students engage in metacognition, *which means thinking about their thinking process*.

Both types of clauses can be **reduced,** which means deleting the relative pronoun and changing or removing the verb:

- Exports are the goods and services ~~*that are*~~ *produced domestically and sold abroad*.
- Recent decades have seen a trend toward globalization, ~~*which is*~~ *the expanding cultural, political, and economic connections between people around the world*.

Activity 3.3: Practice the Language

Write definitions for key words from a recent reading or another class using some of these sentence frames with relative clauses.

1. ____________ is/are __________________ that __________________________.

   Example: *Primary sources are original documents that historians study.*

2. ____________ is/are __________________ in/by/during/for which

   ______________.

   Example: *A recession is a period of time in which the economy contracts.*

3. _____________ refer(s) to/ is defined as __________________, which means

   _____________.

   Example: *Globalization refers to the expansion of international relationships, which means there are stronger cultural, political, and economic connections among people.*

4. ____________________ call _______________ ___________________________.

   Example: *Economists call the inverse relationship between price and quantity demanded the law of demand.*

5. ________________________________ is known as _____________________.

   Example: *A period when the economy contracts is known as a recession.*

6. _____________ is a system/process/way/method of _________________________

   in which _______________.

   Example: *Predatory pricing is a way of setting the cost of a good or service in which competition is discouraged because of the threat of sudden price changes.*

Glosses

A gloss (a short definition that is integrated in a sentence) can be an efficient way to explain the meaning of a new term, a non-English word, an acronym, or a technical word. The definition may be in the sentence or in the parentheses. The first sentence of this paragraph contains an example of a gloss; others include:

- ❐ Gross domestic product **(GDP)** measures the size of total production in an economy.
- ❐ The research was conducted *in situ* **(that is, in a natural setting)**.
- ❐ Most organizations form two types of committee: short-term **(or, *ad hoc*)** task forces and permanent **(or, standing)** committees.

Activity 3.4: Writing Glosses

Imagine you are writing for an audience that has very little knowledge of technology. Add glosses to the italicized words in the paragraph by inserting either a technical term or its definition in the parentheses. Look up any unfamiliar terms in an online dictionary.

> *Social media* (interactive websites for creating and sharing information) have had enormous influence on almost every aspect of society. Social media include *online journals* (or, ①____________), *vlogs* (②____________), and *social networks* (③____________). Users create a *profile* (④____________) with which they can share ideas, personal messages, and other content, and some sites encourage users to post with an *avatar* (⑤____________). A key feature of social media is that *some content is shared quickly across vast networks* (it is said to go "⑥____________").

WRITING TASK 3.1: Write a Paragraph with Glosses

Continue the text from Activity 3.4 with another paragraph that explains how a particular social network or course website that you use functions. Write glosses for terms that may be unfamiliar to a reader who has never used the site (e.g., *post, like, favorite, comment, discussion board*).

Categories in Definitions

So far, you have read and written one-sentence definitions of terms. However, many definitions in academic writing are much longer because the terms are complex (see Activity 3.1). One common form of definition is a *taxonomy*, or a number of categories or parts that comprise the technical term. For example:

> Business ethics exists on **three levels**: the individual, the organizational, and the societal. At the **organizational and societal** levels, laws, regulations, and oversight can go a long way toward curtailing illegal activity. Business ethics motivates managers to (1) meet legal and industry governing and reporting requirements and (2) shape corporate culture so that corrupt practices such as bribery have no place in the organization. At the **individual** level, when corruption takes place, it is a matter of conscience. (Byars & Stanberry, 2020)

In this type of definition, the categories are introduced first, and then each category—or group of categories—is explained. In the business ethics example, the writers use the same sentence pattern to introduce all the categories: *At the organization and societal levels, At the individual level.* This repetition reminds the reader of the three "levels" of business ethics and avoids the need for transition words such as *first, second, third.*

WRITING TASK 3.2: Write a Definition with Categories

Choose one of the terms listed or a term from a topic you are currently studying in this or another class. Write a clear one-sentence definition and explain the term using a taxonomy (two or more categories), as in the business ethics example. Gloss any additional technical terms for a non-specialist audience.

- ☐ Biology: *the cell* (suggested parts: membrane, cytoplasm, nucleus)
- ☐ Computer science: *hard drive* (suggested types: hard disk drive, solid state drive, hybrid)
- ☐ Business: *stocks* (suggested types: common, preferred)
- ☐ Literature: *drama* (suggested categories: comedy, tragedy, history)
- ☐ Engineering: *engineers* (suggested categories: mechanical, chemical, electrical, computer)

Using Sources in Definitions

You may need to cite one or more sources in a definition if:

- ☐ You found the definition in a reading.
- ☐ You want to quote a dictionary definition.
- ☐ The term was coined (that is, invented) or used in a specific way by a particular author or in a particular discipline.
- ☐ The term is **contested**—that is, different sources define the term in different ways.

In general, you should try to **paraphrase** rather than **quote** definitions (that is, rewrite the definition from the source in your own terms), especially if the purpose of the assignment is to demonstrate your understanding of a topic. For example:

> **Textbook definition of universal values**: "ethical principles that apply everywhere despite differences in time, geography, and culture" (Byars & Stanberry, 2019)
>
> **Paraphrased definition**: In ethics, universal values are the beliefs and standards which apply in all places, historical eras, and societies (Byars & Stanberry, 2019).

However, a direct quotation is preferable if there is a technical definition that you do not want to change because a paraphrase might be less accurate. For example:

> In physics, work is defined as "the product of the component of the force in the direction of motion times the distance through which the force acts" (Urone & Hinrichs, 2012).

In other situations, a source's definition may be so elegant or interesting that you want to preserve the original language, such as Carolyn Miller's well-known definition of genre as "typified rhetorical actions based in recurrent situations" (Miller, 1984, p. 159).

Sometimes, it can be difficult to decide whether definitions are shared knowledge (which do not need quotation marks and citations) or specific to a source, which would require paraphrasing or quoting and citing. For example, a Google Scholar search for a definition of the term "body-mass index" ("weight in kilograms divided by height in meters squared") revealed more than 16,000 exact matches, suggesting that a source is not needed because knowledge of this term is broadly shared. If in doubt, try searching for the term or asking an expert in the field.

If you quote a dictionary definition exactly, however, always use quotation marks. For example, the Merriam-Webster dictionary defines a paraphrase as "a restatement of a text, passage, or work giving the meaning in another form."

See the Online Source Use Appendix for more advice on paraphrasing and quotation.

Language Box: Defining Verbs

The verb *define* is very flexible and can be used with a direct quotation or paraphrase:

- Media multitasking **is defined as** "the simultaneous use of and switching between unrelated forms of media (e.g., tablet, smartphone, computer, smartwatch, etc.)" (Lopez et al., 2018).
- Lopez et al. (2018) **define** media multitasking **as** using different devices at the same time.
- **As defined by** Lopez et al. (2018), media multitasking is "the simultaneous use of and switching between unrelated forms of media."

Other options include:

- [term] **means** [definition]
- [term] **refers to** [definition]
- [definition] **is referred to as** [term]
- [source] **calls** [term] [definition]
- [definition] **is called** [term]
- [definition] **is known as** [term]

Note that the choice of verb and form (passive or active) allows you to focus the sentence on the term, the definition, or the source of the definition. The verb tense also makes a difference: present simple (*is defined as*) suggests an uncontested definition, whereas *has been defined* (present perfect tense) suggests that different people may define the term differently. You can also control your level of confidence in the definition by using modal verbs and adverbs:

- [term] is **sometimes** defined as [definition]
- [term] **can/may/could** be defined as [definition]
- [term] is **commonly / sometimes / now** known as [definition]

Activity 3.5: Practice the Language

How would you complete these definitions using verbs from the Language Box? Try to use a different verb for every example. Add a modal verb or adverb if appropriate.

1. Demography _____________ the study of population.
2. Development that occurs without damaging the natural environment _____________ sustainable development.
3. E-waste _____________ old devices and machines that are thrown away.
4. A person who has been forced to leave their home country due to disaster or conflict ________________ a refugee.
5. The level of an organization immediately below the senior executives _____________ middle management.
6. A small business _____________ an independent business with fewer than 500 employees.

Review your definition in Writing Task 3.2. Can you improve it by using any of the verbs from the Language Box?

Contested Definitions

You have already seen that some definitions require more than a sentence because they comprise several categories. Other terms are difficult to define because experts disagree or define the terms in different ways. We call these **contested definitions**. When writing about such terms, you will often want to discuss the range of possible meanings. Depending on the task, you might select a working definition from your sources. Here is an example of a contested definition from a textbook on intercultural communication (Jason et al., 2019):

> *Culture* is an important dimension of diversity for community psychologists to examine. In general, culture has been challenging to define, with modern definitions viewing culture as a dynamic concept that changes both individuals and societies together over time. Further, culture in today's society refers to more than just cultural and ethnic

groups but also includes racial groups, religious groups, sexual minority groups, socio-economic groups, nation-states, and corporations. While numerous definitions for culture are available, there are key defining components, such as shared meanings and shared experiences by individuals in a group that are passed down over time with each generation. That is, cultures have shared beliefs, values, practices, definitions, and other elements that are expressed through family socialization, formal schooling, shared language, social roles, and norms for feeling, thinking, and acting (Cohen, 2009).

In this paragraph, the author rejects a simple definition of culture ("just cultural and ethnic groups") and recognizes that "numerous definitions for culture are available." However, after synthesizing all these definitions, the textbook writer chooses to use Cohen's (2009) "key defining components" of culture, as paraphrased in the last sentence.

Activity 3.6: Plan a Contested Definition

Read these definitions of plagiarism, an important concept in North American universities. In a group, discuss which definitions are similar and which contain ideas or attitudes that are not found in the other texts.

Text A: "to steal and pass off (the ideas or words of another) as one's own: use (another's production) without crediting the source" (*Merriam-Webster Dictionary*)

Text B: "plagiarism is an act of fraud. It involves both stealing someone else's work and lying about it afterward." (plagiarism.org)

Text C: "In an instructional setting, plagiarism occurs when a writer deliberately uses someone else's language, ideas, or other original (not common-knowledge) material without acknowledging its source." (Kent State University)

Text D: "Plagiarism is the inclusion of someone else's words, ideas, images, or data as one's own. When a student submits academic work that includes another's words, ideas, images, or data, whether published or unpublished, the source of that information must be acknowledged with complete and accurate references and, if verbatim statements are included, with quotation marks as well. By submitting work as one's own, a student certifies the originality of all material not otherwise acknowledged. Plagiarism includes, but is not limited to:

1. The quotation or other use of another person's words, ideas, opinions, thoughts or theories (even if paraphrased into one's own words) without acknowledgment of the source; or

2. The quotation or other use of facts, statistics or other data or materials (including images) that are not clearly common knowledge without acknowledgment of the source." (University of Delaware Code of Conduct)

Text E: "*Plagiarism* is defined as the use of work or concepts contributed by other individuals without proper attribution or citation. Unique ideas or materials taken from another source for either written or oral use must be fully acknowledged in academic work to be graded." (Carnegie Mellon University Academic Integrity Policy)

Text F: "Plagiarism is defined as the act of incorporating ideas, words, or specific substance of another, whether purchased, borrowed, or otherwise obtained, and submitting same to the university as one's own work to fulfill academic requirements without giving credit to the appropriate source. Plagiarism shall include but not be limited to:

- submitting work, either in part or in whole, completed by another.
- omitting footnotes for ideas, statements, facts, or conclusions that belong to another.
- omitting quotation marks when quoting directly from another, whether it be a paragraph, sentence, or part thereof.
- close and lengthy paraphrasing of the writings of another.
- submitting another person's artistic works, such as musical compositions, photographs, paintings, drawings, or sculptures.
- submitting as one's own work papers purchased from research companies."

(San Diego State University Policy)

Text G: "Plagiarism is the representation of a source's words or ideas as one's one. Plagiarism occurs when a writer fails to supply quotation marks for exact quotations; fails to cite the sources of his or her ideas; or adopts the phrasing of his or her sources, with changes in grammar or word choice. Plagiarism takes three different forms—cheating, non-attribution of sources, and patchwriting." *Patchwriting* is further defined as "writing passages that are not copied exactly but that have nevertheless been borrowed from another source, with some changes" (Howard, 1995).

Which text(s) incorporate these ideas and attitudes in their definition of plagiarism?

a. Plagiarism is a criminal behavior: ___________

b. Some types of weak paraphrasing can be plagiarism: ______________

c. Plagiarism is always a form of cheating: ____________

d. Cheating is a category of plagiarism: ________________

e. Plagiarism applies to work submitted for a grade or course requirement: ____________

f. Common knowledge is excluded from the definition of plagiarism: ___________

g. Plagiarism is always deliberate: _____________

h. Plagiarism may be deliberate or accidental: ______________

i. The purpose of plagiarism policies is to ensure that students' work is original: ________

j. Plagiarism applies to non-written university assignments: _______________

k. It is sufficient to cite the source of words and ideas to avoid plagiarism: _______

Activity 3.7: Complete a Model Contested Definition

How would you complete this contested definition with references to the texts in Activity 3.6? Use informal citations (e.g., San Diego State University; plagiarism.org).

Although plagiarism is widely accepted as a serious issue for students in U.S. higher education, the term is not consistently defined. Definitions vary from highly legal to more educational. On one extreme, plagiarism is presented as criminal activity: theft (Merriam-Webster's dictionary) or even "fraud" (①__________________). From this perspective, the plagiarist is guilty of "stealing someone else's work and lying about it afterward" (plagiarism.org). These definitions leave no doubt that plagiarism is always an intentional form of cheating. Some university policies support this view. For example, at Kent State University, plagiarism occurs when a student "deliberately" misuses source material.

However, at other universities, the plagiarism policy focuses more on the mechanics of source use, emphasizing the importance of citation, quotation, and even footnotes (University of Delaware; ②__________________; ③__________________). This approach aligns with Howard's (1995) explanation that there are three different forms of plagiarism: deliberate cheating, a lack of proper referencing, and "patchwriting." Patchwriting is broader than the dictionary definition of plagiarism because it refers to weak paraphrasing, or making minor changes to a source text. Patchwriting is included in some universities' plagiarism policies (e.g., ④__________________), while others are more concerned with use of exact wording or missing citations (e.g., ⑤__________________). Some policies make exceptions for "common knowledge" (⑥__________________; ⑦__________________), and Carnegie Mellon University appears to suggest that a student can only be accused of plagiarism in graded assignments.

The writer could conclude this contested definition in different ways depending on the purpose of the writing task. Match the suggested conclusions with the contexts from the list and discuss the reasons for your answers. Context options are:

policy proposal research paper introduction short-answer test question.

a. In conclusion, since there is so much variation, students should take care to fully understand their university or college's plagiarism policy and pay careful attention when using sources in their writing and other assignments.

b. Because the definitions are confusing, our university should revise its policy to clearly explain our understanding of plagiarism.

c. The purpose of this study is to address this variation by investigating universities', faculty's, and students' understanding of plagiarism.

WRITING TASK 3.3: Contested Definition

A. Choose a contested term from the list, your current reading, or another class, and plan a short paper of one or two paragraphs summarizing as many different definitions as you can find. Optionally, conclude by saying which definition is most useful or should be preferred, in your opinion.

- ☐ excellent teaching
- ☐ a successful college, university, or graduate student
- ☐ a good leader
- ☐ severe asthma
- ☐ genre
- ☐ the sharing economy

B. Before you write, consider these components of the Rhetorical Planning Wheel that are relevant to the task.

1. **Audience**: How much does the reader know about the topic?
2. **Purpose**: What is your goal in this text?

3. **Sources**: Who defines this term differently? What are appropriate sources to support the different definitions?
4. **Structure**: What is the best way to organize the different definitions in your paper?
5. **Language**: Which language strategies from this unit can you use?
6. **Conventions**: How does your instructor want you to cite sources in this task?

C. Peer Review: After you draft your contested definition, share it with one or two partners. Use these questions to give peer feedback:

1. What are the different definitions of the contested term?
2. Can you easily identify which sources agree with each other and which disagree?
3. Is the information well organized?
4. Are the sources cited, paraphrased, and/or quoted appropriately?
5. What can the writer do to improve the definition?

D. Self-Review: Revise your definition using your peers' feedback. Have you done everything on this checklist?

- ☐ I have used several appropriate sources that define the term in different ways.
- ☐ I have clearly structured the different definitions.
- ☐ I have cited, paraphrased, and quoted correctly.
- ☐ I have used relative clauses, defining verbs, and glosses correctly, if appropriate.
- ☐ I have concluded by saying which definition is most useful or should be preferred for some reason.

What else do you need to work on? Make further revisions to your definition if necessary.

Process Explanations

Another group of extended definitions describe **processes**: either the process of an event that happened in the past (e.g., the events leading to the 2020 pandemic), the stages in a natural phenomenon (e.g., the water cycle), or the steps you took to conduct a piece of research (e.g., the Methods section of a research paper). Process explanations describe **how** something happens or happened.

Activity 3.8: Analyze Process Explanations

Read the excerpts from two longer texts: Text A is from the Methods section of an undergraduate research study on the use of American Sign Language (ASL). Text B is from an online article summarizing research on how the body protects itself from cold weather. As you read, think about the sequence of stages in each process. Then discuss the questions.

Text A: (Shipley & Cripps, 2018)

Pre- and post-research questionnaires were used to assess the professionals at the beginning and end of the research process. The SLP's [Speech-Language Pathologist's] interviews were conducted through oral/spoken language. The ASL [American Sign Language] specialist's interviews were conducted through ASL. All interviews occurred one-on-one with the researcher. The researcher video-recorded the interviews with the professionals and took notes after reviewing the videotaped interviews to select certain information following the three research questions.

During the in-person observations, field notes were collected by the primary investigator. The observational data was collected approximately once a week over the span of six to seven hours for three months during a semester. After conducting the observations, the researcher reviewed her field notes to analyse and report the selected professional-student interactions that reflect the research questions in this study.

Text B: (Smith, 2019)

Your blood flows through your body carrying nutrients, oxygen and other important substances. This delivery system also brings heat from the muscles to the skin, where it's released. When you enter a cold environment, your body redistributes blood to the body, protecting and maintaining the warmth of the vital organs there. At the same time, your body reduces blood flow to the skin. Narrowing the roads to the skin means less heat can make the journey, so less heat is lost to the environment. And minimizing how much blood goes to the skin – which is in closest proximity to the cold – means you can hold onto more of your internal heat longer.

1. **What is the structure of the information in each of the texts (e.g., process of an event, steps in a procedure, or stages in a phenomenon)?**
2. **Which words and phrases help the reader follow the sequence of the processes?**
3. **Look at the subjects and main verbs in each sentence. What differences between the two texts do you notice? What aspects of the context may explain these differences (see Unit 2)?**

Language Box: Process Connectors

Connectors are words and phrases that make an explicit transition or logical connection between ideas, such as *and, because, however, due to*. When you choose connectors, you need to pay attention to **form**, **function**, and **context**. The connectors in this Language Box help you connect stages in a process. Other Language Boxes in this book list connectors with other functions, such as cause and effect.

There are four grammatical categories of connectors. Each type requires a different sentence structure and makes different types of logical connections:

1. **Coordinating conjunctions** (e.g., *and, but, or, so*) join independent clauses to make sentences. Use a comma before the conjunction unless the subject or verb is missing from the second clause. The two clauses are equally important, so coordinating conjunctions are especially useful for listing ideas or stages in a process.
   - Narrowing the roads to the skin means less heat can make the journey**, so** less is lost to the environment.
   - The researcher recorded the interviews, **and** an assistant took notes.

2. **Subordinating conjunctions** (e.g., *because, when, while, before, after*) join an independent clause with a dependent clause. Most writers use a comma only when the dependent clause starts the sentence. The independent clause carries the main idea of the sentence or stage in the process. The dependent clause adds information such as time, reason, or condition that explains the step in the process.

   - **When** you enter a cold environment, your body redistributes blood to the body.
   - The surveys were distributed **after** the course had ended.

3. **Sentence connectors** (e.g., *first, then, next, also, in addition, however*) show the relationship between ideas in two separate sentences. Do not join sentences with a comma and a sentence connector. Be sure to choose the sentence connector that expresses the correct sequence of events in the process.

   - **At the same time**, your body reduces blood flow to the skin.
   - **Then**, the surveys were distributed.
   - ***INCORRECT:** Most participants answered all the questions, **however** some of them did not complete the survey.

4. **Phrase connectors** (e.g., *during, because of, due to, in the process of*) must be followed by a noun, pronoun, or *-ing* verb. Like sentence connectors, phrase connectors show the relationship of ideas across separate sentences. Note that some words can be used as subordinating conjunctions or phrase connectors (e.g., *before, after*).

   - **During the observations**, field notes were collected.
   - **After conducting the observations**, the researcher reviewed her field notes.

For more information on the grammatical terms in this Language Box, see the Grammar Glossary.

Activity 3.9: Practice the Language

Complete the sentences about the water cycle with connectors from the Language Box that are logically and grammatically appropriate.

1. __________ water evaporates from the ocean, it lowers the surface temperature.
2. Oceans reduce the effect of global warming __________ they absorb heat from the atmosphere.
3. Water vapor is carried by the atmosphere __________ it condenses as clouds and falls as rain.
4. Water mostly evaporates from tropical areas with few clouds. __________, rain and snow occur in places that are far away from the oceans.
5. __________ falling as rain, the water flows into rivers.
6. __________, the rivers flow into the oceans.

WRITING TASK 3.4: Explain a Process

A. Choose a process that you are familiar with or that you can easily research. You might explain how something works or how to do something in your major, your educational institution, or your home community. Alternatively, you could explain a recipe from your family or home culture. Write two *separate* explanations for two *different* situations (that is, you will write two explanations, each for a different audience and context). For instance, you might choose two situations from the list or your own ideas.

- ☐ an email to a friend or family member
- ☐ a traditional or family recipe
- ☐ the Introduction or Methods section of a research paper
- ☐ a general-interest print or online magazine
- ☐ instruction manual, laboratory handbook, or user guide
- ☐ a test question in a college or university class
- ☐ your approach to an academic writing assignment

B. Go online to the companion website and download the chart for this task. Complete the chart with an analysis of the Rhetorical Planning Wheel components for each explanation you are planning. How are the components similar and different in the two genres?

C. Peer Review: Draft your two explanations and share them with one or two partners. Use these questions to give peer feedback:

1. Is each text appropriate for its audience and context?
2. Is the writer's role clear and appropriate?
3. Is each text clearly organized? Can the intended reader easily follow the explanation?
4. Has the writer defined any terms that need definition?
5. Did the writer use connectors effectively?
6. How else could the writer improve these texts?

D. Self-Review: Revise your two explanations using your peers' feedback. Have you done everything on this checklist?

- ☐ Each explanation is suitable for its audience in its structure, language choices, and conventions.
- ☐ Each explanation clearly explains the process using logically and grammatically correct connectors.
- ☐ I have defined technical terms that the readers might not know.

What else do you need to work on? Make further revisions to your explanation if necessary.

Cause-and-Effect Explanations

The final type of explanation discussed in this unit asks you to write about causes and/or effects. In these explanations, you are explaining **why** something happens or happened (known as the **phenomenon**). While you may be asked to make an argument for particular causes or effects, usually the purpose of these assignments is to **explain** all the relevant causes or effects. These texts go beyond process explanations by explaining why and not just describing how.

Language Box: Cause-and-Effect Language

There are many language choices that can express cause and effect, including all four categories of connectors as well certain verbs and nouns (see pages 70–71):

- Coordinating conjunctions: *so, for*
- Subordinating conjunctions: *because, since, as*
- Sentence connectors: *therefore, thus, as a result, consequently, for this reason*, etc.
- Phrase connectors: *due to, because of, as a result of*, etc.
- Verbs: *lead to, result in, come about, produce, cause, make something happen, change, affect, stem from*, etc.
- Nouns: *result, cause, effect, consequence, outcome, impact*, etc.

Activity 3.10: Analyze Cause-and-Effect Explanations

Read these cause-and-effect explanations from a business ethics textbook, a biology textbook, and a college success textbook. As you read, think about the ways that the writers signal the causes and effects. Then discuss the questions.

A. Acculturation refers to the cultural transmission and socialization process that stems from cultural exchange. The effects of this blending of cultures appear in both the native (original) culture and the host (adopted) culture. Historically, acculturation has often been the result of military or political conquest. Today, it also comes about through economic development and the worldwide reach of the media. (Byars & Stanberry, 2018)

B. Genetic diversity in a population comes from two main mechanisms: mutation and sexual reproduction. Mutation, a change in DNA, is the ultimate source of new alleles, or new genetic variation in any population. The genetic changes that mutation causes can have one of three outcomes on the phenotype. A mutation affects the organism's phenotype in a way that gives it reduced fitness—lower likelihood of survival or fewer offspring. A mutation may produce a phenotype with a beneficial effect on fitness. Many mutations will also have no effect on the phenotype's fitness. We call these neutral mutations. (Clark, Douglas, & Choi, 2018)

C. If someone tries to tell you that test anxiety is *all in your head,* they're sort of right. Our thinking is a key element of anxiety of any sort. On the other hand, test anxiety can manifest itself in other parts of our bodies as well. You may feel queasy or light-headed if you are experiencing test anxiety. At its worst, test anxiety can cause its sufferers to experience several unpleasant conditions including nausea and shortness of breath. Some people may feel as though they may throw up, faint, or have a heart attack, none of which would make going into a testing situation a pleasant idea. (Baldwin, 2020)

1. **Use the Cause-and-Effect Language Box and a dictionary to identify the language choices in each text that show causes and effects.**
2. **Which of the texts describe causes? What are the causes?**
3. **Which of the texts describe effects? What are the effects?**

Activity 3.11: Write a Cause-and-Effect Explanation

Read these sentences that describe causes and effects of the decline of traditional retail shopping. Does each sentence contain a cause or an effect?

1. **Online shopping has grown dramatically.**
2. **More consumers have moved away from downtown areas where many retail stores are located.**
3. **Many department stores were too big and paying high rent, which made them unprofitable.**
4. **Employment opportunities have shifted from well-paying retail jobs to lower-paying warehouse jobs.**
5. **Some retailers have developed websites that support the stores.**
6. **There are food deserts (neighborhoods without access to fresh-food stores) in some inner-city areas.**

7. Certain e-commerce sites have even opened brick-and-mortar stores to take advantage of the benefits of traditional retail.

Now rearrange the sentences and add appropriate cause-and-effect language to write an explanation of this phenomenon. Your paragraph could start with this sentence:

> Brick-and-mortar, or physical, stores are in decline in the United States and other countries.

Share your paragraph with a partner. Did you make different choices in organizing your explanation? Discuss the differences.

WRITING TASK 3.3: Answering Test Questions

A lot of test questions, such as short-answer or ID questions, ask for an explanation of a concept you studied in the course (see Unit 1) requiring a definition, process, or cause-and-effect explanation. Here is one way to structure an explanation when answering a test question:

- ☐ **Definition:** one-sentence definition plus a taxonomy, process, or cause
- ☐ **Example(s):** one or more good examples; if you write a taxonomy, you could give an example of each category
- ☐ **Significance:** why is the concept important? What are its effects? Does everyone agree with it?

A. Read this example of a response to a test question which you might find in a course on linguistics or sociology. The question is: What is the Sapir-Whorf hypothesis? As you read, identify the **definition, example,** and **significance**. Discuss your findings with a partner or small group.

> The Sapir-Whorf hypothesis is a theory of language and culture which claims that the language a person speaks determines the way they think about the world. According to Whorf, because languages have different features and words, the speakers of those languages see the world differently. For example, some languages use direction words (north, south, east, west) instead of prepositions like *in front of* or *behind.* As a result, people who speak those languages have an excellent sense of direction. Today, many linguists criticize the Sapir-Whorf hypothesis because it does not explain linguistic variation and can lead to harmful stereotypes about cultures.

B. Now choose one of the questions listed and conduct some quick research so that you can answer it. If you are using a textbook for another class that has practice short-answer questions, you could choose one of those instead.

- ☐ What are Porter's Five Forces?
- ☐ What is cultural lag?
- ☐ What is the difference between a technophile and a Luddite?
- ☐ What are the United Nations' Sustainable Development Goals?
- ☐ What types of objects orbit the sun in our solar system?

C. Plan your answer by taking notes on the definition, one or more examples, and the significance.

D. Discuss your plan with a partner. Ask and answer questions to improve your answers.

E. Write your response in one paragraph. Be sure to read your response carefully and correct any errors before submitting it to your instructor.

Pedagogical Genre: Extended Definition

An extended definition combines a one-sentence definition with additional information about the topic, which may include processes, causes, effects, history, applications, and other relevant details to provide a more complete understanding of a complex topic. Encyclopedia entries are examples of extended definitions, and you will often read other examples in textbooks. You may need to write an extended definition as part of a longer paper or in a test question asking you to display your knowledge of the course material.

A. Read this extended definition of a supercomputer and identify the categories of information.

applications
contrast with something familiar
disadvantages
history
one-sentence definition example
physical characteristics

A supercomputer is a type of very high-performance computer that is immensely quick in calculating and processing large amounts of data. Unlike desktop or laptop computers, supercomputers can have hundreds of thousands of processors and are more powerful than an ordinary user would ever need. The Blue Waters supercomputer at the University of Illinois can perform the same number of calculations in a second that would take a human millions or even billions of years (NCSA, 2020). The first supercomputers were created in the 1960s by governments for military purposes and were much more powerful than the early computers available for commercial use (Graham et al., 2005). Today's supercomputers can be massive and much more powerful. For example, one machine in a physics laboratory in Tennessee covers the area of two tennis courts and is believed to be the fastest supercomputer in the world (Bryner, 2018).

Supercomputers are mostly used by researchers in fields such as cyber-security, astronomy, meteorology, biology, and physics. Blue Waters, for instance, is simulating black holes, studying the COVID-19 virus, and developing "smart farms" that will produce fewer greenhouse gasses (Wurth, 2020). Supercomputers are very expensive to design, build, and maintain: the supercomputer in Tennessee cost over $200 million (Bryner, 2018). In addition, access to supercomputers may be limited to governments and senior researchers. However, thanks to new artificial intelligence programs, supercomputers promise to make enormous contributions to science and the quality of human life.

References

Bryner, J. (2018, June 14). *This supercomputer can calculate in 1 second what would take you 6 billion years*. LiveScience. https://www.livescience.com/62827-fastest-supercomputer.html

Graham, S.L., Snir, M., & Patterson, C.A. (Eds). (2005). *Getting up to speed: The future of supercomputing.* National Academies Press.

Wurth, J. (2020, January 22). *DOE project at U of I will measure bioenergy crop carbon emissions.* https://sustainability.illinois.edu/doe-project-will-measure-bioenergy-crop-carbon-emissions/

B. A good way to organize an extended definition is from **general to specific** (Swales & Feak, 2012). What is the most general information in the extended definition of a supercomputer? What is the most specific information?

C. Choose a term from your current area of study in this or another class or one from the list.

- ☐ social media
- ☐ culture shock
- ☐ a liberal-arts education
- ☐ self-driving cars
- ☐ natural selection
- ☐ the Search for Extraterrestrial Intelligence (SETI)
- ☐ motivation
- ☐ corporate social responsibility

Now, which types of information can you include in your extended definition? Conduct online or library research if needed. You will not know or need all these categories for every topic.

1. Category
2. One-sentence definition
3. Components
4. Causes
5. Effects
6. History or development
7. Similar or contrasting concepts
8. Uses or applications
9. Examples
10. Counter-examples
11. Other information

D. Draft your extended definition in one or more paragraphs. Consider structuring your information from general to specific.

E. Peer Review: Ask one or two partners to read your extended definition. Use these questions to give peer feedback:

   1. After reading the extended definition, do you feel you fully understand the concept?
   2. What other information would help you understand it?
   3. Is any information in the definition not relevant?
   4. Is the definition text clearly organized, for example, from general to specific?
   5. What else can the writer do to improve the extended definition?

F. Self-Review: Revise your extended definition using your peers' feedback. Have you done everything on this checklist?

   - ☐ The paper starts with a one-sentence definition of the term.
   - ☐ There are enough types of information to fully define the term.
   - ☐ The information is logically organized, for example from general to specific.
   - ☐ I have used appropriate defining language.
   - ☐ I have used connectors that are logically and grammatically appropriate.

What else do you need to work on? Make further revisions to your extended definition if necessary.

Genre in Action: Language Blog

Most dictionaries host a blog in which they discuss new words or new meanings of words. Many of them also choose a "word of the year" and write blog posts about it. These articles are good examples of explanatory writing about specialist information for a general audience.

You can read examples of these posts by visiting the website of any major dictionary or searching for "word of the year." Although there is considerable variation, you should notice some or all of these types of information, but not necessarily in this order.

- ❒ definition of the word, including older meanings if relevant
- ❒ history of the word, including its etymology (roots)
- ❒ explanation of the process by which it acquired a new meaning
- ❒ reasons the word was chosen
- ❒ contexts in which the word is used, and who uses it
- ❒ other words that it is similar to (or different from)
- ❒ social, cultural, or historical trends that are reflected in the development of the word (i.e., possible reasons why the word has emerged or why you think it is important)
- ❒ effects of using this word
- ❒ related words and phrases with their meanings

Here is an example of an entry from dictionary.com's blog:

adulting [uh-DULT-ing]

What does adulting mean?

Adulting is an informal term to describe behavior that is seen as responsible and grown-up. This behavior often involves meeting the mundane demands of independent and professional living, such as paying bills and running errands.

Where does adulting come from?

Adulting is based on a verbal extension of the word *adult* (i.e., "to adult" or "behave in the manner of an adult"). While there are older, unrelated instances of the form *adulting*, contemporary use began on social media in 2008–2009. The American Dialect Society nominated *adult* as a "Most Creative" word of 2015, and the term saw a major surge in 2016; its Twitter use increased by 700%.

The concept behind *adulting* may stem from the fact that members of the rising millennial generation are going through major life stages (such as getting married, having children, buying a home, etc.) at much later ages than previous generations. This has caused the term to become somewhat ridiculed in popular media. It doesn't help that there are even classes that teach elementary adult skills ranging from personal finance to how to properly fold laundry—skills once traditionally taught in home economics.

Who uses adulting?

Adulting is often used by millennial-aged people to self-consciously and humorously acknowledge the performance of boring tasks associated with being an adult, frequently in the form of the hashtag "#adulting." Others may ironically use the term to mock millennials's delayed mastery of such responsibilities.

Some cultural critics have argued that the entire concept of *adulting* is a broader condemnation of society as seen by the rising generation of young adults who equate "being an adult" with participation in meaningless, capitalistic labor.

A. Choose a word you would like to write about. It might be:

- ☐ A new word or new meaning of a word that has recently started to spread;
- ☐ A word, phrase, or acronym that has a particular meaning in your community or on your campus;
- ☐ A word that has a particular meaning in your field of study that the general public might not know;
- ☐ A word from another language or variety of English that users of standard English might be interested in.

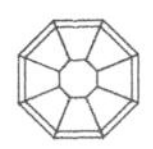

B. Plan your blog post for a dictionary or language website about your word using questions from the Rhetorical Planning Wheel.

1. **Writer:** What is your position, role, or persona as writer?
2. **Audience**: Who will read the text? What do the readers already know? What do they need to know from your text?
3. **Purpose**: Why do people read and write this genre?
4. **Context**: Where will people find this blog post?
5. **Structure**: What patterns of organization are possible? Approximately how long should your explanation be?
6. **Language**: What level of technicality should you use? Should you write impersonally or interactively? How confident are you about your interpretations?
7. **Sources**: What kind of information should you include? Where will you find it?
8. **Conventions**: What are the conventions of the blog where this text might appear? How do you refer to other sources in a blog?

C. Conduct research. Search the internet and (if relevant) academic databases for examples of the word in use or discussions about the development of the word or phrase. Keep track of the information you find and consider how you will cite and use it. For example, in an academic paper, you will need to use a formal reference style. However, on a blog, a link to the original source might be more appropriate.

See the Online Source Use Appendix for advice on finding and evaluating sources from the internet and library databases.

D. Draft your explanation, keeping the rhetorical planning notes in mind.

E. Peer Review: Ask one or two partners to read your blog post. Use these questions to give peer feedback:

1. Do you understand the word that is featured in the blog? What helps you to understand the word?
2. What other information would you like to know if any?
3. Is the blog post clearly and effectively organized? What is the organization?
4. Is the register appropriate for the genre?
5. How could the writer improve the post?

F. Self-Review: Revise your blog post using your peers' feedback. Have you done everything on this checklist?

- ☐ The post provides enough interesting details about the word.
- ☐ The post has a clear and logical structure.
- ☐ I have provided citations or links to any sources I used.
- ☐ The post is written is a style that is accessible to a general audience.

What else do you need to work on? Make further revisions to your blog post if necessary.

References

Adulting (n.d). In *dictionary.com slang dictionary*. Retrieved September 26, 2021 from https://www.dictionary.com/e/slang/adulting/

Baldwin, A. (2020). *College success*. Open Stax. https://openstax.org/details/books/college-success

Byars, S. M., & Stanberry, K. (2018). *Business ethics*. Open Stax. https://openstax.org/details/books/business-ethics

Clark, M. A., Douglas, M., & Choi, J. (2018). *Biology* (2nd ed.). Open Stax. https://openstax.org/details/books/biology-2e

Greenlaw, S. A., & Shapiro, D. (2017). *Principles of economics* (2nd ed.). Open Stax. https://openstax.org/details/books/principles-economics-2e

Howard, R.M. (1995). Plagiarisms, authorships, and the academic death penalty. *College English, 57*, 788-806.

Jason, L. A., Glantsman, O., O'Brien, J. F., & Ramian, K. N. (2019). *Introduction to community psychology*. https://press.rebus.community/introductiontocommunitypsychology/

Lopez, R.B., Salinger, J.M., Heatherton, T.F., & Wagner, D.D. (2018). Media multitasking is associated with altered processing of incidental, irrelevant cues during person perception. *BMC Psychology, 6*(44). https://doi-org.udel.idm.oclc.org/10.1186/s40359-018-0256-x

Miller, C. R. (1984). Genre as social action. *Quarterly Journal of Speech, 70*, 151–167. https://doi.org/10.1080/00335638409383686

Shipley, E. P., & Cripps, J. H. (2018). Exploring signed language pathology: A case study of professionals working with deaf students who have delay/disorders in signed language development. *Reinvention: An International Journal of Undergraduate Research, 11*(2). https://warwick.ac.uk/fac/cross_fac/iatl/reinvention/archive/volume11issue2/Shipley

Smith, J.E. (2019). *It's cold! A physiologist explains how to keep your body feeling warm*. The Conversation. http://theconversation.com/its-cold-a-physiologist-explains-how-to-keep-your-bodyfeeling-warm-108816

Urone, P. P., & Hinrichs, R. (2012). *College physics*. Open Stax. https://openstax.org/details/books/college-physics

4 Summarize

Goals

- ❒ Write academic summaries of various lengths and types: informational, problem/solution, and argument, responding to classroom tasks
- ❒ Chart texts for purpose, main ideas, and language use
- ❒ Understand the relationships between a source text and a summary
- ❒ Effectively use category nouns
- ❒ Pedagogical Genre: Write a summary of an academic article
- ❒ Genre in Action: Write a press release

What Is the Action?

Summarizing may be the most common of all the actions you will take in academic writing. A **summary** is a text that is shorter than the original, capturing the original's main ideas in your own words. However, summaries come in a variety of types, depending on the writer's purpose, the audience, the context, and the task at hand. Depending on the occasion, you might write:

- ❒ a stand-alone summary of an assigned reading
- ❒ a short note about an article for an annotated bibliography
- ❒ a summary of your class lecture notes as you prepare for an exam or paper
- ❒ a summary of a film, activity, or book, followed by a response
- ❒ a summary of an online class discussion for a classmate who has been ill
- ❒ a summary of what you have written (i.e., an abstract or executive summary)

Summaries also come in a variety of lengths. In an exam, you might write a one-sentence summary of a key term or idea. A stand-alone summary assignment will often have a required length. Abstracts may be limited to 75 or 150 words. Therefore, it is important to understand the assignment and plan your writing carefully.

Examples of assignment prompts that require or include summary:

- ❒ Write an annotated bibliography with a one-paragraph summary of each source.
- ❒ Find an article about a biological issue that interests you and write a one- or two-page summary in your own words.
- ❒ A college psychology professor has solicited your help in deciding whether or not this article should be included in a required reading list for her research methods course. Summarize the main idea of the article in three sentences or less, critique the method described in the article, and recommend that the article be included or omitted from the professor's required reading list.

Activity 4.1: What Do You Know?

Read these statements about summaries. Do you think they are always, sometimes, or never true? Discuss your answers with a partner or small group.

1. Summaries are much shorter than the original text.
2. A summary should indicate the source of the text.
3. A summary should be mostly in your own words.
4. The information in the summary should be structured in the same way as in the original text.
5. You can quote words directly from the original text in your summary.

Charting

Charting is an activity where you identify the function of each sentence, paragraph, or section of a text (**what it does**) and the content to be summarized (**what it says**). Charting is an important first step in summary writing because it shows you the structure of the original text as well as what the writer is **doing** and **saying**. As you will learn, different genres (types of text) often have different typical structures, so you need to approach each text with an open mind and not expect, for example, the thesis (the major claim) to always be stated at the beginning.

When you chart a text, you look at each section (sentence, paragraph, group of paragraphs, or sub-heading) and write:

- ❐ One or two verbs that indicate what this section of the text is *doing*.
- ❐ A sentence that summarizes what the section is *saying* (that is, the main idea).
- ❐ Key words that helped you find the purpose and main idea of the section.

For example, here is the first paragraph from an article by a professor of psychology in response to the question "Is 'technology addiction' a valid diagnosis?" (Ferguson, 2018):

> There is little question that a small percentage of individuals, likely 1 percent or less, overuse technology. But it is less clear that this is due to an addiction in the same sense as over-dependence on alcohol, nicotine or illicit drugs.

Here is how we might chart this short section:

WHAT IT DOES	WHAT IT SAYS	KEY WORDS
Challenge or question an idea	Although a small number of people use technology too much, it is wrong to call them "addicted."	*Little question, small percentage, but, less clear*

This is an introductory paragraph, but the purpose is more than just to introduce the article: the author is answering the question by challenging the use of the word *addiction* to refer to the overuse of technology. The phrase *there is little question* shows that the author recognizes a widely held idea. The conjunction *but* at the start of the next sentence shows that the author strongly disagrees, and he sets up his actual argument by telling us that *it is less clear* that technology is addictive.

TABLE 4.1:
Common Text Functions

Explain	*Summarize*	*Synthesize*
Define a term Describe a process Give an example Tell a story	Summarize research Quote/cite an expert	Compare ideas Contrast ideas Connect ideas
Report and Interpret	***Argue***	***Respond***
Present data Interpret data Draw conclusions	Make an argument Support a claim Challenge an idea	Give an opinion Support an opinion Evaluate an idea
	Analyze	
	Analyze a concept Apply a theory to practice Categorize information	

There are many possible verbs you might use to chart the functions of a text because writers take many actions. Some examples of functions that align with the essential actions of academic writing are shown in Table 4.1.

Activity 4.2: Charting Practice

A. Read the rest of the article about technology addiction from the pro/con section of a report on *CQ Researcher*, a well-respected source for unbiased research reports, often found in academic libraries (Ferguson, 2018).

> ①There is little question that a small percentage of individuals, likely 1 percent or less, overuse technology. But it is less clear that this is due to an addiction in the same sense as over-dependence on alcohol, nicotine (cigarettes) or illicit drugs.
>
> ②Technology use doesn't have the same biochemical processes as substance use, and there are no clear parallels to the tolerance (needing more to get the same high) and withdrawal (physical symptoms that result from stopping use) typical of substance abuse. Some scholars have tried to find ways to make tolerance and withdrawal fit into conceptualizations of technology misuse, but these don't seem to work well.

③One misunderstanding arises from the observation that technology use activates some of the same centers of the brain involved with pleasure as does substance abuse. However, these centers are involved in anything fun, so finding that a fun activity (whether technology use, exercising, eating a candy bar, getting an "A" on a test, etc.) activates these areas, just as cocaine and methamphetamine [two illegal drugs] do, is hardly surprising. These are, in fact, natural processes.

④However, illicit substances such as methamphetamine activate these centers to a much greater degree than do normal activities such as technology or exercise. That is what makes these substances dangerous, a detail often left out of these discussions.

⑤Although groups such as the American Psychiatric Association and World Health Organization have proposed technology addiction diagnoses, these have been controversial, with many scholars opposed to such classifications. This is because current evidence suggests these are not unique disorders but rather arise as symptoms of underlying mental health problems, such as depression or attention problems.

⑥Nor is there evidence that technology is uniquely addictive, as other research has focused on everything from exercise to dance addictions. Finally, evidence is clear that on most behavioral indices, youths today are actually pretty healthy. No evidence has emerged to suggest an epidemic of tech-addicted youths.

⑦Every generation of older adults tends to freak out [=panic] about new technology and exaggerate its potential harms. This is something we understand as "moral panic theory." In the 1950s the fear was centered on comic books; in the 1980s, rock music and the game "Dungeons and Dragons."

⑧Current concerns about technology addiction, given the evidence, are better understood as a new moral panic rather than a legitimate concern supported by data.

B. You are going to chart the text in Part A.

Go online to the companion website to download the chart for this activity.

The first row of the chart has been completed for you:

PARAGRAPH(S)	WHAT DOES IT DO?	WHAT DOES IT SAY?	KEY WORDS
1	Challenges the idea of technology addiction	Although a small number of people use technology too much, it is probably not correct to call them "addicted."	*small percentage, but, less clear*

Use the verbs listed to complete the chart.

contrast	explain	support	challenge	offer an alternative	report

Paragraph 2:

Paragraph 3:

Paragraph 4:

Paragraphs 5-6:

Paragraphs 7-8:

C. Now chart a different text that you are reading in this or another class. Explain your chart to a partner or small group.

Planning a Summary

A summary is more than just a list of the actions and main ideas of a source text. It is an original piece of writing with its own writer, audience, structure, purpose, and all the other elements of the Rhetorical Planning Wheel. The ideas from the original text are like a bridge connecting the original source text to your summary.

For instance, if you had to summarize a movie in order to analyze it in a psychology class, you would have to make several choices. The movie was probably made by professional directors and actors for a broad audience for the purpose of entertaining, shocking, or scaring them. However, your summary will be written by a student in the context of a college class for your instructor with the purpose of applying principles from the course to the characters and themes of the movie. Clearly, your summary will be very different from the original movie. Similarly, a summary of a news article, research paper, or annual company report will look very different from the original text.

Activity 4.3: Rhetorical Planning

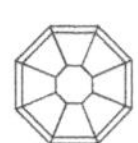

1. Look back at Ferguson's (2018) article about technology addiction in Activity 4.2. Analyze the components of the Rhetorical Planning Wheel that apply to the article. The first one has been completed for you.
   a. Context: *Written at the request of CQ Researcher for a report on internet privacy*
   b. Writer's role:
   c. Audience:
   d. Purpose:
   e. Sources/Evidence:
   f. Language:
   g. Conventions:
2. Your class assignment is to write a short summary of Ferguson's article to share with other students who have not read this article. Analyze the same components of the Rhetorical Planning Wheel for your summary task. For example, your role as a writer is as a student.
3. How does your analysis help you plan your summary? In what ways will your summary be different from the original article?
4. Here are some phrases from the original article. How could you rewrite them so that they are appropriate for the audience, context, and purpose of your summary?
   a. "Technology use doesn't have the same biochemical processes as substance use."
   b. "However, illicit substances such as methamphetamine activate these centers to a much greater degree than do normal activities such as technology or exercise."
   c. "No evidence has emerged to suggest an epidemic of tech-addicted youths."
5. How much of the language of the original text can you use in your summary? Are there any phrases that you can use without quotation marks? Are there any phrases you want to quote directly?

Refer to the Online Source Use Appendix for more advice on paraphrasing and quotation.

Functional Summary

You can turn the chart into a simple summary of a text by listing what each section of the source text does and says. This is called a **functional summary** because it focuses on the **function** of each part of the source text.

Activity 4.4: Analyze a Model

Read this functional summary, a paragraph from a longer article published by an undergraduate student (Cooper, 2014).

> ①Michaela Cullington's essay "Texting and Writing" explores the possible effect of teen texting on formal writing in school. ②Cullington lists three different hypotheses scholars pose about the correlation between the two: those who criticize texting for its negative impact on writing, those who believe texting is actually a beneficial exercise in writing, and those who see no relationship at all. ③Cullington begins her analysis with the first theory, quoting concerned teachers, citing the shocking statistic that "only 25% of high school seniors are 'proficient' writers" (90), and adding testimony from two of her former teachers. ④Cullington then explores the second take on texting and writing by providing contrasting testimony from other teachers who believe that texting is a blessing to their students' writing. ⑤Cullington retrieves support for these two opposing views from interviews and previous studies. ⑥To explore the theory that texting is irrelevant to formal writing, however, she performs her own research, gathering results from seven students, two teachers, and an analysis of students' written work. ⑦Despite the testimonial evidence against and in support of texting, Cullington's own results show that texting has "no effect, positive or negative, on [students'] writing as a result of texting" (95). ⑧Although her study supports the hypothesis that texting and writing have no relationship to one another, Cullington (and the researchers whose work she analyzed) recognizes the significance of new technology and society's evolving modes of communication.

1. **By reading each sentence or group of sentences in the summary, can you infer the functions of the source text (Cullington, 2013)? What key words did you notice?**

   Sentence 1: Cullington asked a research question. Key words: explores, possible effect

   Sentence 2:

   Sentences 3-5:

Sentence 6:

Sentence 7:

Sentence 8:

2. The first five sentences begin with the author's name. How else could these sentences be written to avoid this repetition?

WRITING TASK 4.1: Functional Summary

Use your answers to Activity 4.2 to write a functional summary of Ferguson's article. Follow the example in Activity 4.4: start by summarizing the main idea of the article and then describe each section in one or two sentences each using reporting verbs that reflect the purpose of that section. Some useful verbs may include: *ask, challenge, clarify, explain, contrast,* and *argue.* Paraphrase as much as possible.

Refer to the Online Source Use Appendix for an explanation of reporting verbs and advice on paraphrasing.

Informational Summaries

Functional summaries can sound like a **narrative** of the source text. First, the author writes about one topic; then they write about another topic, followed by another topic. While this is a good way to show you have identified the main parts of the text, it does not usually produce a very clear summary that shows a deeper understanding of the ideas. Thus, most summaries you will write in your academic classes should focus on summarizing the ideas of the text, rather than describing its structure. Since the purpose of these summaries is to communicate information from the original text rather than its functions, we call these **informational summaries.** As the organization of your summary depends on the type of text you are summarizing and the assignment you are completing, we focus in this unit on two of the most common patterns of information you will read in academic contexts: **problem-solution** and **argument** texts.

Language Box: Category Nouns

One way to organize an informational summary is to look for categories of information. For example, your source text might discuss *two problems* or *three reasons* or *four explanations*. However, the author might not directly state this, so you may have to infer the correct category by reading the text carefully.

These terms are sometimes called **categorizing nouns, general nouns,** or more technically, **enumerative nouns.** Examples include:

- The article compares two **approaches** to ....
- There are three **aspects/features/characteristics/types/properties** of ....
- The author describes four **problems / challenges / issues / difficulties**.
- The process occurs in five **stages / phases**.
- _____ has three **parts / sections / components**.
- This policy has had several **consequences / outcomes / results**.
- The author gives three **reasons** for ....
- The argument is supported by two **studies**.

Always check a dictionary to make sure the word fits your context. Note that **non-count nouns** (nouns that do not have a plural form) cannot easily be used as categorizing nouns. For example, it is not correct to write about *three evidences*, *several supports*, or *two researches.* However, you can write about *three statistics, several arguments,* or *two studies* because they are countable nouns.

Once you have established a number of categories, you can then refer to them as *first*, or *the second reason*, or *another problem*.

Activity 4.5: Practice the Language

Read these extracts and decide which categorizing nouns from the Language Box you would use in a summary.

1. Plants are adapting to climate change by regulating the amount of carbon dioxide they absorb and the amount of water they release. This may cause the soil to become more saturated with water, increase the amount of rain that runs into rivers, and eventually lead to more frequent flooding.

2. Kenneth Carter, a professor of psychology at Emory University, is fascinated by the question of why people seek out thrills, adventures, and scary experiences. His research looks into the stories of these "thrill seekers" and attempts to understand what is happening inside their heads.

3. Artificial intelligence (AI) has many applications but it has also been criticized for allowing biases to affect the analysis of data sets. For example, some AI systems have been found to discriminate against people on the basis of race. Others only have data from North America and so do not produce results relevant to other countries.

Activity 4.6: Paraphrase Practice

An essential skill in summary writing is paraphrasing because you are expected to rewrite the ideas from the source text in your own words. If you use too much of the original text, you may be accused of plagiarism, which can be a serious problem.

Use the paraphrasing techniques discussed in the Online Source Use Appendix to paraphrase these sentences from an introduction to video-game addiction in *CQ Researcher* (Ladika, 2018). As shown in the Online Appendix, you should start by identifying key words that you do not need to change, synonyms and alternate forms of other words, the logical relations between the ideas, and different ways to express those connections. The first paraphrase has been completed as an example.

1. While experts have yet to define technology overuse as an addiction, internet gaming disorder could be included in future versions of the American Psychiatric Association's *Diagnostic and Statistical Manual of Mental Disorders.*

Key words	*technology overuse, internet gaming disorder, Diagnostic and Statistical Manual of Mental Disorders*
Synonyms and alternate word forms	*experts* = psychologists; *future versions* = new editions; *included* = recognized; *addiction* = being addicted to; *define* = definition; *overuse* = excessive use of
Logical relations	*while* (concession: the author recognizes an alternative view but wants to make their own argument) → *even though, despite* (+ noun), *however, nonetheless, the lack of*
Paraphrase	New editions of the *Diagnostic and Statistical Manual of Mental Disorders* might recognize "internet gaming disorder" despite the current lack of a definition for the excessive use of technology (Ladika, 2018).

2. Some addiction specialists say the obsessive use of technology, including virtual reality headsets, can affect the brain in the same way an overdependence on alcohol or drugs does.

3. Eighth-graders who use social media heavily increase their risk of depression by 27 percent.

Language Box: Introducing Sources

A clear way to introduce a source article in a summary is **author + reporting verb (purpose of the source text) + main idea, claim, or thesis of the source article.** For example:

- Bristol (2016) **argues that** smartphones have changed communication habits.

Other options include:

- **According to** Bristol (2016), smartphones have changed communication habits.
- **In her article** "Screens and scream," Bristol (2016) **argues that** smartphones have changed communication habits.

When you introduce a source, you need to answer these questions:

1. Are you going to use an integral or non-integral citation?
2. Are you going to use first name and last name, or just last name? (In formal writing, the choice is made by your style guide: in APA style, use last names, but in MLA style, use both names.)
3. Do you need to include the title of the article? Usually, it is not necessary because you will list the title in your references, but sometimes the title might make your writing stronger and make the intent and focus of the source article clearer. If you include the title, write it in quotation marks.
4. Do you want to include the source for the article, such as *The New York Times* or the *Journal of the American Medical Association*? In most academic writing, we do not provide this information in the text itself, but sometimes you might want to emphasize that you are using a reliable source.
5. Which verb tense should you use? Summaries are often written in present tenses, but you could use past tenses to emphasize that a text was written in the past, especially if you think the ideas are no longer relevant today.

Do not use a reporting verb after *according to* since the source is already clear:

- *According to* Bristol (2016), ~~the author argues that~~ smartphones have changed communication habits.

Refer to the Online Source Use Appendix for an explanation of integral and non-integral citations, reporting verbs, and style guides.

Activity 4.7: Practice the Language

The reporting verb you use to introduce a source often tells the reader the purpose of the original article. It can also show whether you want to **align** the reader with the source (that is, show your agreement), **distance** the reader (that is, show that you do not agree), or stay **neutral** (Martin & White, 2005). Which verbs listed should be used when you want to align? Which verbs show distance? And which verbs are neutral? Explain your choices to a partner or small group.

argue	assume	claim	consider
contend	discuss	hypothesize	propose
prover	report	review	suggest

Problem-Solution Summaries

Texts that can be summarized using a problem-solution structure are very common in a number of academic disciplines, including social work, engineering, business, and all fields of medicine. They are also found in professional genres such as some opinion editorials, reports, and most proposals.

As with other types of summaries, you need to create a bridge between the original text and the summary that you are writing so that the summary you create is actually your writing but is still true to the original. Writing a summary also requires you to paraphrase ideas from the original text, except technical words or special terms used by the author, which you may need to quote.

Refer to the Online Source Use Appendix for more advice on paraphrasing and quotation.

In a problem-solution summary, you need to chart the four key functions of the source text:

Situation	What is the context or background to the problem?
Problem	What exactly is the problem? Why? For whom?
Solution(s)	What solution(s) does the author suggest?
Evaluation(s)	Does the author think the solutions will solve the problem? Why?

WRITING TASK 4.2: Problem-Solution Summary

A. Read this article about "summer loss" or "summer slide," which refers to the information and skills that students forget between the end of the school year in June and the start of the next year in August or September. Note that the original article contained many links to sources and research, which are not included here. As you read, think about the structure of a problem-solution text (situation, problem, solution, evaluation).

What Advice Articles Miss about "Summer Loss"

Kelly Chandler-Olcott
Professor for Teaching Excellence, Syracuse University
June 10, 2019, *The Conversation*

①When the end of the school year arrives, internet articles and TV talk shows sound the annual alarm about preventing summer learning loss. They advise parents to purchase hot new reads for their children, take them to museums, and sign them up for science camp.

②As a literacy educator for the past 27 years—and the parent of two teenagers—I've tried many of these recommendations myself. I understand why such tips are appealing. Who doesn't want young people to spend their summers more productively than sleeping and playing video games?

③But it's high time we question the assumptions about the so-called "summer slide."

④It's hard to blame parents for anxiety about summer loss given a century's worth of research that shows young people can lose up to several months' worth of school-year learning over summer break. Studies also show older students have greater gaps than younger students, and summer loss is greatest for low-income students. These findings are worrisome.

⑤However, the loss-prevention recommendations reflect biases because they assume an audience with disposable income, employment flexibility and English fluency that not all families have. For example, suggesting that families who can't afford summer camps create their own using online resources ignores variation in parental education, literacy levels and technology access. Also troubling is the assumption that families, not educators, should promote learning in specialized areas such as mathematics, reading and science. Although families from all walks of life promote varied kinds of learning in everyday life, most parents lack preparation to address academic subjects, and their work doesn't end just because school is out for their children.

⑥Given these complexities, I believe that solutions to the summer slide should not fall on students and their families. Instead, schools must step up to design summer-learning supports that respond to community needs. For example, schools might offer no- or low-cost programs that combine academics with a mix of activities such as dance, drama, or meditation.

⑦For four years, I served as director of a summer writing institute that was meant to ease middle schoolers' transition to high school. The three-week program was free and open to all students. Students pursued individual and collaborative projects in both print and digital forms, and guest authors from the community spoke about how and why they write.

⑧Programs like the writing institute require considerably more time and money than sending home a one-page menu of suggestions for families. But if such programs engage students without stigmatizing them and help teachers refine their craft, that investment could be well worth it.

B. Read the article again and divide it into sections: Situation, Problem, Solution 1, Evaluation 1, Solution 2, Evaluation 2. For each section, answer the questions.
   1. What does the section say?
   2. What are the key words that helped you understand what the section does and says?

C. Write a summary of the article. You could adapt the structure shown in Figure 4.1 using information from your analysis of the text.

FIGURE 4.1:
Structure of a Problem-Solution Summary

Introduce the source	Chandler-Olcott (2019) discusses the problem of ________ ________
State the situation	"Summer slide" occurs because ________
Explain the problem	This is an important problem for ________ because ________
Present current solutions	Some of the solutions to the problem of summer slide include ________
Evaluate solutions	However, these do not work for every family because ________
Present new solution	Therefore, the author recommends ________
Evaluate new solutions	According to the author, this solution is effective because ________

D. Peer Review: Ask one or two partners to read your summary. Use these questions to give peer feedback.

1. Does the summary accurately represent all the main ideas of the original text?
2. Are the sections of the problem-solution text clear for the reader?
3. Is the summary effectively paraphrased in the writer's own words?
4. What else can the writer do to improve the summary?

E. Revise your summary using your peers' feedback.

Argument Summary

In an argument summary, your focus is on the major claim (thesis) and the supporting evidence. In many cases, the role of the source writer is also important since the writer's identity may give them authority and credibility. It is a good idea to start your summary with a restatement of the author's major claim like this (the element in parentheses is optional):

> **Author (+ author's position, job, or source of authority) + reporting verb of purpose + paraphrase of the major claim or thesis**

For example:

> Ferguson (2018), a professor of psychology at Stetson University, argues that technology addiction is not a true disorder but an example of "moral panic."

Arguments are structured differently across academic disciplines. In general, however, you can summarize an argument after the thesis by identifying and explaining the author's main reasons and supporting evidence. Your conclusion, if needed, will probably paraphrase the source writer's conclusion.

Activity 4.8: Analyze a Model

Read this summary of Ferguson's argument about technology addition (Activity 4.2).

> ①Ferguson (2018), a professor of psychology at Stetson University, argues that technology addiction is not a true disorder but an example of "moral panic." ②A moral panic occurs when adults are afraid of new trends that are highly popular with the younger generation, causing them to overestimate the risk of harm. ③Excessive use of technology, which is probably very rare, is an example of this fear. ④It is not a real addiction for three reasons. ⑤Addictions greatly increase activity in certain parts of the brain that respond to enjoyment. ⑥Technology naturally engages the same parts of the brain but only in the same way that any enjoyable action does. ⑦It is only very high levels of activation associated, for example, with illegal drugs, that are considered dangerous. ⑧The second reason is that overuse of technology may be the

result of another psychological problem like depression rather than a separate condition. ⑨Finally, if technology were a real addiction, then so would be other normal teenage interests that adults are not worried about, such as exercise. ⑩Since the research does not support widespread addiction to technology and since technology does not meet the psychological definition of addiction, Ferguson concludes that there is no reason to worry about teenagers' use of technology.

Discuss these questions with a partner or group.

1. How is this summary different from the informational summary you wrote of the same text in Writing Task 4.1? Look at the components of the Rhetorical Planning Wheel to answer this question.
2. How does the writer remind the reader that this is Ferguson's argument and not the summary writer's?
3. What information does Sentence 1 include?
4. What is the purpose of Sentence 4 in the summary? Is there a sentence or paragraph that directly expresses this idea in the original text?
5. What is the purpose of Sentence 10 in the summary? Is there a sentence or paragraph that directly expresses this idea in the original text?
6. Why is the phrase "moral panic" in quotation marks in Sentence 1?
7. The chart shows some phrases from the original text and their paraphrases in the summary. What strategies did the writer use to paraphrase and summarize the original text? The first one is answered for you as an example.

ORIGINAL	PARAPHRASE / SUMMARY	STRATEGIES
A small percentage of individuals, likely 1 percent or less, overuse technology	Excessive use of technology is probably very rare.	Change the verb overuse into an adjective (excessive) and noun (use); change the statistic (likely 1 percent or less) into an adjective of frequency (rare).
However, illicit substances such as methamphetamine activate these centers to a much greater degree than do normal activities such as technology or exercise. That is what makes these substances dangerous.	It is only very high levels of activation associated, for example, with illegal drugs, that are considered dangerous.	
This is because current evidence suggests these are not unique disorders but rather arise as symptoms of underlying mental health problems, such as depression or attention problems.	The second reason is that overuse of technology may be the result of another psychological problem like depression rather than a separate condition.	
No evidence has emerged to suggest an epidemic of tech-addicted youths.	The research does not support widespread addiction to technology.	

 Go to the companion website to complete the chart for Activity 4.8.

Pedagogical Genre: Summary of a Source

A. Choose a text from a magazine, news source, professional journal, website, or other appropriate source in your current area of study (or your instructor will choose one for you).

B. Read the text carefully and divide it into meaningful sections.

C. Identify the structure and purpose of the text (e.g., argument, problem-solution, etc.).

D. Go to the companion website and complete the chart to analyze your text.

E. Write the first sentence of your summary (author + optional information about the author's credibility + reporting verb of purpose + overall purpose, theme, claim, problem, or main idea of the article).

F. Identify some categorizing nouns that help you understand the organization of your source text (see Language Box, p. 91).

G. Plan your summary. Choose the information you will include and the organization of your summary, based on your chart. Your instructor will tell you how long your summary should be (one paragraph or multiple paragraphs).

H. Draft your summary.

I. Use the checklist to review your summary and/or ask a peer for feedback.

- ☐ The first or second sentences include the author, purpose, and main idea.
- ☐ All the main ideas from the original text are included accurately.
- ☐ I have paraphrased ideas from the original text in my own sentences.
- ☐ I have chosen an appropriate organization for the summary and used categorizing nouns.
- ☐ I have presented the author's ideas without my own opinions.
- ☐ The summary is an appropriate length for the assignment.
- ☐ I have edited my summary using the language boxes for this unit: categorizing nouns and introducing sources.

What else do you need to work on? Make further revisions to your summary if necessary.

Genre in Action: Press Release

A press release is a short article that universities, companies, and other organizations send to journalists to announce a new research discovery, a new project, a successful event, or a future activity. Universities use press releases to promote the work of their faculty and communicate with the public about the benefits of their research. A press release is, therefore, a summary written for non-experts with a very specific purpose: to show off the work of the organization.

A. The website www.futurity.org republishes press releases from universities around the world. Here is an example of the start of an article about engineering research at Iowa State University (Krapfl, 2018). What is the function of each paragraph of the text? For example, the purpose of the headline (Paragraph 1) is to attract the reader to a new solution.

> ### ①Graphene Ink Could Lead to Washable Electronics
>
> ②New graphene printing technology can produce electronic circuits that are low-cost, flexible, highly conductive and water repellent, researchers report.
>
> ③The nanotechnology "would lend enormous value to self-cleaning wearable/washable electronics that are resistant to stains," according to the new paper.
>
> ④"We're taking low-cost, inkjet-printed graphene and tuning it with a laser to make functional materials," says Jonathan Claussen, an assistant professor of mechanical engineering at Iowa State University and the corresponding author of the paper in the journal Nanoscale.
>
> ⑤The paper describes how Claussen and the nanoengineers in his research group use inkjet printing technology to create electric circuits on flexible materials ....

FIGURE 4.2:
Structure of a Press Release

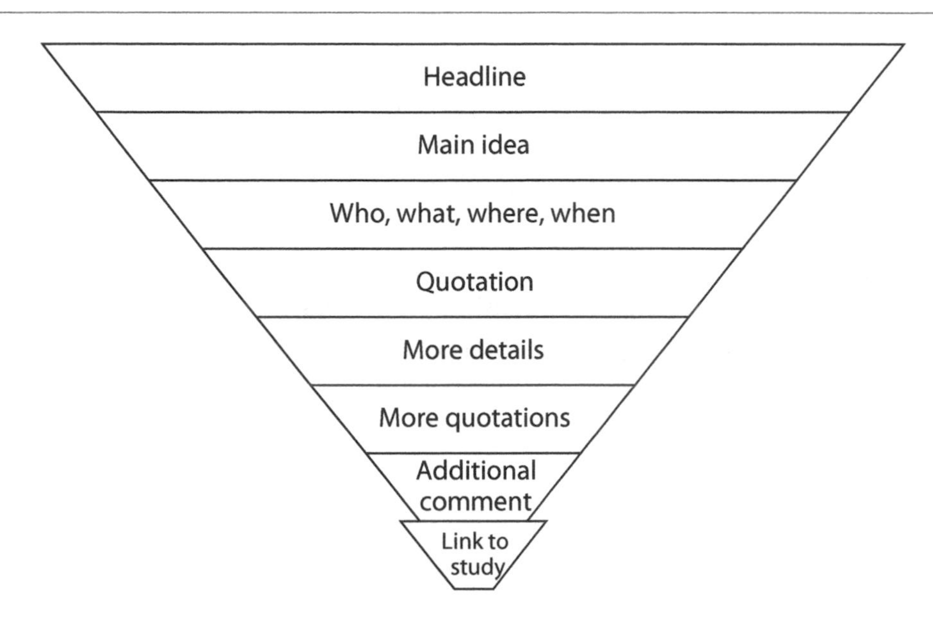

B. Many guides to writing press releases describe the structure of this genre as an inverted pyramid, shown in Figure 4.2.

C. Find the steps from Figure 4.2 in the graphene ink press release.

D. What differences in language use do you notice in these extracts from the press release about graphene ink and the abstract in the academic journal *Nanoscale*? What do they tell you about the context, purpose, and audience of the press release compared to the scientific journal article?

PRESS RELEASE	SCIENTIFIC ARTICLE ABSTRACT
"We're taking low-cost, inkjet-printed graphene and tuning it with a laser to make functional materials."	Solution-phase printing of exfoliated graphene flakes is emerging as a low-cost means to create flexible electronics for numerous applications.
New graphene printing technology can produce electronic circuits that are low-cost, flexible, highly conductive and water repellent.	Herein, we demonstrate how the energy density of a direct-pulsed laser writing (DPLW) technique can be varied to tune the hydrophobicity and electrical conductivity of the inkjet-printed graphene (IPG).

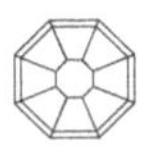

E. Analyze the components of the Rhetorical Planning Wheel for the press release genre:

1. Audience
2. Writer's role
3. Purpose
4. Context
5. Structure
6. Sources and data
7. Language
8. Conventions

F. You are going to write a press release for a college or university press office to announce:

- ☐ a recent piece of research in your field of study or interest
- ☐ a textbook written by a member of the faculty
- ☐ an event or activity that took place recently.

Make a list of the **talking points**—the most important information that readers should notice in your press release. Remember that one purpose of a press release is to promote the research and faculty of the university! Then, refer back to Figure 4.2 and use it to outline your press release.

G. Draft your press release, using the examples from www.futurity.org and other academic press releases as models, taking into account your Rhetorical Planning Wheel analysis and outline.

H. Peer Review: Ask one or two partners to read your press release. Use these questions to give peer feedback:

1. Does the press release quickly and clearly give you the main idea of the research or event?
2. Is the press release written in a register of language you can understand?
3. Does the press release have a logical organization?
4. What else can the writer do to improve the press release?

I. Self-Review: Revise your press release using your peers' feedback. Have you done everything on this checklist?

   - ☐ The press release follows an inverted pyramid structure, starting with the most important information.
   - ☐ I summarize the research/event clearly for a non-expert audience.
   - ☐ I quote researchers and experts and punctuate them correctly.
   - ☐ I write in the present tense to describe recent research to make it sound more immediate.

What else do you need to work on? Make further revisions to your press release if necessary.

Language Box: Using Direct Quotation

In press releases, it is common to quote members of the research team and other experts. Direct quotation like this is somewhat unusual in academic writing except in the humanities (e.g., literature, history, philosophy), but it is useful in a press release and in reporting on conversations and interviews. To introduce a direct quotation, use a reporting verb such as *say, explain,* or *write*. Note that press releases often use present simple tense (*says, explains, writes*) even though the interview was given in the past. This makes the quote sounds more immediate. Pay attention to the punctuation and capitalization:

- "We're micro-patterning the surface of the inkjet-printed graphene," Claussen says.
- Clausen explains, "We're micro-patterning the surface of the inkjet-printed graphene."
- "We're taking low-cost, inkjet-printed graphene and tuning it with a laser to make functional materials," says Jonathan Claussen, an assistant professor of mechanical engineering at Iowa State University.

Note that the speaker and reporting verb can be inverted as in the last example (*says Jonathan Claussen)*. This is especially useful when you want to state who the speaker is, as the information can then directly follow the name.

References

Chandler-Olcott, K. (2019). *What advice articles miss about "summer loss."* The Conversation. http://theconversation.com/what-advice-articles-miss-about-summer-loss-118430

Cooper, J. (2014). A response to Michaela Cullington. *Young Scholars in Writing, 11*, 91–93.

Ferguson, C.J. (2018). Con: Is "technology addiction" a valid diagnosis? In S. Ladika (Ed.), *Technology addiction*. CQ Researcher. http://library.cqpress.com/cqresearcher/cqresrre2018042006

Krapfl, M. (2018, January 25). *Graphene ink could lead to washable electronics*. Futurity. https://www.futurity.org/graphene-printing-electronic-circuits-1662932/

Ladika, S. (2018). Technology addiction. *CQ Researcher, 28*, 341–364.

Martin, J., & White, P. (2005). *The language of evaluation: Appraisal in English*. Palgrave Macmillan.

5 Synthesize

Goals

- ❒ Understand how and why to synthesize source texts
- ❒ Write comparative/contrastive and informational syntheses
- ❒ Use categorizing language to organize a synthesis
- ❒ Synthesis information using general-to-specific and specific-to-general organization
- ❒ Pedagogical Genre: Write an integrative synthesis of an academic reading and a book or movie
- ❒ Genre in Action: Write a literature review

What Is the Action?

Synthesis is the action of integrating ideas, evidence, claims, examples, or data from two or more sources. Among the many reasons you might synthesize sources are:

- ❒ to show how the ideas in two sources are similar and/or different
- ❒ to summarize information from multiple sources
- ❒ to discuss a text (including a movie, song, or book) using ideas from another source
- ❒ to review previous research to frame your own research question.

A good synthesis is not just a collection of summaries, discussed one after the other. Synthesis requires you to show the connections between the sources, which means you have to carefully choose information from the sources and show interesting themes, relationships, similarities, and/or differences.

You might be asked to write a synthesis as an entire assignment. You will also use synthesis as part of many longer assignments, especially those that require library research. This unit focuses on two common types of synthesis: a **comparative/contrastive** synthesis in which you write about the similarities and differences between ideas in your source texts, and an **informational** synthesis, which brings together information from multiple sources to answer questions and demonstrate your understanding of a topic.

Activity 5.1: What Do You Know?

Are these statements sometimes, always, or never true? Discuss your answers with a small group.

1. Any paragraph with two or more different citations is a synthesis.
2. When you plan a synthesis, you should mostly look for sources that disagree with each other.
3. You can show whether you support a source in your choice of reporting verbs and other language around the citation.
4. In a good synthesis, each paragraph should mostly summarize a separate source.
5. If you find two sources that support an idea, you can cite them both.
6. In a synthesis, it is important to summarize all the details from all the sources.

Comparative-Contrastive Syntheses

In a comparative-contrastive synthesis, your task is to find similarities and differences between the ideas in two or more sources. This is a common action in academic writing since you will often meet ideas on which experts agree and disagree. A comparative-contrastive synthesis allows you to show that you understand the different sides of an issue.

When you read articles or use lectures and textbooks for this kind of synthesis, you should take notes that help you see the connections and relationships between the sources in ideas, arguments, examples, and data. This will help you write a synthesis that goes beyond a simple summary of the two sources.

Activity 5.2: Analyze a Model

Read this excerpt from a final-year undergraduate student's report on Attention Deficit Hyperactivity Disorder (ADHD) from the Michigan Corpus of Upper-level Student Papers (MICUSP). *Dopamine*, mentioned in the report, is a chemical sent by certain nerve cells in the brain to other parts of the brain. As you read, pay attention to the sources that are cited.

> According to the biological perspective, ADHD has a strong genetic component (Faraone et al., 2005). Adoption studies have also shown that children that develop ADHD are more likely to have biological parents who suffered from ADHD and less likely to have adoptive parents with ADHD (Sprich et al., 2000). Moreover, abnormalities in dopamine have been implicated as the biological cause for the development of ADHD. Gene association studies have identified the gene that may be the cause of reduced dopamine activities and the onset of ADHD (Hawi et al., 2002). Furthermore, neuroimaging studies have identified areas of the brain responsible for sustaining attention which show decreased levels of activity in children with ADHD (Durston, Totterham, & Thomas, 2003).
>
> While the biological perspective focuses on the role of genes and brain abnormalities as the root cause of ADHD, the family systems perspective emphasizes the role of family relations in the onset of ADHD. Often children with ADHD have families that are unstable financially and emotionally with parents suffering themselves from depression or ADHD (Bernier & Siegel, 1994). Furthermore, the severity of family dysfunction is linked to the degree and severity of ADHD symptoms in the child (Hansell & Damour, 2005). However, familial dysfunction and bad parent-child interactions may not necessarily cause ADHD but instead be the result of the difficulties of caring for a child with ADHD.

Answer these questions, and then discuss your answers with a partner or small group.

1. **Which sources support the two perspectives on the cause of ADHD?**
2. **What language choices show the similarities and differences between the sources?**
3. **Which perspective does the writer seem to support (biological or family systems)? What language choices help you answer this question?**

Preparing to Synthesize

When you read sources that you are going to synthesize, it is helpful to take notes in a chart of some sort so that you can see how the information in your readings is connected. In the top row, write information about the source, such as the author, year, and title of each article. You will need this information to write references and citations later. Underneath that, write any relevant information about the author. In the main section of your chart, write information that will be useful for your assignment. Be sure to paraphrase or use quotation marks to indicate exact words and phrases from the sources. Here is an example of the first part of a synthesis chart:

Dynarski (2017), "Laptops are great. But not during a lecture or a meeting." *New York Times.*	**Numer (2017),** "Don't insult your class by banning laptops." *Chronicle of Higher Education.*
Author: Professor of education, public policy, and economics, University of Michigan	Author: Professor of human sexuality at Dalhousie University, Canada
Does not allow most students to use laptops, tablets, or cell phones in her classes	Laptops and other devices are not only used for notetaking: they encourage all students to participate in class, especially during uncomfortable discussions.

Next, try adding arrows or color-coding to highlight points that are **similar, different,** or **related** between the texts. You do not need to limit yourself to differences. Although contrasts between sources can be interesting, so can areas of agreement. Sometimes you will also find that one source supports the ideas in the other. For example, you might find examples, data, and evidence in one source that support the arguments, claims, and ideas in another source.

Activity 5.3: Note-Taking Practice

Find two articles on a topic you are currently studying in this or another class. Try news sources, magazines, professional journals, or library databases. Take notes in a chart using the techniques described to show the connections and contrasts between the information and points of view in the articles.

Language Box: Comparing and Contrasting Connectors

There are at least four types of connectors you can use to compare sources by showing similarities or differences:

1. **Coordinating conjunctions** (especially **but** and **yet**), which join equally important ideas. *Yet* shows a stronger contrast or feeling of surprise than *but*.
   - ADHD has a strong genetic component, **but/yet** it is also connected to family experiences.
2. **Subordinating conjunctions** (e.g., **while, whereas, although, even though**) create dependent clauses that add contrasts and concessions to the main clause. Note that most writers use commas before these conjunctions of contrast and concession but not other subordinating conjunctions when they follow the independent clause:
   - **While** the biological perspective focuses on the role of genes, the family systems perspective emphasizes the role of family relations.
   - Family dysfunction is linked to ADHD symptoms, **although** it may be the result of the difficulties of caring for a child with ADHD.
3. **Sentence connectors** (e.g., **furthermore, also, however, in contrast**) show the reader the logical connection from the previous sentence or paragraph. Most transition phrases are used at the start of a sentence, but *also* is more common after the subject or verb:
   - Researchers have isolated the gene that may be the cause of the onset of ADHD. **Furthermore**, studies have identified areas of the brain responsible for sustaining attention. Other areas of the brain are **also** affected by ADHD.

4. **Phrase connectors** (e.g. *like, unlike, similar to, in contrast to*) are especially helpful for creating clear connections between ideas in different sentences:

   - *Unlike* the biological perspective, the family systems perspective considers social factors in the development of ADHD.

It is important to check the meaning of the words to carefully control the types of comparisons you are making. Some common ways to express three patterns of meaning are shown.

MEANING / FORM	SIMILARITY	CONTRAST	CONCESSION
Coordinating Conjunction	*and*	*but*	*yet*
Subordinating Conjunction		*whereas, while*	*although, while, even though*
Sentence Connector	*in addition, moreover, furthermore, similarly, also, too*	*in contrast, however, on the other hand,*	*admittedly, surprisingly, unusually, improbably*
Phrase Connector	*like* *similar to*	*unlike* *in contrast to*	

The language of concession recognizes one point of view (in the *although* clause) but emphasizes the position in the main clause. For this reason, it may be too evaluative for a synthesis if you are expected to maintain a neutral stance.

Activity 5.4: Practice the Language

This chart contains notes on two sources that present different perspectives on banning laptop and tablet computers in college classrooms. Where do you find connections, similarities, and contrasts between the columns?

Dynarski (2017), "Laptops are great. But not during a lecture or a meeting." *New York Times.*	**Numer (2017),** "Don't insult your class by banning laptops." *Chronicle of Higher Education.*
Professor of education, public policy, and economics, University of Michigan	Professor of human sexuality at Dalhousie University, Canada
Does not allow most students to use laptops, tablets, or cell phones in her classes.	Laptops and other devices are not only used for note-taking: they encourage all students to participate in class, especially during uncomfortable discussions.
Students are easily distracted from the lecture when laptops are used for notetaking, according to "unequivocal" research (i.e., all the research agrees).	Students should be treated as adults who can choose whether to concentrate on a lecture or do something else online.
Using a computer to take notes in class is a type of "visual pollution" because it distracts students sitting near the computer user, even if they are taking notes by hand.	It is the professor's responsibility to engage learners using "active learning" methods so that they are not distracted.
Studies show that students who use electronics, even when they are only taking notes and not using other apps, still earn lower grades that students who are not allowed to use their devices.	In Numer's own research, he used an app in his class; students reported that they found the class more engaging and that it improved their "critical-thinking skills."
When students take handwritten notes, they have to think about the material and choose what to write down, which produces better notes.	Students can also use laptops in class for research and collaboration as well as to access online textbooks and other resources.
Students with learning disabilities should be allowed to use electronic devices if needed.	Because undergraduate students have grown up using the internet, colleges need to teach differently.

Write five to eight sentences about the information in the chart using language of similarity, contrast, or concession from the chart in the Language Box. You could use some of these sentence frames.

1. Dynarski argues that ____________. However, according to Numer, ____________.
2. Unlike Dynarski, Numer suggests ______________________________________.
3. Whereas Numer ______________________, Dynarski __________________________.
4. Although laptops can __________________, _______________ .

WRITING TASK 5.1: Contrastive Synthesis

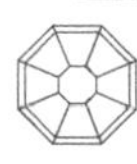

A. Read this introduction to a synthesis of the two articles in Activity 5.4 in response to the prompt: Is a laptop ban a good policy, according to university professors? Then, complete the components of the Rhetorical Planning Wheel, based on your analysis of the prompt and the introduction. A few have been done as examples.

> In most university classrooms, a laptop or tablet computer is an essential piece of equipment for students. However, college faculty are divided on whether to encourage or restrict the use of laptops during class. Dynarksi (2017), a professor at the University of Michigan, argued in a *New York Times* op-ed column, that laptops should be banned, except for students with disabilities. However, Numer (2017), a professor at Dalhousie University, responded that Dynarski's policy is an "insult" and defended his students' use of laptop computers in his class. The main areas of disagreement are the potential for distraction and the impact of digital devices on learning.

1. **Writer's Role:** Student
2. **Audience:** Instructor
3. **Purpose:**
4. **Context:** After reading the two articles for a class
5. **Structure:**
6. **Language:** Comparison and contrast connectors; mostly paraphrasing the sources; some limited quotation

B. The last sentence of the introduction suggests that the synthesis will continue with at least two more paragraphs. Individually or with a small group, write one or both of these synthesis paragraphs using information from both sources summarized in the table in Activity 5.4:

1. **Distraction**: Do laptops affect students' concentration, or is maintaining students' focus the responsibility of the instructor?
2. **Learning:** Can laptops and other devices be used as tools for learning, or do they lead to less learning and lower grades?

C. Choose the information from each article you will use in your paragraph. Use the Language Box to add appropriate compare/contrast language as you write.

D. Peer or Self-Review: Share your synthesis with one or two partners or another group. Use these questions to give peer feedback or review your own writing:

1. Does the paragraph refer to both sources?
2. Does the paragraph present both sides of the argument accurately, without taking a side?
3. Is comparative and contrastive language used correctly?
4. How could the writer improve the paragraph(s)?

Informational Syntheses

Many university writing assignments are informational, asking you to summarize information from a textbook or lecture. Sometimes, though, your answers have to draw on multiple sources. Unlike a comparative or contrastive synthesis, the goal in an **informational synthesis** is to demonstrate your understanding of the topic rather than show how the sources are similar and different. An informational synthesis can also form part of a larger assignment if you need to provide background information for a proposal, report, or argument. In some classes, you may write library research papers (sometimes called *term papers*) that are almost entirely syntheses of articles you have read on a particular topic. Finally, if you write an original research paper, an important stage is the **literature review**, in which you synthesize the previous research on your topic (see Genre in Action p. 128).

FIGURE 5.1:
General-to-Specific and Specific-to-General Organization

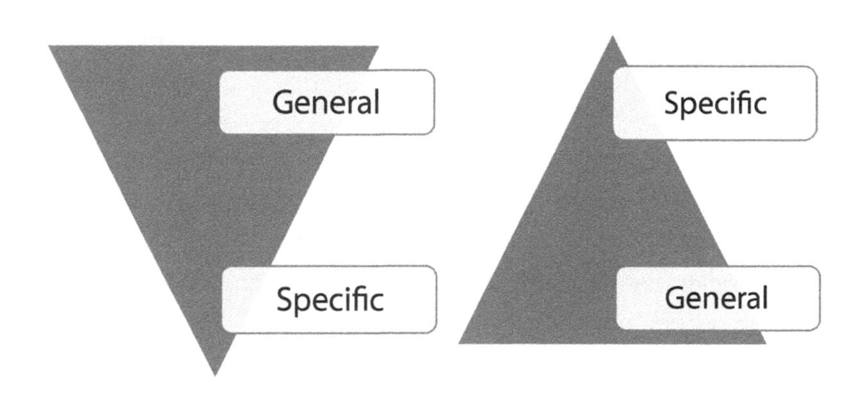

In an informational synthesis, you may see two common patterns of organization (Figure 5.1): from general to specific or from specific to general (Swales & Feak, 2012, pp. 55–92). In **general-to-specific** organization, the paragraph starts with the focus or major claim (often with citations to the sources of this idea) and continues with supporting details and examples that become increasingly specific, perhaps ending with a detailed example, statistic, or research finding. In **specific-to-general** organization, the paragraph starts with examples, statistics, or details, and concludes with the main idea, focus, or claim.

Activity 5.5: Analyze a Model

Read these paragraphs from the Literature Review section of a research article on students' use of information computer technologies (ICT) in the classroom—that is, laptops, tablets, and smartphones (Vahedi et al., 2019).

> ①Few studies have examined students' views regarding policies on ICT use in the classroom; however, the results of these studies indicate that students are generally not supportive of restrictive policies regarding their ICT use (e.g. Jackson, 2013; Santos et al., 2018; Tindell and Bohlander, 2012). ②Students are opposed to policies completely banning ICT use in the classroom. They are also opposed to policies aimed at reducing non-academic ICT use in classroom, such as sending text messages during a class lecture (McCoy, 2016; Santos et al., 2018). ③This opposition is perhaps not surprising if a

major factor in non-academic ICT use is boredom. ④Simply taking away the ICTs would do nothing to make classes more interesting, and instead removes students' preferred means of coping with a boring class. ⑤However, students' attitudes contrast with those of instructors, who are more likely than students to support restrictive policies [for] ICT use, including a complete ban of all electronic devices from classrooms (e.g. Baker et al., 2012). ⑥For example, Santos et al. (2018) reported that compared to instructors, students were significantly *less* likely to agree with policies that would restrict their non-academic ICT uses (such as social media) and significantly *more* likely to support policies that would allow them to continue to use their ICTs while minimizing disruption (e.g. to use them in silent mode).

1. **Which sentence expresses the most general claim or focus of the paragraph?**
2. **Is this paragraph organized from general to specific (main idea then details and examples) or from specific to general (examples then main idea)?**
3. **Which word or phrase in each sentence shows its connection to the previous sentence?**
4. **How many different sources are cited in this paragraph?**
5. **How does the writer use sources in this paragraph? Choose all the correct answers from the list, and identify the sources used for each purpose.**
   a. to show the sources of the paragraph's main claim
   b. to define key terms
   c. to give examples of research findings
   d. to give a counter-example that disagrees with the main claim of the paragraph

Continue reading the literature review.

> ⑦Although several studies have assessed participants' attitudes toward *hypothetical* restrictive policies, Elliott-Dorans (2018) assessed the impact of an actual laptop ban on students' performance. ⑧Several sections of a course were randomly assigned to a "laptop" or "laptop ban" condition. ⑨Elliott-Dorans reported that students who were banned from using their laptops had lower class attendance and lower grades on both papers and examinations compared to students who were permitted to use their laptops. ⑩In another study by Hutcheon et al. (2019), students in two sections of a course were allowed to use ICTs in the classroom, whereas those in two other sections were banned from using their ICTs. ⑪They found no significant differences between the two groups on students' exam grades, professor–student rapport, or interest in the course. ⑫However, students in the technology-ban sections reported significantly lower levels of engagement in the course. ⑬Taken together, these results suggest that restricting ICT use may not be the best solution to reducing negative outcomes associated with technology in the classroom. ⑭Banning ICTs may simply disengage students, or drive them away from class, resulting in poorer learning outcomes.

6. Which sentence or sentences contain the author's main claim in this paragraph about restricting ICT use?
7. Is this paragraph organized from general to specific or from specific to general?
8. How many different sources are cited in this paragraph?
9. How does the writer use sources in this paragraph? Choose all the correct answers from the list, and identify the sources used for each purpose.
    a. to show the sources of the paragraph's main claim
    b. to define key terms
    c. to give examples of research findings
    d. to give a counter-example that disagrees with the main claim of the paragraph

Activity 5.6: Integral and Non-Integral Citations

Refer to the Online Source Use Appendix for an introduction to integral and non-integral citations.

The examples in this unit have demonstrated that syntheses typically use both integral and non-integral citations. While the preference for integral or non-integral citations depends on the academic discipline, writers can often choose the type of citation that is most effective for their text.

These sentences are adapted from a review of the research on different types of note-taking (Jansen et al., 2017). In each pair of sentences, one uses an integral citation, while the other uses a non-integral citation. Which sentence in each pair do you find more effective, and why?

1. a. Aiken et al. (1975) examined the effects of note-taking and lecture speed on memory.
   b. A study has examined the effects of note-taking and lecture speed on memory (Aiken et al., 1975).
2. a. According to Di Vesta and Gray (1972), there are two types of benefits of note-taking on memory.
   b. The benefits of note-taking on memory have been classified into two groups (Di Vesta & Gray, 1972).
3. a. Mueller and Oppenheimer (2014) and Peverly et al. (2007) have showed that the effects of note-taking depend on the experimental conditions.
   b. Some studies have showed that the effects of note-taking depend on the experimental conditions (Mueller & Oppenheimer, 2014; Peverly et al., 2007).
4. a. Note-taking is common among students (Carrier et al., 1988).
   b. Carrier et al. (1988) found that note-taking is common among students.
5. a. Laptop note-taking has seen a rapid increase in the past years, warranting interest in its effects on note-taking and memory for lecture content (Grahame, 2016; Mueller & Oppenheimer, 2016; Numazawa & Noto, 2016).
   b. Some researchers including Grahame (2017), Mueller and Oppenheimer (2016), and Numazawa and Noto (2016) have observed that laptop note-taking has seen a rapid increase in the past years, warranting interest in its effects on note-taking and memory for lecture content .

Language Box: Framing Sentences

In Unit 4, you saw how to organize a summary with **category nouns**, which are general nouns that help the reader see how the ideas in the source text are related (e.g., two opinions, three applications, or four solutions). You can use similar language to organize your points in a synthesis. Your synthesis—or sometimes individual paragraphs within a synthesis—will often benefit from framing sentences. A **framing sentence** is a topic sentence that signals the type of information in the forthcoming synthesis, often by stating the categories you have used or showing the connection from the last paragraph to the new one. The choice of frame—whether contrasting, classification, or overview—will depend on the information you are summarizing and will often indicate how you have organized your synthesis. For instance:

- While **the biological perspective** focuses on genetic differences, the **family systems perspective** emphasizes the social environment. (*contrasting frame*)
- Renewable energy faces **three major challenges**. (*classification frame*)
- Different **theories** have been discussed to explain the incidence of ADHD. (*overview frame*)

Once you have framed your synthesis, you can refer back to the categories at the start or end of subsequent paragraphs. In most tasks involving synthesis, you will not want to organize your ideas using a simple *first, second, finally* pattern because these connectors do not give the reader any information about the relationships between the ideas you are synthesizing. Some widely used language choices for referring back to frames in academic writing include:

Another	example
A different, alternative, alternate	study
A complementary, further, additional, similar	way (that ... / for ...)
A/The major, important, primary, compelling, underlying	reason
A possible, plausible, common	possibility
The final, last	factor
	problem, challenge, concern, issue
	approach, method, strategy
	explanation
	consideration
	aspect, type (of ...)
	benefit

Activity 5.7: Practice the Language

Choose a category noun to start the second sentence in each extract. The first one has been done for you as an example

1. Smith (2012) found that grades suffered when students used laptops in class. However, *another study ....*
2. Traffic can be reduced by pedestrianizing streets in downtown areas. An alternate __________
3. Urbanization has caused air and water pollution. One __________
4. Technology bans are unfair because they discriminate against students with certain learning disabilities. Another __________
5. Regular exercise improves physical health and fitness. The final __________

WRITING TASK 5.2: Informational Synthesis

Write a synthesis in answer to the question "What are the challenges of reducing the use of fossil fuels?" Your sources are two texts about climate change and the challenges of reducing the use of fossil fuels (or, *decarbonization*). The first source (Text 1) is a report from a National Research Council committee on strategies to reverse the effects of climate change. The second source (Text 2) is an extract from a textbook on sustainability, specifically from the chapter on renewable energies.

Refer to the Online Source Use Appendix for a guide to citing sources in your synthesis.

Text 1: Scientific Report (National Research Council, 2015)

①Global energy use is conservatively projected to rise between 15 percent and 30 percent by 2035 from 2011 levels, adding to the challenge of decarbonizing global energy. In addition to the electric power sector, the transportation, industrial, and residential and commercial sectors currently account for the majority of energy use in the United States. Energy input into electricity is only about 35 percent of U.S. total energy consumption. Most of the remainder involves the direct combustion of fossil fuels in transportation, heating and cooling of buildings, and industrial processes. In order to decarbonize the entire energy system, all of these applications will also need to be converted to systems that emit little or no carbon dioxide, in many cases by converting them to run on cleaner sources of electricity.

②Because they produce varying and intermittent power, it is thought that wind and solar cannot currently be the sole replacement for conventional fossil fuel–fired power plants. Although estimates indicate that it may be possible to achieve a decarbonized energy system, great uncertainties remain due to factors such as costs, technology evolution, public policies, and barriers to deployment of new technologies (NRC, 2010b). Furthermore, simply accounting for the emissions from existing fossil fuel energy facilities over their remaining lifetime commits the planet to an additional 300 billion tons of CO_2 (Davis and Socolow, 2014). With whatever portfolio of technologies the transition is achieved, eliminating the carbon dioxide emissions from the global energy and transportation systems will pose an enormous technical, economic, and social challenge that will likely take decades of effort to achieve.

Text 2: Sustainability Textbook (Theis & Tomkin, 2015)

> Renewable energy faces several barriers to its widespread deployment. Cost is one of the most serious. Although the cost of renewables has declined significantly in recent years, most are still more expensive than traditional fossil-fuel alternatives. A second barrier is public opinion. Renewable energy is not a choice that *individual* consumers make. Instead, energy choices are made by government policy makers at city, state and federal levels, who balance concerns for the common good, for "fairness" to stakeholders, and for economic cost. Nevertheless, public acceptance is still a major factor in balancing these concerns: a strongly favored or disfavored energy option will be reflected in government decisions through representatives elected by or responding to the public. However, the difference in the public acceptance and economic cost of alternative energies (wind, solar, hydroelectric) is striking: solar is at once the most expensive alternative and the most acceptable to the public. In addition, the geographical distribution of useable renewable energy is quite uneven. Sunlight is concentrated in deserts where cloud cover is rare. Winds are up to 50 percent stronger and steadier offshore than on land. Hydroelectric potential is concentrated in mountainous regions with high rainfall and snowmelt.

A. Make a list of the challenges to using renewable energies in response to climate change appearing in each text.

B. Where are the ideas in the two texts connected? There is no need to write a comparison in an informational summary. Instead, you can cite both sources to show that the idea has wide support. For example, "One obstacle to renewable energy is cost (NRC, 2015; Theis & Tomkin, 2015)."

C. Organize your synthesis. Decide how many paragraphs you will write and the order of the information you will present.

D. Write your synthesis. You might start with a framing sentence such as:
   - ☐ There are ______ major obstacles to replacing fossil fuels with renewable energy sources.
   - ☐ Decarbonizing the world's electricity supply will be difficult for ________ reasons.
   - ☐ Although renewable energy is more sustainable than carbon-based fuel, implementing green energy production will be very challenging.

E. Draft your synthesis, using the Language Box on Framing Sentences to frame the problems or challenges. Choose whether to use general-specific or specific-general organization in your paragraph(s).

F. Peer Review: Share your synthesis with one or two partners. Use these questions to give peer feedback.

1. Does the writer use general-specific or specific-general organization? Is it effective?
2. Has the writer used categories to organize the problems or challenges effectively?
3. Has the writer selected appropriate information from both sources to answer the question: What are the challenges of reducing the use of fossil fuels?
4. What can the writer do to improve the synthesis?

G. Self-Review: Revise your synthesis using your peers' feedback. Have you done everything on this checklist?

- ☐ I referred to both sources in all paragraphs of my synthesis.
- ☐ I paraphrased and/or quoted and cited sources correctly.
- ☐ I used framing sentences to structure my paragraphs.
- ☐ I used general-specific or specific-general organization patterns.
- ☐ I included enough information to fully respond to the prompt.

What else do you need to work on? Make further revisions to your synthesis if necessary.

Pedagogical Genre: Integrative Synthesis

Sometimes an assignment might ask you to use ideas, theories, or frameworks from your academic readings to write about a movie, play, or popular book. This can be a good way to demonstrate your understanding of key concepts from a course while applying them to a piece of art, literature, or popular entertainment. This kind of **integrative synthesis** is a pedagogical genre (that is, you would probably only write it for a class), but some professional movie and book reviews will also make reference to research and theories from fields such as psychology, sociology, anthropology, or cultural studies.

A. Choose one of these tasks, or a topic related to this or another course you are taking:
   1. Research the "five stages of grief," a widely used theory that explains how many people react after the death of a loved one. Then, explain whether characters in a book or movie follow those stages, making specific reference to both the theory and the book or movie.
   2. Research a historical period and read a book or poem or watch a movie about it. How is the historical period or event represented in the book or movie?
   3. Watch a movie or read a book that deals with a physical or mental illness, disability, or difference. Research the condition and discuss the extent to which it is accurately represented, both medically and socially.

B. Plan your integrative synthesis using a chart similar to this example using the Five Stages of Grief (Kübler-Ross & Kessler, 2005) and *The Outsiders* (Hinton, 1964). Start with the main concepts, facts, or events from your academic sources in the first column. Then look for examples, scenes, and quotations from your book or movie. In the last column, note your observations. Does the book movie show the academic concept? Do you see any interesting variations? What do you learn from the comparison?

CONCEPT, FACT, OR EVENT	EXAMPLES FROM BOOK/MOVIE	MY OBSERVATIONS
Five Stages of Grief (Kübler-Ross & Kessler, 2005)	*The Outsiders* (Hinton, 1964)	
First stage of grief: denial. "The world becomes meaningless and overwhelming ... .We go numb ... .To believe at this stage would be too much." (p. 10)	Dally doesn't accept that Johnny is dead. Ponyboy refuses to accept Dally's death. He almost starts a fight with another teenager and says that he feels nothing.	The teenagers in *The Outsiders* display the first stage of grief, denial.
Second stage of grief: Anger. "Underneath anger is pain: *your* pain .... Scream if you need to. Find a solitary place to let it out .... Do not bottle up anger inside." (p. 15-16)	Dally screams at the nurse when Johnny dies and runs out of the hospital. He lets out his anger, with tragic results. Ponyboy turns his grief inward and allows it to "bottle up."	The characters express the second stage, anger, in different ways with different outcomes. A key stage in the process?

C. Organize your synthesis using appropriate framing categories (see Language Box on page 125). You may be able to use the concepts or observations column from the chart to help you plan your paper.

D. Draft your synthesis. Be sure to refer to both the concepts and the book or movie in each paragraph and paraphrase or quote and cite your sources correctly. For example:

> Once the grieving person has overcome their denial and understands the reality of their loss, they enter the second stage of anger. In this stage, they encounter the pain of grief (Kübler-Ross & Kessler, 2005). In *The Outsiders*, Johnny's death causes a great deal of pain. Once Dally realizes his friend is dead, he seems to follow Kübler-Ross and Kessler's advice: "Scream if you need to" (p. 15) by shouting at the nurse and rushing out of the hospital. Pony, on other hand, does indeed "find a solitary place" (p. 16), but his anger turns inward and his body responds physically with a fever that leaves him unconscious for several days. However, while Ponyboy does not "bottle up anger inside," he works through all the stages of his grief, unlike Dally, who lets out his anger on the world, leading to his own death. Therefore, for the characters in *The Outsiders*, the ways they express anger in this second stage of grief seem key in determining their ultimate outcomes.

Refer to the Source Use Appendix for a guide to paraphrasing, quotation, and citation.

E. Peer Review. Ask one or two partners to read your synthesis. Use these questions to give peer feedback:

1. Does the writer refer to both the academic reading and the book or movie in each paragraph?
2. Does the writer make effective connections between the sources?
3. Are the paragraphs clearly framed and organized?
4. What else could the writer do to improve the synthesis?

F. Self-Review: Revise your integrative synthesis using your peers' feedback. Have you done everything on this checklist?

- ☐ I make connections between the academic reading and the movie or book in every paragraph.
- ☐ I organize the synthesis using category words (if appropriate).
- ☐ I use integral and/or non-integral citations to highlight the most important information.
- ☐ I use connecting language to show the relationship between ideas and punctuate it correctly.

What else do you need to work on? Make further revisions to your synthesis if necessary.

Genre in Action: Literature Review

A **literature review** is a required section of many larger writing projects, including most empirical (that is, data-driven) research papers, where it may be part of the Introduction. The Literature Review section synthesizes previous research to show what experts in your field already know and what they do not know about the area of your investigation, leading to the "gap" or question that is the focus of your research. Literature reviews may also be assignments by themselves, in which you need to demonstrate your knowledge on a particular subject. In some professional writing (e.g., proposals, reports), you may also need to provide a synthesis of existing knowledge on a topic as part of an introduction.

Here are some possible literature reviews you might write for this assignment:

1. Choose a controversial topic in your academic or professional field, or a controversial issue of public interest on your campus or in contemporary culture. Synthesize the arguments made by experts on different sides. This task does not necessarily call for your own opinion, though you might express an opinion after studying and synthesizing the literature.
2. Develop a research question or hypothesis in the context of this or another class. Synthesize relevant prior research that shows the current state of knowledge on this topic and identifies a "gap" in the research that your work will fill. This could the introduction to a research paper.
3. As part of a proposal, summarize what others have written or said that would support the project or idea you are proposing.

For example, you could investigate further the laptop bans discussed earlier in this unit and respond to one of these prompts:

1. Synthesize the arguments for and against banning laptops in university classes to educate readers (your peers and instructors) about the issue.
2. Review the literature on banning laptops to introduce your own research (proposal) to be conducted at your college or university.
3. Write a proposal to administrators at your college or university either for or against a laptop ban. Review the literature that supports your recommendation.

Refer to the Online Source Use Appendix for guides to finding, evaluating, and citing sources in your literature review.

A. There are many ways to frame a literature review, including:

- ☐ major theories or approaches (e.g., "There are three main approaches to ________")
- ☐ chronological, or order of time (e.g., "At first, _______ was believed to be ________")
- ☐ stages of a process (e.g., "There are four major stages in this process ...")
- ☐ categories or themes (e.g., "The research on X can be divided into ____________")
- ☐ narrowing from general topics to a specific focus for research (see Activity 5.5 for an example)

Read these excerpts from the introductions of some student-written literature reviews. Which pattern of organization does each text probably follow? What is the purpose of each text? Highlight the framing sentence(s) in each paper.

1. The way in which simultaneous bilingual children acquire the syntax of languages that differ typologically and syntactically and are not genetically related, such as Cantonese and English, is intriguing. One of the most prominent debates concerning the development of simultaneous bilinguals—those who were exposed to both languages regularly since birth—is the number of language systems established in these children's minds. Two of the hypotheses put forward to explain this phenomenon, namely the autonomous development account and the interdependent development account, will be examined in this paper.

   The autonomous development account suggested that....

   On the other hand, the interdependent development account indicated that. ... (Ng, 2018)

2. The essay will begin with a brief historical analysis of plague outbreaks, and then explore plague's geographical distribution, with the goal of understanding where the disease originated and how this might affect population resistance. Then, the organisms involved in plague ecology will be discussed in detail. After understanding the ecology of plague, preventative and control measures at each stage of the infectious cycle and their effectiveness are examined. Finally, social and political questions about plague are raised, particularly its threat as a bioterrorist weapon and the role of international health policy in eradicating this disease. (MICUSP)

3. The literature review highlighted major challenges that young adults with Type I diabetes may experience during transition to adulthood. These challenges included "psychosocial challenges," "life style change," "lack of supportive network," and "delivery of diabetes care." Each of these will be discussed with supportive evidence from literature. (Curtis et al., 2018)
4. The student teaching experience is one of the major steps that all future teachers must go through before entering the classroom. Throughout this experience, the future teacher, also known as the "teacher candidate" interacts with two people: the cooperating teacher and the university supervisor. Together, these three members form a triad whose purpose is to guide the teacher candidate throughout the student teaching process. An essential part of this guidance is the feedback given to the teacher candidate by the cooperating teacher and university supervisor. This feedback allows the teacher candidate to learn and improve teaching skills and practices. This study seeks to better understand the nature of feedback given by university supervisors so as to inform any changes to clinical practice that may better support teacher candidate development. (Vertemara & Flushman, 2017)

   Subheadings:

   - The Importance of University Supervision
   - The University Supervisor's Role
   - University Supervisor Feedback
   - Praise versus Growth

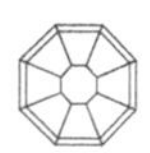

B. Complete the Rhetorical Planning Wheel for the task you have chosen or been assigned. In the Structure component, describe the type of organization from Step A that is most appropriate for your assignment. You may need to do more reading on your topic (Step C) before you can complete this component.

Go to the companion website for the RPW Analysis document.

C. A good literature review can require a lot of reading. Look at the Sources segment of the Rhetorical Planning Wheel and think about the types of sources that are appropriate for your assignment. As you read, keep notes to help you connect the information, ideas, arguments, theories, and results. There are many ways to take notes, depending on the type of texts you are reading:

- ☐ Write detailed notes about each source on a separate piece of paper or computer document.
- ☐ Write each useful piece of information on an index card, and then sort them into categories or themes.
- ☐ Keep a table with one row per source. For example, if you are reading empirical research, your columns might include the methods, participants, results, and implications.

Look for connections between the sources as you did for the syntheses in Writing Tasks 5.1 and 5.2.

D. Draft your literature review. As you write, check that you are paraphrasing and/or quoting your sources correctly, using integral and non-integral citations.

E. Peer Review. Ask one or two partners to read your literature review. Use these questions to give peer feedback:

1. What is the topic, purpose, and focus of the literature review?
2. What pattern of organization did the writer use? Is it effective?
3. Does each paragraph deal with one topic, aspect, or category of information?
4. Are multiple sources cited in each paragraph?
5. Do the paragraphs follow general-to-specific or specific-to-general organization, if appropriate?
6. How can the writer improve the literature review?

F. Self-Review: Revise your literature review using your peers' feedback. Have you done everything on this checklist?

- ☐ I organized the information effectively in each paragraph and between paragraphs.
- ☐ I cited at least two sources in every paragraph.
- ☐ I used integral and/or non-integral citations to highlight the most important information.
- ☐ I used connecting language to show the relationship between ideas and punctuate it correctly.
- ☐ I paraphrased and/or quoted all my sources appropriately, avoiding plagiarism.
- ☐ My literature review meets all the requirements of the assignment, including reference style, length, format, and choice of sources.

What else do you need to work on? Make further revisions to your literature review if necessary.

References

Curtis, M. J., Abdoli, S., & Hall, J. (2018). Young adulthood and unique challenges in living with type 1 diabetes. *Journal of Student Research, 7*(1), 1–5. https://doi.org/10.47611/jsr.v7i1.427

Dynarski, S. (2017, November 22). Laptops are great. But not during a lecture or meeting. *New York Times.* https://www.nytimes.com/2017/11/22/business/laptops-not-during-lecture-or-meeting.html

Hinton. S.E. (1964). *The outsiders.* Viking Press.

Jansen, R. S., Lakens, D., & IJsselsteijn, W. A. (2017). An integrative review of the cognitive costs and benefits of note-taking. *Educational Research Review, 22*, 223–233. https://doi.org/10.1016/j.edurev.2017.10.001

Kübler-Ross, E., & Kessler, D. (2005). *On grief and grieving.* Simon and Schuster.

National Research Council. (2015). *Climate intervention: Reflecting sunlight to cool Earth.* National Academies Press. https://doi.org/10.17226/18988

Ng, J. H. C. (2018). Effects of bilingualism on morphosyntactic development in children: A corpus study. *Reinvention: An International Journal of Undergraduate Research, 11*(2). http://www.warwick.ac.uk/reinventionjournal/archive/volume11issue2/ng

Numer, M. (2017, December 4). Don't insult your class by banning laptops. *Chronicle of Higher Education.* https://www.chronicle.com/article/dont-insult-your-class-by-banning-laptops/

Swales, J. M., & Feak, C. B. (2012). *Academic writing for graduate students: Essential tasks and skills* (3rd ed.). University of Michigan Press.

Theis, T., & Tomkin, J. (Eds.). (2015). *Sustainability: A comprehensive foundation.* Open Textbook Library. https://open.umn.edu/opentextbooks/textbooks/96

Vahedi, Z., Zannella, L., & Want, S. C. (2019). Students' use of information and communication technologies in the classroom: Uses, restriction, and integration. *Active Learning in Higher Education.* https://doi.org/10.1177/1469787419861926

Vertemara, V., & Flushman, T. (2017). Emphasis of university supervisor feedback to teacher candidates. *Journal of Student Research, 6*(2), 45–55. https://doi.org/10.47611/jsr.v6i2.392

6 Report and Interpret Data

Goals

- ❐ Describe the data in a table, graph, or chart
- ❐ Interpret the data in a table, graph, or chart
- ❐ Hedge and boost claims about data
- ❐ Write effectively about numbers
- ❐ Choose appropriate verb tenses to write about trends
- ❐ Pedagogical Genre: Write a data commentary
- ❐ Genre in Action: Write a policy brief

What Are the Actions?

This unit introduces two separate but related actions for writing about data. The first is **reporting** what is in the graph, figure, chart, or table. The second is **interpreting** what the data mean. Some tasks require you just to describe data, while others also expect you to provide an interpretation, that is, your comments about the data you have reported (that is called a **data commentary**). Data commentaries are common in many disciplines, either as short class assignments or part of a longer text, most notably an original research paper. You may also write about graphs and tables in textbook exercises or in professional genres such as reports, articles, memos, and presentations.

Activity 6.1 What Do You Know?

Can you correctly label each type of graphic and the various components shown in Figure 6.1?

bar chart	line graph	pie chart	scattergraph
table	bar	column	dashed line
dotted line	horizontal axis	legend/key	line of best fit
row	segment	solid line	vertical axis

Go to the companion website to access the material for Activity 6.1.

FIGURE 6.1:
Common Types of Graphs

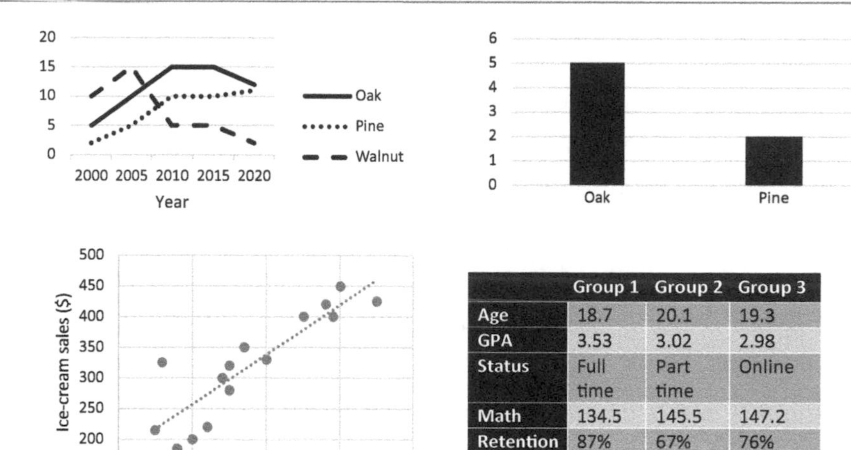

	Group 1	Group 2	Group 3
Age	18.7	20.1	19.3
GPA	3.53	3.02	2.98
Status	Full time	Part time	Online
Math	134.5	145.5	147.2
Retention	87%	67%	76%

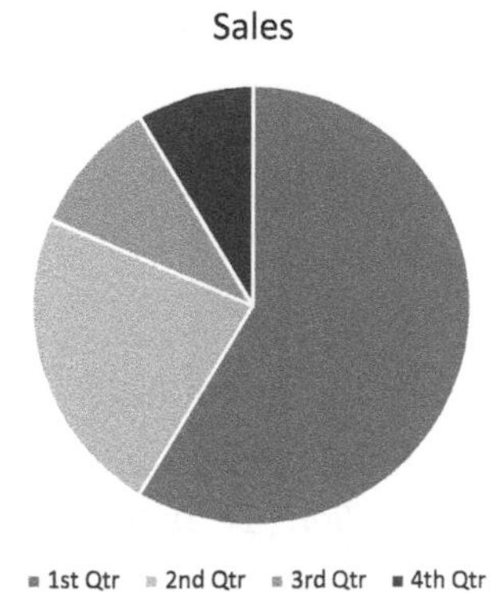

Describing Data

In fields such as economics and business, you often have to describe data by helping readers notice the most important information in a table, graph, or chart. In research papers in most scientific fields, you describe the data in the Results section separately from your interpretations in the Discussion section, a practice that is also followed in some social sciences. However, in all cases, reporting data is rarely completely neutral since the writer chooses which data points to highlight.

Language Box: Writing about Numbers

The conventions for writing about quantitative data (that is, numbers, percentages, and statistics) vary among academic disciplines. The advice provided here follows the APA style guide (7th edition), which is a good starting point for most writers, but your instructor may require you to follow a different style guide.

- Numbers up to nine are written in words (*five students*) unless you are reporting an exact measurement or percentage (*7% of the student body*) or writing about time or money (*children aged 2-5, 7 days, 2 years ago, $5*).
- Numbers 10 and higher are generally written as numerals (10, 20, 500, etc.). Write a comma separating groups of three digits in numbers over 1,000 (*525,600*, etc.).
- You should not start a sentence with a numeral (*Ten students took our survey* not *10 students took our survey*). You can also change the structure of the sentence, for example by using the passive voice (*Our survey was taken by 10 students*).
- Capitalize the word *figure* or *table* when it is followed by a number, e.g. Figure 1, Table 2.
- *Percent* (%) is used with a number (*25% or 25 percent*). *Percentage* means proportion and is not used with an exact number (*the percentage of older people who use a smartphone rose*).
- Sometimes, writers give both a percentage and an exact number for clarity, with one of the two numbers in parentheses. For example: *spending decreased by $47 billion (18 percent)* or *there was an 18 percent ($47 billion) decrease in spending*.

- Write common fractions in words (*half, quarter, two thirds*), and use them when the exact number is less important or to emphasize that a number is large or small. Consider these different ways of expressing the same value. For example, do they make 47% sound large or small?
    - 47% of the students
    - nearly/almost half (of) the students
    - less/fewer than half (of) the students
    - about 50% of the students
    - about half (of) the students
- You can express multiples as *three times, four times as much as*, etc. Instead of *two times*, you can say *twice as much as* or *double*.
- Be careful with *most*. It means "a majority," or more than half. It is not the same as *many*.

Activity 6.2: Practice the Language

Look at Table 6.1, which shows the budget and actual sports-related costs of the Summer Olympic Games from 1992–2020.

TABLE 6.1:
Costs of the Summer Olympic Games, 1992–2020

Games	*Country*	*Budget ($ billions)*	*Cost ($ billions)*	*Overrun ($ billions / %)*
Barcelona 1992	Spain	3.1	11.2	8.1 (261%)
Atlanta 1996	U.S.	1.8	4.7	2.9 (161%)
Sydney 2000	Australia	3	5.7	2.7 (90%)
Athens 2004	Greece	2.2	3.3	1.1 (50%)
Beijing 2008	China	7.7	7.8	0.1 (1%)
London 2012	U.K.	9.8	17.3	7.5 (77%)
Rio 2016	Brazil	10	15	5 (50%)
Tokyo 2020*	Japan	7.4	15.4	8 (108%)
Average		5.6	10.0	4.4 (79%)

Notes: Money is expressed in 2021 U.S. dollars. * The Tokyo 2020 Olympics were postponed until 2021.
Source: Data adapted from Flyvbjerg et al., 2016, www.thesportdigest.com, and AP News.

How would you complete the sentences using data from Table 6.1?

1. The cost of the Barcelona games was $11.2b.
2. The Sydney games cost ____________ (_______________%) more than they budgeted.
3. The budget for the Athens games was about _____________ of the actual final cost.
4. _________ of the summer games between 1992 and 2020 cost at least a billion dollars more than expected.
5. The 2016 Rio games overran the budget by _______________.
6. The lowest _____________ of overrun was achieved by Beijing in 2008.
7. The cost of the London games was _____________ as the Sydney games.
8. The budget for the Rio games was more than __________ that of the Atlanta games.
9. The cost of the Tokyo Olympics was ___________ the original budget.
10. On average, the Olympic Games cost ___________ more than the host country budgets.

Activity 6.3: Analyze a Model

Read this extract from a Pew Research report (Bialik & Fry, 2019) comparing the education of Millennials (people born between 1981 and 1996) with older generations: Generation X (1965–1980), Baby Boomers (1946–1964), and the Silent Generation (1928–1945).

> Figure 6.2 shows the highest level of education attained on average by five generations of Americans. As can be seen, today's young adults are much better educated than their grandparents, as the share of young adults with a bachelor's degree or higher has steadily climbed since 1968. Among Millennials, around four-in-ten (39%) of those aged 25 to 37 have a bachelor's degree or higher, compared with just 15% of the Silent Generation, roughly a quarter of Baby Boomers, and about three-in-ten Gen Xers (29%) when they were the same age.

FIGURE 6.2:
Educational Attainment of 25- to 37-Year-Olds

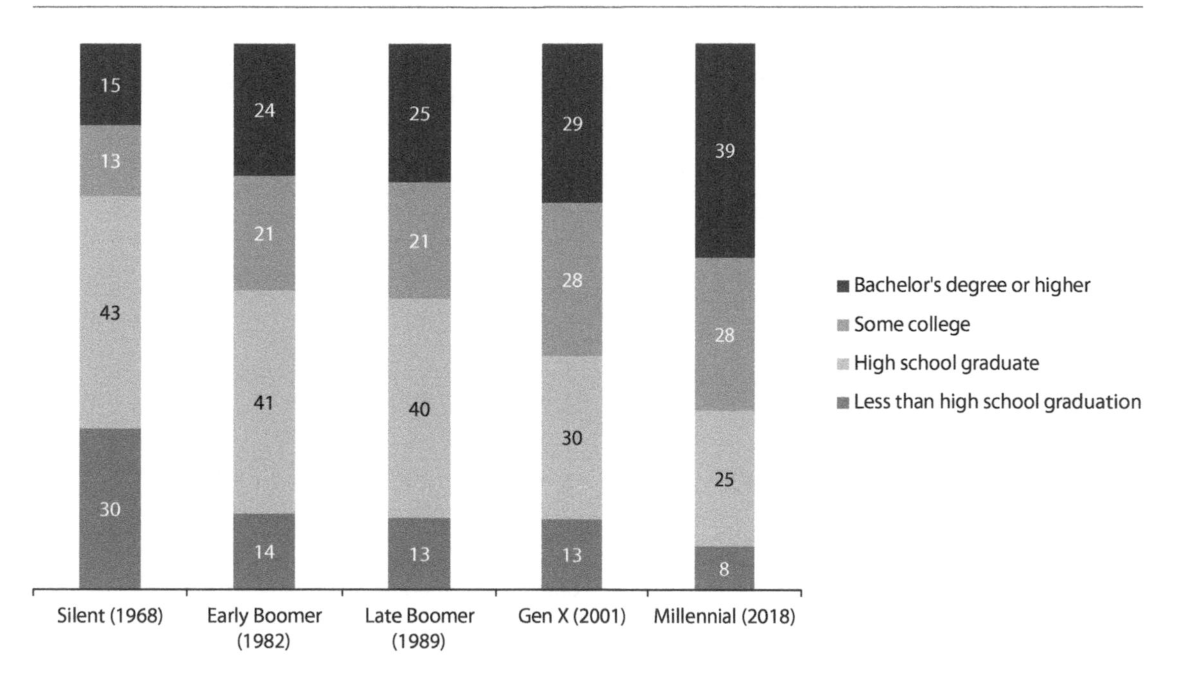

Note: Figures may not add up to 100% due to rounding. "Some college" includes associate (2-year) degrees and those who attended college but did not obtain a degree.
Source: Pew Research Center

Gains in educational attainment have been especially steep for young women (Figure 6.3). Among women of the Silent Generation, only 11% had obtained at least a bachelor's degree when they were young (ages 25 to 37 in 1968). Millennial women are about four times (43%) as likely as their Silent predecessors to have completed as much education at the same age. Millennial men are also better educated than their predecessors. About one-third of Millennial men (36%) have at least a bachelor's degree, nearly double the share of Silent Generation men (19%) when they were ages 25 to 37.

Discuss the questions with a partner or small group.

1. The text does not include all the data from the figures. How do you think the authors selected data from the figures for the report?
2. How is the information organized in the two paragraphs?

FIGURE 6.3:
Percentage of 25- to 37-Year-Olds Who Have Completed at Least a Bachelor's Degree

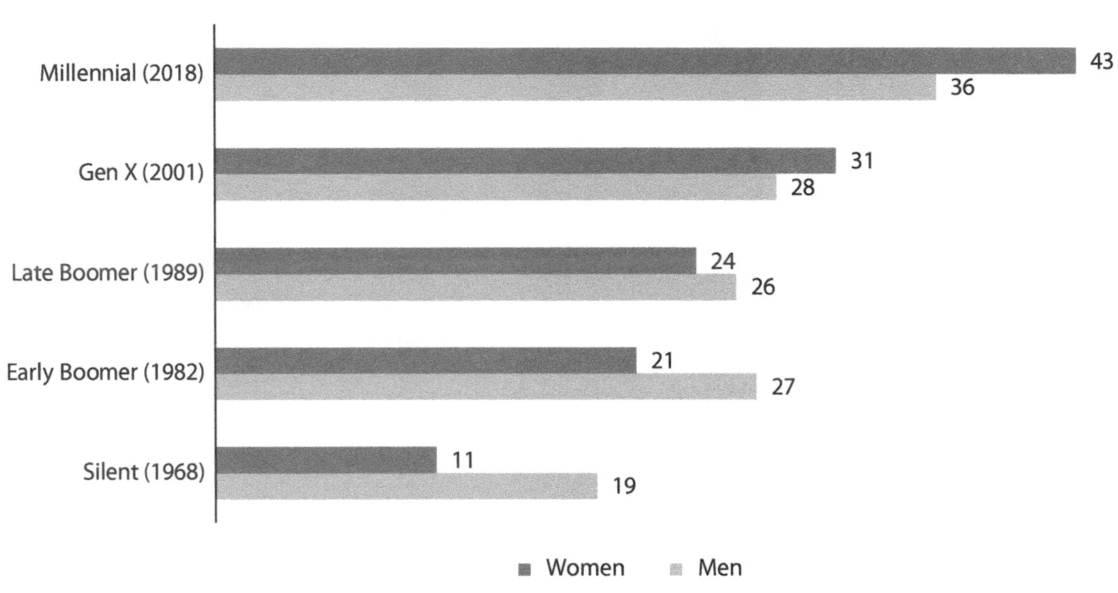

Source: Pew Research Center

3. Highlight all the different ways that the authors refer to numbers in the text. Why do the writers not just use the numerical value (e.g., 11%) for every data point?
4. The second paragraph reports that "only 11%" of women in the Silent Generation earned a bachelor's (undergraduate) degree. How would the meaning of the sentence be different if the authors used these phrases?
   a. more than one in ten women in the Silent Generation
   b. a very small proportion of women in the Silent Generation
   c. as many as 11% of women in the Silent Generation
   d. 11% of women in the Silent Generation
5. Locate all the verbs in the paragraphs. Which tenses are used and why?

Language Box: Verb Tense Use in Writing about Data

Your choice of verb tense is especially important when reporting and interpreting data. Here are the most common tenses that will be useful:

1. **Present simple** (*the graph shows, the largest category is, the change is attributed to*). Use the present simple for facts that have no particular time because you present them as always true. Do not use present simple to indicate something that is no longer true or to discuss changing trends over time. When you give your interpretation of the data, it will often be in the present simple tense.

2. **Past simple** (*the number increased, most respondents reported, the survey was conducted*). Use past simple to narrate events that happened in the past and are complete. Use past tense with most time markers (*in 1997, from 2010-2016, after the recession*) but not *since* or *for*.

3. **Present perfect** (*the rate has fallen, the situation has changed, taxes have been raised*). Use the present perfect tense (*has/have + past participle*) to show a change or development over time, starting in the past and continuing into and sometimes beyond the present. Use present perfect with *since* and *for* (*the cost has increased since 2016; prices have fallen for five years*).

4. **Present progressive** (*the growth is continuing, numbers are falling*). The present progressive means that something *is happening* now. Use the present progressive to emphasize the current situation.

In most registers of academic and professional writing, you should pay attention to these conventions:

- You can change between tenses in a sentence, paragraph, or text, but you need a reason, such as shifting in time or moving from describing the data to interpreting it.
- Be sure to edit for the *-s* ending (including *is* and *has*) with singular subjects.
- The word *data* is technically plural (*the data show ...*), although in less formal registers and in speech, it is often used as a singular noun (*the data shows ...*).

Activity 6.4: Practice the Language

Which verbs best complete each sentence about the graphs in Figure 6.4 from a Pew Research Center study on global smartphone ownership (Silver, 2019)? Discuss your answers with a partner. In many cases, different tenses are grammatical but carry different meanings. Note that although 2018 is now in the past, assume that it still represents the present situation for the purpose of this activity.

1. In Germany, almost all adults under 50 already ________________ a smartphone.

   a. own b. owned c. have owned d. are owning

2. From 2013-2017, smartphone ownership among older adults in Mexico __________ very low.

   a. remains b. remained c. has remained d. is remaining

3. Smartphone purchases __________ fastest among adults over 50 in Germany.

   a. rise b. rose c. have risen d. are rising

4. In 2013, fewer than a third of Mexicans in any age bracket ______ a smartphone.

   a. own b. owned c. have owned d. are owning

5. The proportion of young Mexicans who own a smartphone _____________ since 2013.

   a. more than doubles b. more than doubled c. has more than doubled

   d. is more than doubling

6. Overall, smartphone ownership ____________ much lower in emerging economies like Mexico than developed economies like Germany.

   a. is b. was c. has been d. had been

FIGURE 6.4:
Percentage of Adults Who Own a Smartphone in Germany and Mexico

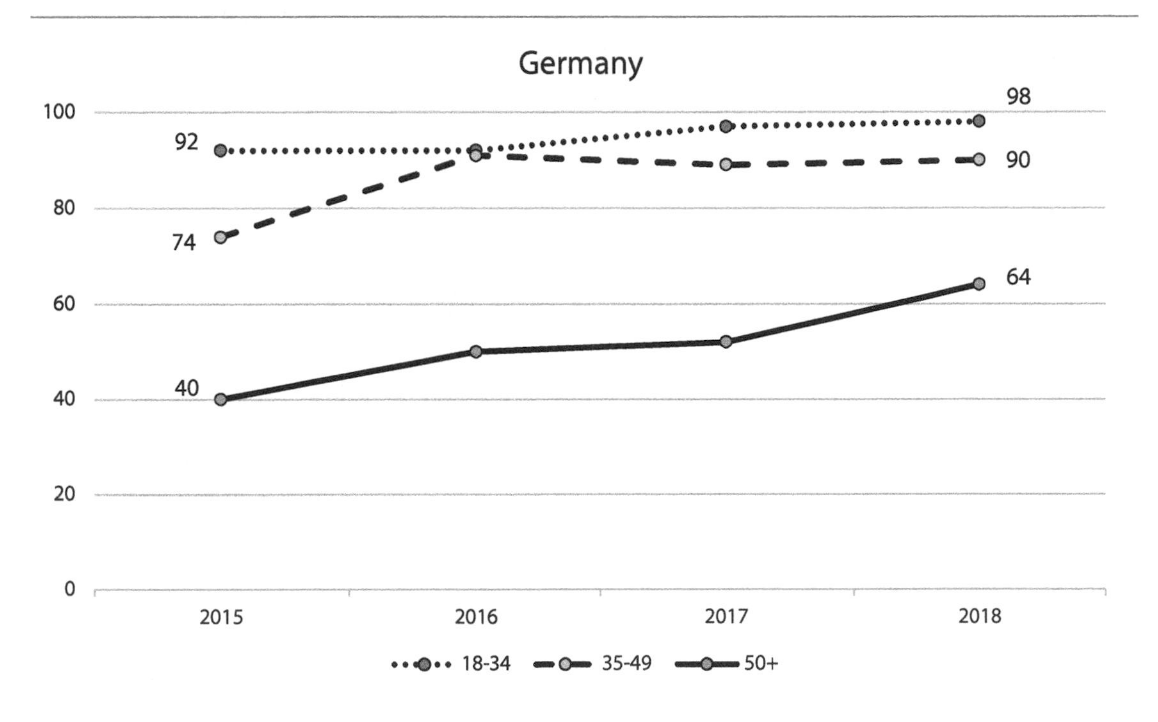

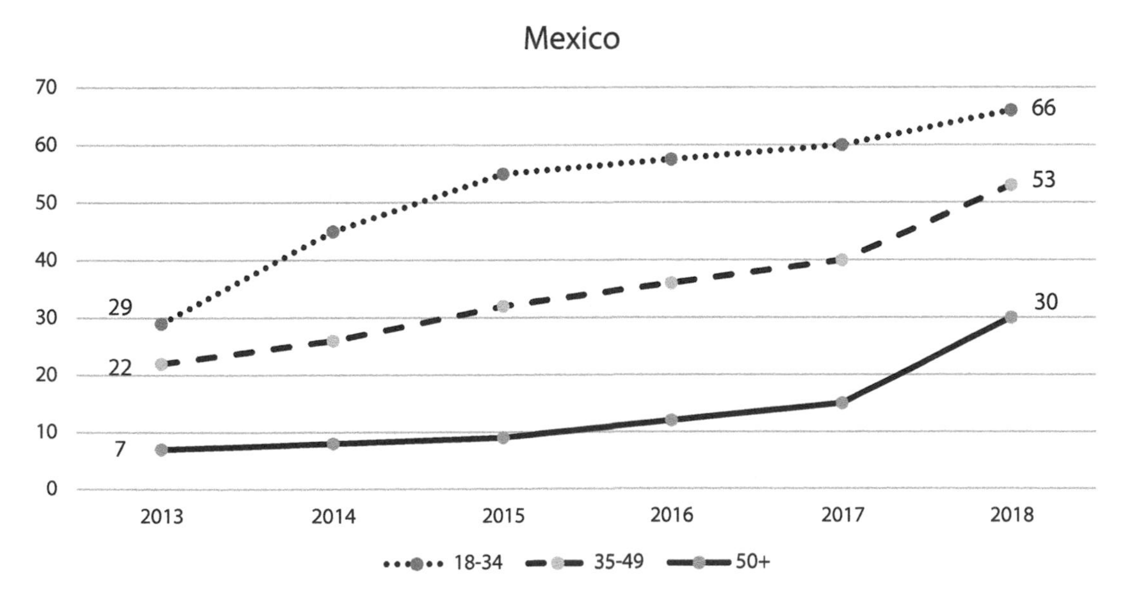

Note: Data not available for Germany before 2015.
Source: Pew Research Centers, Spring 2018 Global Attitudes Survey

WRITING ACTIVITY 6.1: Report Data from a Table

Table 6.2 shows the mean intake (i.e., average consumption) of added sugar by different age groups in the United States. Complete the gaps with data from the table, and then add your own sentences to finish the paragraph about Table 6.2.

TABLE 6.2:
Estimated Mean Intake of Added Sugars per Day, by Age

Age Group	*Added Sugar 2004 / tsp*	*Added Sugar 2016 / tsp*	*Change from 2004–2016 / Tsp (%)*
All	21.0	16.2	4.8 (23%)
2-5	15.4	10.5	4.9 (32%)
6-11	23.3	16.6	6.7 (29%)
12-19	26.5	18.3	8.2 (31%)
20+	20.2	16.2	4.0 (20%)

Notes. Tsp = Teaspoon equivalent (4.2g sugar).
Source: What We Eat in America 2003–2004 and 2015–2016 (U.S. Department of Agriculture).

Overall, Americans are consuming less added sugar. The average daily intake fell by 4.8g (①__________) from 2004 to 2016. Although all age groups saw declines, the largest percentage drops were among children aged ②_____________ and ③______________. The amount of sugar consumed by the youngest children in the survey fell by almost ④____________.

From Description to Interpretation

It is important to recognize whether an assignment is asking you to **describe** and/or **interpret** data. Sometimes, you need to **describe** the trends, patterns, and data set. In other situations, you also have to **interpret** what the data mean. For example, in an economics class assignment or test question, you might need to describe what a graph shows about a particular situation or interpret it using a theory or framework from the course. In a scientific research paper (see Project 3), after reporting the results, the writer interprets them to answer the research question or test the hypothesis. Interpretations can include:

- ❒ **Explanations:** Why do you think this pattern in the data occurred?
- ❒ **Implications:** What does the data tell us about the world?
- ❒ **Recommendations:** What should be done because of this data?
- ❒ **Inferences:** What is probably behind the data? What other explanations are possible?
- ❒ **Conclusions**: What are the results or consequences of the data?

Activity 6.5: Reporting or Interpretation?

Read the sentences from an undergraduate research paper about hedging (Guicehlaar, 2017). Note that "hedging" in these sentences refers to language we use to soften claims, such as *may, perhaps, seems,* or *somewhat.* Do you think the sentences come from the Results (reporting) or Discussion (interpretation) sections? How do you know? Discuss your answers with a partner or small group.

1. As Table 2 demonstrates, students used almost 400 more hedges per million words compared with *CCC* writers. [*CCC* is the name of an academic journal of writing studies.]

2. Students used hedging modal and lexical verbs at a higher frequency.

3. The number of times *seems* was used in the corpus of student papers was 622 times per million compared with the professional academic writers, who only used it 327 times per million.

4. Both groups were also more likely to write about they personally thought or believed over what they doubted.

5. Different audiences and purposes may account for why students use more metadiscourse.
6. Students may purposely use more hedges because they feel they lack authority.
7. Professional academic writers write for their peers, arguing that what they have to say is relevant, new, and interesting.
8. My study reflects how teachers value undergraduate metadiscourse use, despite its difference from professional use.

Activity 6.6: Writing interpretations

Read these statements reporting on data and write one or two interpretations for each one. An example has been done for you.

1. *Report:* In one laboratory study, 43% of people admitted they were guilty of an offense when they were in fact innocent (Iowa State University, 2013).

Interpretation: Admissions of guilt are not completely reliable since innocent people often admit to guilt when they are under pressure.

Other interpretations:

2. *Report:* More people have heart attacks on Monday than any other day of the week (O'Connor, 2006).

3. *Report:* Beef production requires over 15,000 liters of water per kilogram, compared to 322 liters per water for vegetables, 1,644 liters for wheat, and 4,055 liters per kilogram for beans (Mekonnen & Hoekstra, 2010).

4. *Report:* In a 2013 survey, 90% of people who remembered reading online reviews said the reviews influenced their buying decisions (Gesenhues, 2013).

Data Commentary

A **data commentary** is a text or section of a text in which you report and interpret the most important information in a figure, chart, or table of data. A data commentary can be an assignment by itself or part of a longer genre such as a policy brief, project report, or research paper.

Activity 6.7: Analyze Models

Read these data commentaries and discuss the questions that follow.

Text 1 (from a U.S. Department of Agriculture publication; Rhone, 2018)

Between 2009 and 2014, the number of grocery stores in the United States grew from 63,619 to 65,975, an increase of 4 percent. The number of convenience stores grew by 4 percent as well, but their numbers rose from 120,581 to 124,879. The greatest percentage jump in the types of stores available to consumers was for supercenters and warehouse club stores. These stores saw an 18-percent increase in their numbers between 2009 and 2014 but still totaled only 5,307 stores in 2014. Specialized food stores saw a 6-percent decline in store numbers over this period. Preference for one-stop shopping by some consumers may be playing a role in the increase in supercenters and warehouse club stores and the decline in specialized food stores.

Text 2 (from an undergraduate economics paper in MICUSP)

Figure 1 shows the changes in the distribution of family size over time. This graph shows a relatively normal distribution of children born across all years, although this distribution is slightly skewed to the left. Furthermore, this graph shows a clear decline in the number of children born to women in Costa Rica over the three years surveyed. In 1973, approximately 44 percent of women in Costa Rica had at most five births over their lifetime; by 2000 this percentage increased to nearly 78 percent, with 40 percent of those women having only two or three births. This shows quite clearly the women's changing preferences of childbearing over time.

1. Since readers can also see the actual figure or table, what is the purpose of a data commentary?
2. Highlight sentences that report the data in one color and sentences that explain or interpret the data in another color.
3. How confident are the writers in their interpretations? How do you know?
4. How are the texts organized? What strategy do you think the writers used to choose the order of information in each paragraph?
5. What is the function of the first sentence in the second (student) text? Write a different sentence to start this paragraph. How does your sentence change the paragraph?
6. What verb tenses are used in the data commentaries, and why?

Language Box: Referring to Tables and Figures

You can refer to figures and tables using internal references in several ways:

- Figure 1 shows the number of students enrolling in language courses.
- The number of students enrolling in language courses is falling (Figure 1) or (see Figure 1).
- As Figure 1 demonstrates, the number of students in language courses is falling.
- The results are shown in Table 1.

The most common verb for referring to data is *show* (or, in the passive voice, *is shown*), but all the verbs listed are frequently used in research writing for figures and tables.

An important phrase you can use in the source or highlight stage of a data commentary is *as* _____ *(in)*:

- As shown in Figure 1, ...
- As seen in the table, ...
- As can be seen, ...

These phrases are more common in academic writing than *as you can see in Figure 1*, which is appropriate in presentations or other genres where the writer addresses the reader directly (e.g., textbooks).

	ACTIVE VOICE	**PASSIVE VOICE**
	Figure/Table 1 ________ sugar intake in 2004 and 2016.	Sugar intake in 2004 and 2016 is _______ in Figure/Table 1.
Figures	*illustrates* *displays** *depicts**	*illustrated* *seen* *displayed*
Tables	*lists** *contains** *reports* *provides** *summarizes**	*presented* *given* *reported* *listed* *found*
Both	*shows* *presents**	*shown*

Source: Corpus of Contemporary Academic English (Davies, 2020) and Swales & Feak (2012).
* These reporting verbs *cannot* be followed by *that* clauses (for example, "Figure 1 shows *that sugar consumption has increased*" but not "Table 1 summarizes *that sugar consumption has increased*").

Activity 6.8: Practice the Language

How would you complete the sentences with appropriate words from the Language Box?

1. As ________________ in Table 1, attendance at sporting events is decreasing.
2. Figure 1 ________________ the cost of textbooks in three different disciplines.
3. The average global temperature since 1980 can be ________________ in Figure 2.
4. Figure 3 ________________ that sales of large cars are related to the cost of gasoline.
5. As can be ________________, the number of non-English academic journals continues to grow.
6. People who have served prison time can have their voting rights restored in some but not all states (____________ Table 4).

Organizing a Data Commentary

Data commentaries are usually made up of these moves, typically in this order:

- ❒ **Context**: Why is this data relevant?
- ❒ **Source**: Who collected the data? Where should the reader look (e.g., Figure 1, Table 2)?
- ❒ **Focus**: What are the data about? What is the main idea?
- ❒ **Highlights**: What are the most important, interesting, or surprising data points?
- ❒ **Interpretations**: What do the data mean or imply? What can you suggest or conclude? What is missing or unclear?

Look back at the example data commentaries in Activity 6.7. Which moves can you find? An important consideration is the organization of the highlights in a data commentary. Your decision will depend on your rhetorical planning (e.g., what is the purpose of your writing, who is the audience, what is your role?), but here are some options:

- ❒ **General to specific**: Start with the broad patterns, trends, or findings and then focus on specific or technical details (e.g., Activity 6.7, Text 1).
- ❒ **Specific to general**: Highlight the key data and then draw a conclusion from it (e.g., Activity 6.7, Text 2).

- ❒ **Chronological**: Discuss changes over time, from the earliest to most recent, or more recent to earliest data (e.g., "*From 2005–2010 … Between 2011 and 2015 … Since 2015 …*").
- ❒ **Categorical**: Divide the data into categories and discuss them in turn (e.g., the data commentary in Activity 6.3 discusses generations and then gender).

Remember that a data commentary is always selective. You choose the most important data, trends, patterns, or observations to present and interpret.

WRITING TASK 6.2: Scrambled Text

These sentences could be used in a data commentary on the graphs about smartphones in Figure 6.4 (Silver, 2019). What order would you put the sentences in?

a. As smartphone ownership has increased in both advanced and emerging economies, the growth has often been uneven.

b. In Mexico, meanwhile, smartphone data stretches back to 2013, when 29% of 18- to 34-year-olds owned smartphones compared with just 7% of Mexicans ages 50 and older. In the most recent survey, however, smartphone ownership has jumped to roughly two-thirds of young Mexicans but remains at just three-in-ten among those ages 50 and above.

c. Figure 6.4 shows differences in smartphone adoption by age group in a developed (German) and developing (Mexico) country.

d. Three years later, smartphone ownership had ticked up to 98% among younger Germans and grown to nearly two-thirds (64%) of the 50-plus population.

e. Although the gap between developed and developing countries is closing, especially for younger people, the differences that remain need to be further studied to better understand which social groups lack access to modern technology and the advantages it brings.

f. As can be seen, opposite patterns are visible in these two countries. In 2015, 92% of Germans under 35 owned a smartphone, compared with just 40% of those ages 50 and above.

g. Taken together, these graphs suggest that age is a key factor associated with cell phone ownership.

h. In advanced and emerging economies alike, younger people are much more digitally connected than older generations.

Discuss your choices with a partner or small group using these questions as a guide.

1. What moves did you find in this data commentary (you may not find all of them): context, source, focus, highlights, interpretations?
2. How did you choose the order of the sentences? Did you follow a general-to-specific, specific-to-general, chronological, or categorical organization?
3. Does the writer have a positive or negative view about the growth of the smartphone market? How do you know?

Language Box: Hedging Interpretations

When you are interpreting data (and also images, literature, historical events, and other aspects of your studies), you often need to show that you cannot be 100 percent certain of your conclusions. In experimental research, there are always limitations to the findings which mean that writers cannot sound over-confident. Therefore, writers use language techniques called **hedging.** The use of hedging depends on several aspects of your rhetorical planning, such as your role, your audience, the situations, and conventions of the genre.

1. **Modal verbs** used for hedging include *may, might, can, could, should.* They are followed by a base verb (*may suggest, could mean, should result in*). *May* is especially common in academic writing:
   - Education level **may affect** consumer choices.
   - The change **could be** due to new government policies.
   - These results **might suggest** that ....
   - Public art **may** force viewers to see their environment through new eyes.
   - The lower rate in 2008 **may have been caused** by the recession.

Note the **past modal** form in the last example (*may* + *have* + past participle) to indicate a guess about a situation in the past.

2. **Quantifiers** are very helpful when summarizing or interpreting data without giving the exact quantity:
   - **Many** adults / **Much** research
   - **Most** smartphones (= over 50%)
   - **Some** products
   - **Few** respondents / **Little** information
3. **Adverbs** can be inserted either to hedge a claim or to strengthen it (**boosting**):
   - The rate rose **dramatically/quickly/drastically/rapidly/steadily/ quickly.**
   - The population fell **slightly/somewhat/gradually/slowly/rapidly/ substantially/sharply.**
   - The number was **considerably/much/far/substantially/slightly** higher.

If you want to show surprise at a trend in the data, use *actually* or *even*:

- The number of incidents **actually** increased after 2015. (*I expected it to decrease*)
- The proportion of men in higher education is **even** declining. (*not just staying the same*)

Note that the adverb *significantly* has a technical meaning in quantitative research. It means that a difference is statistically unlikely to be due to chance. If you are not sure what this means, avoid the word in your writing! In the arts and humanities, *significantly* is less common but can safely be used as a synonym for *considerably*.

4. Finally, here are some phrases you can use to avoid suggesting that a complex phenomenon has only one cause or result:
   - **One of the reasons** for ... is ....
   - ... is **a factor** in ....
   - **One major/important/notable result** of ... has been ....
   - ... is **partly caused/explained/supported** by....

Activity 6.10: Practice the Language

Put the words in these lists in the order you think best represents the degree of hedging, from weakest to strongest, or smallest to largest. Discuss your ideas with a small group. Use a dictionary to confirm or question your results.

1. dramatically / quickly / drastically / rapidly / steadily / quickly
2. slightly / somewhat / gradually / slowly / rapidly / substantially / sharply
3. much / some / many / few / a lot / most / all / almost all
4. prove / suggest / hint / mean / indicate / show / tend
5. can / may / could / might / will / must

Activity 6.11: Hedging Claims

Using the Language Box and Activity 6.10, write hedges for these claims and make them more reasonable in academic writing.

1. People consume too much sugar.
2. Fast food causes disease.
3. Children are more active than adults.
4. Restaurants do not offer appealing vegetarian options.
5. Healthy food is more expensive than unhealthy food.

Pedagogical Genre: Data Commentary

A. **Re-read the examples of data commentaries in this unit, plus this additional model:**

> ①While the internet is very widely used among Americans, the Pew Research Center found that 10% of U.S. adults are still not online. Figure 1 depicts the demographic profile of U.S. adults who do not use the internet. As can be seen from the chart, age, education, and socio-economic status are major factors in internet access. Adults aged 18 to 29 are all internet users, according to Pew's survey, whereas more than a quarter of adults over 65 live without the internet. Education is another notable point. Almost one in three Americans without a high-school education do not use the internet at all. This may be explained by other demographic categories: the proportion of non-internet users is also higher in rural areas (15%) and low-income communities (18%), where educational attainment tends to be lower. In summary, offline Americans are not distributed equally across the society.
>
> ②Social factors may contribute to the differences among generations in their use of the internet. Millennials probably feel very strong peer pressure to go online. If the survey is representative and 100% of young people use the internet, it may be very isolating to remain offline. However, since almost 30% of Baby Boomers are not online, the internet is clearly less important for making social connections among this older generation. They are probably also less concerned than younger users with the number of reactions they receive to social media posts, which is likely to be another factor that makes the internet almost universal among Americans under the age of 30.

Answer the questions about this data commentary and then discuss them with a partner or small group.

1. **Where are the five moves in the text: context, sources, focus, highlights, interpretations?**
2. **What is the overall pattern of information in this data commentary—chronological, general/specific, or categorical?**
3. **Identify the hedging and boosting language in both paragraphs. Do you think it is effective? Why, or why not?**

4. Which of these framing sentences could start the next paragraph in the data commentary? Why?
   a. There are several consequences resulting from the lack of internet access for working-age adults.
   b. However, technology infrastructure (e.g. home broadband, cell phone towers) is not always available in rural areas.
   c. There are two reasons why more students are choosing computer science majors at university.
   d. This graph will change over the next generation in a number of interesting ways.

B. Choose a graph, figure, or table that is related to a topic you are currently studying, or choose one of interest from a site such as the Pew Research Center (http://www.pewresearch.org/), Gallup (https://news.gallup.com), the United Nations (http://data.un.org/), or Statista (https://www.statista.com/). Your library may also maintain a page of statistical sources you can access, or you might choose data from another course you are taking.

C. Plan your data commentary using this outline:

   Context:

   Source:

   Focus:

   Highlights (order of information?):

   Interpretations:

D. Write a data commentary that highlights the most important data points and offers interpretations. Your instructor might specify the audience and context; otherwise, take on the role of an expert in the field who is explaining the data to an educated but general audience for one of the websites listed in Step B.

E. Peer Review: Ask one or two partners to read your data commentary. Use these questions to give peer feedback:

1. Does the writer clearly identify the context, source, and focus of the data?
2. Does the writer choose interesting highlights?
3. Does the writer discuss implications (e.g., implications, recommendations, conclusions, inferences)?
4. Has the writer hedged interpretations effectively?
5. What is the writer's strategy for organizing the data commentary (e.g., general-to-specific, chronological, categorical)?
6. How else could the writer improve the data commentary?

F. Self-Review: Revise your data commentary using your peers' feedback. Have you done everything on this checklist?

- ☐ My data commentary has all the necessary moves in a logical order with a clear strategy for organization.
- ☐ Verb tenses are well chosen and verb forms are accurate.
- ☐ Claims are appropriately hedged and/or boosted.
- ☐ Numbers are presented using appropriate conventions.

What else do you need to work on? Make further revisions to your data commentary if necessary.

Genre in Action: Policy Brief

A **policy brief** is a professional genre in which writers summarize research (often including data) for an audience of readers who make policies, such as government officials, local councils, company executives, boards of directors, non-profit organizations, or university administrators. In most cases, the writer of the brief is an expert in a particular area, but the readers are not, so the information has to be reported and interpreted for a non-specialist audience. Some policy briefs provide an objective summary (a report) and suggest several possible courses of action (interpretations). Others go further and argue that one solution or policy is best. According to research at the University of North Carolina at Chapel Hill, policy briefs are a common assignment in social science courses because they are important professional preparation (Danielewicz et al., 2018).

Policy briefs are, as the name implies, usually short. For the assignment, you will write a one- to two-page brief on an issue that is important to you or relevant to one of your classes.

A. Read the text of this policy brief published by the Society for Research in Child Development (SRCD), a well-established international professional society in the field of developmental psychology. The original document can be found on the society's website (www.srcd.org). A section titled "What the research says" has been omitted.

Understanding and Addressing the Effect of Digital Games on Cognitive Development in Middle Childhood

Social Policy Report Brief, Volume 32, Number 1 (April 2019)

Why does this matter?

The effects of using interactive media have been well studied among young children and adolescents but remain understudied for middle childhood (ages 6-12 years). Children and youth of this age comprise much of the pre-adult population that uses digital games and apps. The Every Student Succeeds Act [the U.S. federal education law] says that states must give students access to technology and use evidence-based methods of incorporating technology into curricula and instruction, but doesn't speak to digital games directly. Research on digital games in middle childhood can inform the design of games that teach tech-savvy skills and promote cognitive development.

Background

Six- to 12-year-olds are exposed to digital media extensively[1]:

- In 64% of the 4,000 U.S. households sampled recently, at least one person played video games three or more hours a week and nearly 30% of these players were 18 years and under.
- Two-thirds of parents in that survey said they played video games with their children weekly and perceived the games as beneficial.

[1] See the full Social Policy Report for references, including for the surveys that are the sources for the statistics summarized in this section of the brief.

- In a survey of U.S. children under 8, on average, children used interactive games about 25 minutes daily, with little use before age 2. In another survey, interactive game play for children ages 8 to 18 averaged 1 hour, 20 minutes daily.
- In a survey of K-8 [kindergarten to 8th-grade] teachers, 74% reported using digital games for instruction, with 80% indicating that they primarily used educational games and apps.

Yet little research has studied the effects of digital media at these ages:

- Much of what is known about the impact of media on children's development is drawn from research on television-viewing behaviors.
- In two meta-analyses examining the impact of commercial video game use on information processing, only a few of the studies focused on children and youth from 3 to 17 years.

Implications for Practice

- Parents need research-based guidelines to understand how to support their children's learning while using digital media.
- Under-resourced schools need access to digital media and high-speed internet to integrate educational games into curricula.
- Training for teachers should include best practices for developmentally appropriate instruction when using digital games.

Implications for Policy

- Federal agencies should fund technology, app, and game development aimed at fostering students' academic skills, together with research on effects on cognitive development.
- Research-based guidance on what constitutes an educational app is needed. The designation of an app as "educational" is largely unregulated and unmonitored, and is rarely based on research.
- Some [U.S.] states include digital games in their curriculum policies. While 22 states have adopted statewide media literacy standards, they vary widely. Research on how and when digital media use in middle childhood benefits children's cognitive development could inform the further development of state standards.

Answer the questions to analyze the structure and style of the policy brief:

1. What is the purpose of each section (sub-heading)? What are the relationships between the sections?
    a. Why does it matter?
    b. Background
    c. Implications for practice
    d. Implications for policy
2. How and where are data used in the brief?
3. The writers of the brief use no citations except for a footnote to a longer scholarly report published by their organization. Why do you think they do this?
4. What verb tenses are used in the background section, and why?
5. Locate the subjects of the sentences in the two implications sections. Why do you think the sentences are written in this way?
6. What do you notice about the verb tenses in the implications sections?
7. Look up other short policy briefs on this topic or another topic you are interested in. Do they follow the structure of the SRCD brief? What similarities and differences do you find?

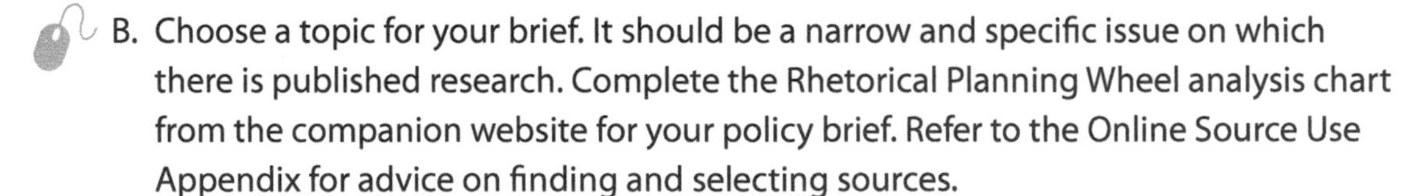

B. Choose a topic for your brief. It should be a narrow and specific issue on which there is published research. Complete the Rhetorical Planning Wheel analysis chart from the companion website for your policy brief. Refer to the Online Source Use Appendix for advice on finding and selecting sources.

C. Use your rhetorical planning notes and the structure you identified in Step A to plan and draft your policy brief. You can see examples of attractive designs and templates online if you would like to present your brief in a visually effective way.

D. Peer Review. Ask one or two partners to read your policy brief. Use these questions to give peer feedback:

1. What is the problem that the brief is addressing?
2. Does the brief present a range of options objectively or advocate for one particular policy solution?
3. Is the brief clear to you as a non-expert reader?
4. Does the brief report and interpret data effectively?
5. How can the writer improve the policy brief?

E. Self-Review: Revise your brief using your peers' feedback. Have you done everything on this checklist?

- ☐ The brief has all the required sections and uses clear sub-headings.
- ☐ Highlights of the data and interpretations are boosted and/or hedged to fit my purpose in this brief.
- ☐ I edited the brief to make it clear and accessible to a non-specialist reader.
- ☐ I chose appropriate verb tenses for each section of the brief.

What else do you need to work on? Make further revisions to your brief if necessary.

References

Bialik, K., & Fry, R. (2019). *Millennial life: How young adulthood today compares with prior generations.* Pew Research Center. https://www.pewresearch.org/social-trends/2019/02/14/millennial-life-how-young-adulthood-today-compares-with-prior-generations-2/

Bowman, S. A., Clemens, J. C., Friday, J. E., Schroeder, N., Shimizu, M., LaComb, R. P., & Moshfegh, A. J. (2018). *Food patterns equivalents intakes by Americans* (Dietary Data Brief No. 20). U.S. Department of Agriculture. https://www.ars.usda.gov/ARSUserFiles/80400530/pdf/DBrief/20_Food_Patterns_Equivalents_0304_1516.pdf

Danielewicz, J., Jack, J., Singer, S., Stockwell, J., & Guest Pryal. (n.d.). *The genre project–A research project from the UNC Writing Program.* http://genre.web.unc.edu/

Davies, M. (2020). *Corpus of contemporary American English.* https://www.english-corpora.org/coca/

Flyvbjerg, B., Stewart, A., & Budzier, A. (2016*). The Oxford Olympics study 2016: Cost and cost overrun at the games* (Said Business School WP 2016-20). https://ssrn.com/abstract=2804554cite

Gesenheus, A. (2013, April 9). *Survey: 90% of customers say buying decisions are influenced by online reviews.* https://martech.org/survey-customers-more-frustrated-by-how-long-it-takes-to-resolve-a-customer-service-issue-than-the-resolution/

Guichelaar, K. (2017). Metadiscourse in professional and student writing: A corpus study. *Young Scholars in Writing, 14,* 6–16.

Iowa State University. (2013, September 10). *ISU researchers examine how stress may lead to false confessions* [Press release]. https://www.news.iastate.edu/news/2013/09/10/falseconfessions

Mekonnen, M.M., & Hoekstra, A.Y. (2010). *The green, blue and grey water footprint of farm animals and animal products* (Value of Water Research Report Series No.48). UNESCO Institute for Water Education. http://waterfootprint.org/media/downloads/Report-48-WaterFootprint-AnimalProducts-Vol1_1.pdf

O'Connor, A. (2006, March 14). The claim: Heart attacks are more common on Mondays. *New York Times.* https://www.nytimes.com/2006/03/14/health/the-claim-heart-attacks-are-more-common-on-mondays.html

Rhone, A. (2018, May 2). County-level data show changes in the number and concentration of food stores. *Amber Waves.* https://www.ers.usda.gov/amber-waves/2018/may/county-level-data-show-changes-in-the-number-and-concentration-of-food-stores/

Silver, L. (2019). *Smartphone ownership is growing rapidly around the world, but not always equally.* Pew Research Center. https://www.pewresearch.org/global/2019/02/05/smartphone-ownershipis-growing-rapidly-around-the-world-but-not-always-equally/

Society for Research in Child Development. (2019). *Understanding and addressing the effect of digital games on cognitive development in middle childhood* (Social Policy Report Brief, Vol. 32, Issue 1). https://www.srcd.org/research/understanding-and-addressing-effect-digital-games-cognitive-development-middle-childhood

Swales, J. M., & Feak, C. B. (2012). *Academic writing for graduate students: Essential tasks and skills* (3rd ed.). University of Michigan Press.

7 Argue

Goals

- ❒ Write arguments appropriate to different academic disciplines with claims and support
- ❒ Write claims with different degrees of confidence and authority
- ❒ Choose effective and appropriate supporting evidence, including citations, examples, and counterarguments
- ❒ Pedagogical Genre: Write an argument essay
- ❒ Genre in Action: Write an opinion editorial (op-ed)

What Is the Action?

In academic writing, argument rarely involves expressing a personal opinion or disagreeing with someone else. Instead, you will be asked to take and defend a position based on your readings, data, class lectures, and sometimes your own experience. Arguments in college writing are supported by the evidence appropriate for a specific class assignment and academic discipline. However, not every piece of writing you will do is an argument. Reports, summaries, and most short-answer questions are basically informational and not argumentative.

In this unit, we focus on two key components of argumentative writing—making claims and supporting them with appropriate evidence. As always, you need to consider all the components of the Rhetorical Planning Wheel as you write. Your argument is only effective if you have taken into account your role, your audience(s), your purpose(s), the context, appropriate sources, an effective structure, and the relevant conventions.

Although you will need to make arguments in a wide range of assignments, the way you argue varies in different academic disciplines and classes. In particular, the placement of claims within the text and the types of evidence required are different. For example, in most argumentative writing in the humanities (English, history, philosophy), the major claim (or **thesis**) is usually made near the beginning of the paper, supported by references to other texts in the body and often restated in the conclusion. But in other disciplines such as the sciences and business, the evidence often comes from data, theories, equations, and previous research. In these fields, the major claim frequently comes at the end of the paper after the data have been analyzed and discussed.

Assignments that ask you to argue include:

- ❒ many and varied tasks referred to as *essays*
- ❒ editorials and opinion columns
- ❒ literary interpretations
- ❒ historical arguments
- ❒ the discussion section of an empirical research paper
- ❒ business proposals
- ❒ some discussion board posts

Activity 7.1: What Do You Know?

Do you agree or disagree with these statements? Explain your reasons to a partner or small group.

1. Arguments must always have three supporting points.
2. It is acceptable to use personal experience and examples in arguments. The first person *I* can be used.
3. The major claim (thesis) for an argument always appears in the introduction to a paper.
4. Most arguments are stronger when the writer considers multiple perspectives on claims.
5. Arguments can present both sides of an issue without showing preference for one of them.

Argument in Academic Writing

Argument in academic writing varies widely depending on the discipline, genre, and even the class in which an argument task is assigned. The purpose of an argument might be to claim that something is important, correct, incorrect, or possible based on evidence, which might include research, examples, data, or other sources. Some arguments are written to change readers' thinking, while others are calls to action. However, in all cases, the **claims** about the writer's topic are supported by **evidence**. In addition to selecting appropriate types of evidence, you need to consider the audience, your role as a writer, and the conventions of the genre. All of these will impact the way you structure your argument and the language you choose.

Consider history and biology: History belongs to the humanities, whereas biology is one of the natural sciences. The purpose of argumentative writing in history is to evaluate evidence in support of one or more perspectives on a historical issue. Like most academic writing, historical arguments are based on sources, but these sources might include other historians' writing as well as original documents, images, and videos. Research shows that there are four keys to effective historical argumentation (Wineburg, 2001):

1. **Sourcing:** evaluate the reliability of each source you use.
2. **Contextualization:** consider the historical context of each source.
3. **Corroboration:** ask what other sources say about the evidence you have found.
4. **Close reading**: examine the language, claims, and reasoning of the source carefully.

Meanwhile, experts in scientific argumentation suggest that there are three different components to a scientific argument (McNeill & Knight, 2013):

1. **Claim:** an answer to a question, a solution to a problem, a scientific idea, theory, practice, or hypothesis, often appearing, well-hedged, at the end of a text.
2. **Evidence:** scientific data that supports the claim, usually empirical (from direct observation and experimentation) but sometimes also citing evidence and claims from other sources.
3. **Reasoning**: using scientific principles, explaining whether and how the evidence shows that the claim is accurate or inaccurate.

A distinctive feature of scientific argumentation is its use of data and specific scientific reasoning. For example, if you are arguing why a golf ball sinks, your personal experience with dropping golf balls in the water is not relevant, but a table of data showing the density of the golf ball is relevant because the scientific reasoning is that objects with greater density than water will sink (McNeill & Knight, 2013).

Whatever subject you are studying, ask these questions:

1. What kinds of claims can I make in this assignment, in this class, or within this discipline?
2. What counts as acceptable evidence in an argument for this context?
3. What type(s) of sources should I use for this task?
4. Do I need to evaluate these sources, or are they considered reliable?
5. What do I do with sources that present a different argument or interpretation?

Activity 7.2: Analyze Models

Read these extracts from arguments in history and biology, both of which deal with the topic of sleep. The first is from a paper published in the *Journal of Undergraduate Science and Technology*, which reviews the research on the effects of sleep deprivation (i.e., lack of sleep). The second text is from a paper published in *History Matters: An Undergraduate Journal of Historical Research*. This paper examines the myth of "super soldiers" in World War II (1939–1945), in particular the use of stimulant drugs to combat sleep deprivation. Note that the texts use different citation and reference styles. Most references and footnotes have been omitted here for clarity.

Text 1: Biology (Karimikonda, 2017)

Both sleep quality and duration have been shown to have a direct impact on health.[4] Many studies show that sleep deprivation impairs learning and memory processes, both of which play crucial roles in an individual's academic performance.[4] In addition to poor academic performance, sleep deprivation has also been linked with obesity. A study involving fourteen healthy individuals subjected to either four nights of healthy sleep or sleep deprivation found that those who were deprived of sleep felt hungrier and consumed twice as much fat and protein as the control group. These food cravings were explained through amplified endocannabinoid levels, which were involved in food cravings and led to hunger pangs.[5]

Text 2: History (Racine, 2019)

Sleep deprivation can have profoundly negative impacts on overall functioning. The average adult human requires roughly eight hours of sleep to maintain proper physical and mental health. According to Derickson, 85 percent of American soldiers in the Italian campaign [in World War II] slept fewer than 6 hours, while 31 percent slept fewer than 3 hours per night. Sleep-deprived individuals are more prone to task errors, experience higher levels of psychological stress, are less likely to properly follow orders, are more likely to take shortcuts in decision making, and suffer from potential loss of muscle. The need to overcome fatigue was a challenge, one that needed a fast-acting solution. For many governments, psychostimulant drugs would answer the call.[4]

Note 4 in Text 2 refers the reader to the article by Derickson and adds "for more information on the biological and psychological effects of sleep deprivation, see . . ." where four more sources are listed.

Answer the questions with a partner or small group about the two texts.

1. What is the claim in each text? That is, what point is the writer trying to argue?
2. Where in each text is the claim stated?
3. What are the claim, evaluation, and scientific reasoning in the biology extract?
4. What are examples of sourcing, contextualization, corroboration, and close reading in the history extract?
5. What differences in the use of sources do you notice between the two texts?

Claims and Evidence

A **claim** is a position that a writer takes on a particular issue. In academic writing, claims must always be supported by authoritative **evidence,** such as examples, citations, quotations, data, or logical reasoning. In everyday conversation, you might hear someone claim that air travel is the safest form of transportation, but in an academic context, the reader would expect the writer to provide appropriate support for that claim in the form of statistics, examples, or explanations.

In a typical argumentative essay, a common pedagogical genre in a range of disciplines, you will make one major claim, called the **thesis**. You might then break this down into a number of smaller claims, or **sub-claims**. Each of these must have evidence to defend it. Together, your claims build an argument. Sometimes, you will write one sub-claim and its supporting evidence per paragraph. However, sometimes you will need several paragraphs of evidence to support a claim in your writing.

Activity 7.3: Analyze Models

Read the first paragraph from an undergraduate student's argument essay for a writing class. The title of the essay is "Progress Built on a Wasteland: Consumerism and the Dangers of E-waste" (Schlusser, 2020). As you read, look for the thesis, or major claim, that the writer will make. (Citations follow MLA style, 9th edition.)

> Stepping into an Apple store is like looking at the future. The architecture, with its glass walls and white interior, is ripped from a twentieth-century science fiction novel, and the orderly rows of devices, glowing with crisp retina displays and humming with soft electricity, provoke childlike wonder. Across the globe, one can find other scenes ripped from science fiction, but in this future, everything has gone horribly wrong. In a quaint Chinese village, crop failures, diseased livestock, and poisonous drinking water have forced everyone to relocate (Kaiman par. 3). In Ghana, fires smolder and spew thick smoke across a blackened landscape littered with shiny green circuit boards and the emptied plastic shells of laptops (McElvaney). Tragically, these circumstances are brought about by humanity's technological progress. More specifically, they are a result of mass consumption and disposal of the byproducts of technological progress. According to a United Nations report, 41.8 million tons of e-waste was generated in 2014, a sharp rise from

> 33.8 million in 2010. In 2018, it is projected that 49.8 million tons will be produced (Baldé et al. 24). The world consumes more electronics every year. The increased consumption of electronics that is fueling ecological damage is attributable to a consumer culture that promotes constant replacement of devices and deemphasizes repair and longevity. Society's obsession with newer, faster, and better devices is creating an ecological nightmare overseas that can only be mitigated by a massive change in cultural mindset.

1. **Identify the thesis of the essay (the major claim in this paragraph).**
2. **What language choices in this paragraph indicate that the writer is making an argument and not just presenting information?**
3. **Why does the writer start his essay with his experience of going into an electronics store?**

Now read a paragraph from another first-year student's argument essay from the same course. The topic is the use of methacrylates, a group of chemicals found in some cosmetics products, especially for nails (Soukaseum, 2018). (Citations appear in APA style, 6th edition.)

> A case examined by Dan Slodownik and Jasen D. Williams demonstrates the negative effects of exposure to methacrylates through the experience of a thirty-three-year-old woman who developed paresthesia a feeling of burning in her fingers after receiving acrylic nail treatments (Slodownik et al., 2007). As explained by Donaghy, Rushworth and Jacobs, if applied directly to the hands over an extended period of time, methacrylates will cause nerve damage (Donaghy et al., 1991). People go to nail salons with intentions of self-pampering and relaxation, not mutilation or painful allergic reactions. Therefore, it does not make sense for strong polymerizing chemicals historically used in dentistry to be used in nail products.

4. **What is the claim in this paragraph?**
5. **What language choices in this paragraph indicate that the writer is making an argument and not just presenting information?**
6. **What types of evidence does the writer provide to support the claim?**

Language Box: Controlling the Strength of Claims

Although argumentative writing asks you to defend a claim, position, or opinion, in most cases, you are not expected to insert your own voice directly (e.g., *I believe that* or *in my opinion)*. Instead, the strongest form of a claim is a statement in a present tense using a linking verb (such as *be*) or a causal verb (*causes, results from, leads to, create,* etc.). If you write your claim in this way, you are taking full responsibility as the writer for the truth of the claim and not allowing any disagreement, so you should only write like this if you are confident about your claim or if the assignment calls for you to express a strong opinion:

- These circumstances **are brought about** by technological progress.
- They **are a result** of ....
- Society's obsession with newer, faster, and better devices **is creating** an ecological nightmare.

You can also make claims stronger by **boosting** them, for example:

1. Use a modal of obligation (*should, must, need to*).
2. Use an adjective to emphasize urgency (it is *necessary, important, vital, urgent* to ...).
3. Use an adverb to intensify a claim (*absolutely, clearly, precisely, certainly, particularly, extremely, only*).

In all these cases, you are emphasizing your own voice, which may be appropriate if your role is to show your personal commitment to the argument. In other types of writing, however, the writer is expected to be distant from the text, so you should avoid additional boosting.

On the other hand, you can modify the strength of your claims by introducing other voices that share responsibility for the claim or which cast the claim as an opinion rather than an uncontested fact. This is called **hedging**. Common hedging techniques in academic writing include:

1. Attribute the claim to a source:
   - The chemicals in nail polish are harmful to the skin **(Donaghy et al., 1991)**.
   - **According to Donaghy et al. (1991)**, the chemicals in nail polish are harmful to the skin.

2. Use a modal verb (*can, could, may, might*) to recognize that other readers and experts might have different views:
   - Using nail polish **can** be harmful to the skin.
   - These circumstances **may** result from the disposal of e-waste.
3. Use a verb like *seem* or *appear* to show that the claim is not a fully settled fact and open the space for readers to disagree:
   - **It appears that** the chemicals in nail polish are harmful to the skin.
   - Consumers **seem** unwilling to pay more for environmentally friendly products.
4. Choose words that do not suggest direct cause/effect or limit the scope of the claim:
   - E-waste is **one factor in** the environmental disaster.
   - **Some** chemicals in nail polish **have been associated with** painful skin conditions.

Activity 7.4: Practice the Language

Read each group of sentences (a–c) and number them 1 through 3 in the order of strength, with 1 being the strongest claim of the three. Which words helped you determine the order? Then discuss your rankings and the language used with a partner or small group.

1. a. __ According to technology experts, social media has changed the way we understand privacy.

   b. __ Social media has fundamentally changed our perceptions of privacy.

   c. __ It seems that social media has had an effect on our understanding of privacy.

2. a. __ Cybercriminals may use social media to steal credit card information.

   b. __ Credit card information is being stolen from social media by cybercriminals.

   c. __ Cybercriminals can steal credit card information using social media (Baron, 2019).

3. a. __ Governments should regulate social media companies like traditional media.

   b. __ Some activists have suggested that governments should regulate social media.

   c. __ One possible solution would be for governments to regulate social media.

Activity 7.5: Text Revision

These sentences make very strong claims because they are adapted from a student newspaper editorial (Streicek, 2019). Most academic assignments do not make claims that are so strong. Rewrite the sentences for an academic assignment by making less confident claims, using the Language Box on pages 175–176.

1. The system of recycling in California is broken and in need of reform.
2. Essentially our money-hungry state government has turned what is supposed to be a noble effort to reduce pollution and boost sustainability into yet another way of taxing us all into poverty.
3. Economics have turned against this critical aspect in preventing the destruction of our planet's environment.
4. A simple way to create more demand for recycled plastic is to subsidize the private sale of recycled plastic and other materials to American industrial companies.
5. It is critical to not extend this subsidy to any foreign organizations, as we do not want to subsidize foreign industry.
6. This solution will ensure the material is actually recycled.
7. It is vital that we recycle.
8. The current situation is unacceptable, and there is absolutely something that can be done.

Supporting Claims

The way you support your claims will depend on the topic, assignment, and subject area as well as rhetorical considerations including your role, audience, purpose, and context. Some general strategies that might support your arguments include:

- ❒ giving examples
- ❒ imagining a hypothetical situation
- ❒ citing or quoting authorities (use the SIFT method in the Online Source Use Appendix to make sure you are citing reliable authorities.)
- ❒ considering and rejecting a counterargument
- ❒ examining logical sequences, such as causes and effects
- ❒ providing statistics and discussing trends

In most academic assignments, some other argument strategies are usually **not** effective, including:

- ❒ **emotional appeals:** These work very well in advertising and fundraising campaigns but not in most academic writing. Consider, for example, *If you don't recycle, you are personally responsible for killing the planet!* Although writers may be passionate about their arguments, claims involving logic, authorities, and examples are usually preferable.
- ❒ **exaggeration:** Academic arguments are expected to be reasonable, which means that boosting a claim too much can make it less effective, especially when the reader might be familiar with the evidence that limits the claim. Consider, for example, *Recycling is a complete waste of time and effort.*
- ❒ **personal examples:** There is no reason to avoid *I* in all academic writing. However, you should always ask whether you have enough authority to use yourself as an example. For example, if you are an international student making an argument about support for international students, your personal experiences may be relevant. However, if you are writing about animal testing and you have never conducted scientific research, they probably are not. For the same reason, phrases like *as I know* and *as we know* are not common in effective student writing.

WRITING TASK 7.1: Supporting a Claim

A. Choose one of the claims listed, or write a claim about a topic you are working on for this or another class. Find three to five pieces of supporting evidence for or against the claim. For each piece of evidence, write a paragraph explaining why you are confident that the support is reliable and accurate.

Open the Online Source Use Appendix, and read about the four SIFT strategies for evaluating online information (Caulfield, 2019).

1. A college or university degree increases a graduate's lifetime earnings.
2. Young people are less trusting of institutions than older generations.
3. Immigration strengthens the country to which people move.
4. Climate change will make countries around the world less stable.
5. English is the language of international scientific research.

B. Read a partner's claim and evidence. Use the four SIFT strategies to fact-check the information for yourself. Do you agree that the evidence is reliable and accurate? Does it effectively support or counter the claim? Write a response, memo, or email to your partner with your conclusions.

Choosing Examples

In most writing situations, examples are an important way to support claims, and readers will expect specific examples to support more general claims. Examples can fill many functions in an argument, including:

1. providing a specific case as an example to support a general claim
2. using a research result as an example to support a claim
3. challenging a commonly held position in order to introduce a claim
4. hypothesizing about possible situations as examples of a claim

Language Box: Introducing Examples

It is important to signal the start of an example so that the reader can recognize the transition from your claim to its support. You may also need to give a signal that you are explaining, interpreting, or connecting the example to your argument.

The two easiest phrases for introducing examples are *for example* and *for instance*. You can also use *such as*, but be aware that it is a preposition.

- Academic discussions now frequently take place on social-media platforms *such as* Twitter and Facebook.
- Academics often discuss their ideas on social media. ~~Such as~~ *For example/instance*, there are weekly Twitter chats for teachers of English learners.

Other ways to introduce examples include:

- X is a prime/excellent/good example of Y.
- A striking/notable example/case (of X) is ....
- The best-known/clearest example (of X) is ....
- (Source) cites/gives/provides an example of (Y / this phenomenon / this problem / etc.).
- This (situation / problem / issue / etc.) can be illustrated by ....
- Experts/Scientists/Researchers argue/claim/suggest that ....
- According to ...

After you have given an example, you can explain its connection to your argument using verbs such as:

- This example *illustrates / shows / demonstrates / suggests / reveals /* etc. ...

As always, the choice of verb indicates the strength of your confidence in your interpretation. The verbs *illustrate, show, demonstrate,* and *reveal* all show that you believe in the interpretation, but the verb *suggest* creates room for doubt.

Activity 7.7: Practice the Language

Read this argumentative paragraph, which makes a claim about plant-based meat alternatives (adapted from Kirschenbaum & Buhler, 2019). Choose the word or phrase that best completes each blank.

according to	*experts*	*for instance*
provide	*suggest*	*the best-known example*

① ______________ a United Nations (2019) estimate, the global population will reach 9 to 10 billion in 2050. Hunter et al. (2017) ② ______________ an important consequence of this increase: the world food supply will need to increase sharply from today's levels (Hunter et al., 2017). This concern has led a number of biotechnology startups to create plant-based meat alternatives. ③ ______________ is the "Impossible Burger," which uses an ingredient created in the lab from natural sources to mimic the texture of a rare meat burger. The success of the Impossible Burger has attracted a number of major food manufacturers. ④ ______________, Kellogg and Hormel are launching their own plant-based product lines (Brown, 2019). These cases ⑤ ______________ that plant-based meat alternatives are a successful innovation that could spread around the world and alleviate the unsustainable global demand for animal-based protein. Therefore, ⑥ ______________ argue that biotechnology can help feed the world's growing population with fewer resources.

Now discuss these questions about the paragraph:

1. **Where is the main claim stated in the paragraph?**
2. **What is the purpose of the first sentence?**
3. **What is the overall organization of information in the paragraph?**

WRITING TASK 7.2: Claims and Examples

Look again at the claim and evidence you collected in Writing Task 7.1. Write one or two paragraphs supporting or countering the claim. Conduct additional research to find further examples if necessary. Check all your sources using the SIFT method (see the Online Source Use Appendix). Connect your sentences using strategies from the Introducing Examples Language Box on page 180.

Language Box: Hypothetical Examples

You can sometimes support an argument by imagining what would happen if a condition were satisfied. This is a useful strategy if you do not have a specific example, but you can draw logical conclusions from a set of conditions. Note the verb forms used in these hypothetical examples:

- If this growth in demand **continues**, there **may be** a lack of labor in developing countries.
- Most farmers **would remain** profitable if they **stopped** using genetically modified seeds.
- If the university **made** its email directory private, it **would be** more difficult for hackers to access.

The choice of verb form indicates your degree of confidence in the prediction, as shown in the chart.

IF (CONDITION) CLAUSE	MAIN (RESULT) CLAUSE	MEANING
Present simple (*happens, increases, continues*)	*will* (*will improve, will change, will fail*)	The writer is completely confident in the outcome.
Present simple	*may/might/could* (*may improve, might change, could fail*)	The writer is not completely confident, but the outcome is strongly possible.
Past simple (*stopped, decreased, went*)	*would* (*would succeed, would be better, would improve*)	The situation is not real (it hasn't happened yet), but the writer is confident about the outcome.
Past simple	*might/could* (*might succeed, could improve*)	The situation is not real and the writer recognizes other possible outcomes.

Writing about hypothetical situations in the past—known as **counterfactuals**—requires more care, especially if you are writing in the field of history because it is impossible to know for certain what *would have happened* if something else *had happened* (although in reality it did not).

- If the government **had cut** taxes, some companies **might have hired** more workers.
- The patient **would probably have survived** the operation if she **had been healthy**.

Activity 7.8: Practice the Language

How would you add one or more hypothetical examples to each argument based on your experience and imagination?

1. One of the strongest reasons for attending a university far from home is to develop independence. *If young people have to make their own decisions, they learn to be more responsible.* In addition, if . . .
2. Students should not always be punished for turning in assignments late. For example, if . . . .
3. Opponents of animal testing argue that computers can more accurately model the effect of a medication or allergies to a cosmetic product on humans. If . . . .
4. Today, many electronic devices such as cell phones are only designed to last for a few years. However, if. . . .
5. When the first cars were made, the gas-powered engine was not the only option. In fact, many early cars ran on batteries. Since the internal-combustion engine has caused so much pollution and made such a large contribution to global warming, it is worth imagining a world in which batteries or electricity, not gasoline, powered cars, trucks, and airplanes. If electric vehicles. . . .

Counterarguments and Contradictory Findings

Many arguments in the humanities and social sciences are stronger when the writer considers and rejects different views, known as **counterarguments**. A counterargument introduces another source, perspective, or idea that disagrees with your own argument. Then, you **rebut** (or **refute**) the counterargument—that is, you respond to the opposing idea and reinforce your thesis or claim. Counterarguments and rebuttals show that you recognize ways in which the reader might disagree with you and that you can answer their objections.

In scientific writing, you also should not ignore research findings that differ from your own or contrast with your conclusions. Since all research builds on previous results, it is important to show the ways in which your results and arguments are different from earlier work. You might argue that your research is more specific, more careful, or somehow an improvement on contradictory findings. Alternatively, you may need to acknowledge that different studies have produced different results and suggest the need for further research.

Activity 7.9: Analyze Models

Read this excerpt from an argumentative essay about newspaper and magazine rankings of colleges and universities (Vedder, 2011).

> It is true, as some critics assert, that sometimes rankings lead colleges to allocate resources in a manner to maximize their standing, regardless of whether that appears optimal from an educational perspective. Some rankings are based in part on spending on inputs, which encourages a spending frenzy that arguably contributes to rising higher-education costs. That criticism, however, does not mean rankings are bad. It may mean that more emphasis needs to be placed on outcome-based, student-centered rankings.

1. Does the writer support or oppose university rankings?
2. What is the counterargument that the writer uses?
3. Identify the language choices that signal the counterargument and the author's rebuttal (that is, the response to the counterargument).
4. Do you think this excerpt comes from the start or end of the essay? Why?

In this excerpt from the Discussion section of a published undergraduate research paper in neuroscience (brain science), the writers explain why their results contrast with some previous research. Genova and colleagues (2018) found that student athletes who had previous suffered a concussion (a hard hit to the head) did not score worse on memory tests than athletes who had never been concussed. In fact, they even scored higher on some measures. This was an unexpected result.

> ①It appears that there is a general pattern in the previous literature that suggests multiple concussions may cause more serious lingering cognitive deficits. ②It is possible that because our study utilized a majority of participants who had only experienced a single concussion (60%), our results failed to show that concussion history produced performance deficits.
>
> ③Our results go beyond the findings of previous studies by exhibiting potentially superior performance on a memory distortion task by concussed individuals when compared to non-concussed individuals. ④No previous studies have displayed a result similar to this. ⑤It is difficult to explain this phenomenon, but an answer could possibly be found in the differences our study possesses when compared to previous research. ⑥One possible explanation of our results was the subject group. ⑦All of our subjects came from Middlebury College. ⑧Several studies have shown that exposure to higher education alters the brain (Yen et al., 2004; Tun and Lachman, 2008; Lachman et al., 2010) in areas involved with memory and language (Kim et al., 2015). ⑨In our study, the participants' exposure to higher education may have negated the possible long-term effects of the concussions and allowed them to do just as well, and in some cases better, than the subjects who had never been concussed before.

5. How did Genova et al.'s results contradict previous research findings?
6. In which sentence do the authors acknowledge that the reason for the difference might be a limitation in their research design?
7. What is the function of the second paragraph?
8. How confident are the authors in the explanation that the participants' level of education affected the results? How do you know?
9. How do the authors use citations in this extract?

Language Box: Countering Language

When you introduce a counterargument or contradictory results, you should carefully **distance** your reader from the idea you do not agree with (the counterargument) and attempt to **align** the reader with your position (the rebuttal or refutation).

Counterargument

- Admittedly / Certainly,
- It is (admittedly / certainly) true that ....
- Supporters / opponents / critics of X point out / might argue / suggest / claim that ....
- However, previous research has found that ....

Rebuttal

- However,
- In fact,
- In reality,
- In contrast to earlier studies, this research reveals that ....
- However, the present study suggests that ....
- This study extends the previous research by ....

You can also combine the counterargument and rebuttal in a single sentence:

- *Although / While* (counterargument), (rebuttal).
- *I agree/recognize/accept/admit that* (counterargument), *but* (rebuttal).
- *It is not correct that* (counterargument), *but rather* (rebuttal).

Activity 7.10: Practice the Language

Choose one of these arguments or another argument you are working on, and develop a counterargument and rebuttal. For example:

> *Argument*: University tuition should be free.
>
> *Counterargument*: Graduates earn more than non-degree holders, so taxpayers should not have to fund their studies.
>
> *Rebuttal*: Those graduates pay their communities back in their income and other taxes, so increased access to university ends up supporting the entire community.

Then, write a short paragraph for each counterargument and rebuttal using the Countering Language Box (p. 182).

1. *Argument*: Animal testing is wrong.

   Counterargument: Some life-saving medications would not have been developed without animal testing.

2. *Argument*: Banning plastic straws discriminates against some people with disabilities.
3. *Argument*: Children should be exposed to at least two languages before they are five years old.
4. *Argument*: With growing hostility between countries, it has become increasingly difficult to travel.
5. Argument: Professors should value teaching over research at every academic level.

Pedagogical Genre: Argument Essay

We have tried not to use the common term *essay* often in this textbook because it is a vague label that could cover many different genres. However, we cannot avoid the word completely since you may take courses where an assignment is called an argument essay, a persuasive essay, or a thesis-driven essay. Essays may also be found in some publications in which a writer develops and defends a position on a topic of personal importance. For example, some op-ed columns in the *New York Times* are now called "guest essays."

Wingate (2012) identifies three features of an argument essay in academic contexts:

- ❒ The writer develops a position on the topic, called a **thesis** (the major claim).
- ❒ The thesis is developed by connecting a series of **sub-claims** to build the argument.
- ❒ The claims are supported by relevant **information, evidence, and examples** from sources that are appropriate for the discipline (academic subject) and context.

Most readers in North American colleges and universities expect students to state their thesis near the start of an argument (although other types of argument will end with the thesis). The thesis can best be understood as the core answer to the question that is asked in the essay prompt. Each paragraph or group of paragraphs will then develop one step in the argument, which may involve introducing many more claims and perhaps some counterarguments. At the end, the writer may reiterate—but not repeat—the thesis and look ahead to the implications or limitations of the writer's position.

A. Read this argument essay by an undergraduate student, Ziang Zhou, about collaborative learning, and answer the questions that follow each paragraph. The writer uses the APA 7th edition style guide.

Collaborative Learning Is Necessary for a Better Future

① Collaborative learning is an educational process in which students work in groups to achieve common learning goals. Since collaboration involves group work in which teams can share information, resources, brainstorming, and understanding, students in collaborative classrooms can work together to challenge, share resources, and assist each other (Center for Teaching Innovation, n.d.). This collaboration gives rise to student initiative, creativity, and effective interpersonal connections. However, some students are resistant to collaborative learning because they may feel limited, forced to compromise, frustrated by groupmates' behavior, or required to devote too much time to the process (Center for Learning Experimentation, Application, and Research, n.d.). Actually, these complaints touch on the very strengths of collaborative learning. Although collaborative learning has its disadvantages, this educational approach has been proven to advance students' learning.

1. **What is the purpose of this paragraph?**
2. **Where is the thesis (the major claim) of the essay?**

② Group work can seem like a waste of time, simply a social hour compared to the focus and efficiency of individual study (Center for Learning Experimentation, Application, and Research, n.d.). However, it is actually the connected study with others that advances learning. A survey by Ku et al. (2013) found that students like collaborative learning because it allows them to communicate and exchange ideas and to think broadly about how to use each other's individual input for the "greater good" (p. 926). What is especially valuable compared to working independently is that students can share and exchange ideas and resources and give and receive immediate feedback. This process quickly identifies students' shortcomings so they can be quickly corrected. Collaborative learning therefore improves individual work and is more efficient and effective in the long term than traditional learning alone.

3. **What is the sub-claim in Paragraph 2?**
4. **How is the claim linked to the thesis?**
5. **How does the writer use sources to support the claim?**
6. **What is the purpose of the first sentence in the paragraph?**

③ Collaborative learning not only promotes individual achievement, but it also develops the ability to work with others, which is one of its many strengths (Kapp, 2009). Teamwork is crucial in the working world, and it is therefore vital that students gain interpersonal skills. Employers consistently rate teamwork as one of the most valuable "career competencies" (National Association of Colleges and Employers, 2019). However, if collaboration is not taught as a skill in college, teams may fail because teammates do not participate or "hijack" the group (Kapp, 2009, p. 139). In collaborative learning, students should learn how to get along with other members to reach the team's goal. If students have different ideas from others, they can argue for their ideas or discuss with others the strengths and weaknesses of all the ideas. This team discussion leads to more creative and solid conclusions. For example, Macdonald (2003) found that in a well-structured team task that includes ongoing assessment, students learn about collaborative management and are motivated to build team rapport. In this way, collaborative learning contributes to lifelong success.

7. **What is the sub-claim in Paragraph 3?**
8. **What types of support are provided in this paragraph?**
9. **How is Paragraph 3 connected to Paragraph 2 and to the thesis of the essay?**

④ Perhaps most importantly, students who study cooperatively learn more, achieve higher grades, and show greater productivity than those who study alone (Kapp, 2009). According to a study of students' evaluation of collaborative learning, a majority of students (60%) reported that working together reduced their tendency to procrastinate and improved performance (Kitchen & McDougall, 1999). However, Kitchen and McDougall (1999) note that it is still important to set clear expectations and criteria with time limits, but the final grade should not be the only motivation. Collaborative work definitely helps students improve their work and develop their knowledge.

10. Why do you think the writer chose to introduce this sub-claim as the last body paragraph in the essay?

⑤ Collaborative learning in college advances student learning and performance. Collaborative learning has not yet received full acceptance, but research-based methodology addresses the problems. If goals are clear and well-defined, activities are shared by all group members, and communication is continual, colleges should transition to more collaborative learning. The world needs everyone to work together to solve its serious problems.

References

Center for Learning Experimentation, Application, and Research. (n.d.) *Student resistance to engaged learning.* University of North Texas Teaching Commons. https://teachingcommons.unt.edu/teaching-essentials/engaged-learning/student-resistance-engaged-learning

Center for Teaching Innovation. (n.d.). *Collaborative learning.* https://teaching.cornell.edu/teaching-resources/engaging-students/collaborative-learning

Kapp, E. (2009). Improving student teamwork in a collaborative project-based course. *College Teaching, 57*(3), 139–143. https://doi.org/10.3200/CTCH.57.3.139-143

Kitchen, D., & McDougall, D. (1999). Collaborative learning on the Internet. *Journal of Educational Technology Systems, 27*(3), 245–258. https://doi.org/10.2190/5H41-K8VU-NRFJ-PDYK

Ku, H. Y., Tseng, H. W., & Akarasriworn, C. (2013). Collaboration factors, teamwork satisfaction, and student attitudes toward online collaborative learning. *Computers in human Behavior, 29*(3), 922–929. https://doi-org.udel.idm.oclc.org/10.1016/j.chb.2012.12.019

Macdonald, J. (2003). Assessing online collaborative learning: process and product. *Computers & Education, 40*(4), 377–391. https://doi-org.udel.idm.oclc.org/10.1016/S0360-1315(02)00168-9

National Association of Careers and Employers. (2019, March 29). *The four career competencies employers value most.* https://www.naceweb.org/career-readiness/competencies/the-four-career-competencies-employers-value-most/

11. What is the purpose of Paragraph 5?
12. Do the references appear to be reliable sources? How do you know?

B. Choose a topic you are currently studying or one of these questions. Conduct research to investigate possible claims, counterarguments, refutations, examples, and other types of evidence.

- Do you agree that the only responsibility of a business is to make profit?
- Should college and university faculty be allowed to require students to purchase books they have written themselves?
- Do you believe that all elementary school students should learn a second language?
- Should universities, colleges, and schools stop giving grades?

Review the Online Source Use Appendix for guidance on finding and evaluating sources.

C. Write an outline of your argument essay.

D. Write a thesis, using your answers to the questions above to guide you.

E. Draft your essay using the model and your planning notes.

F. Peer Review: Ask one or two partners to read your essay. Use these questions to give peer feedback:

1. What is the thesis, or statement of the major claim?
2. Are you persuaded by the argument? What additional information or support would help you accept the writer's argument?
3. Does each paragraph or group of paragraphs make a sub-claim that supports the argument?
4. Does the essay have or need a counterargument and rebuttal?
5. Are the sources reliable and persuasive?
6. What else can the writer do to improve the essay?

G. Self-Review. Revise your essay using your peers' feedback. Have you done everything on this checklist?

- ☐ I have checked the reliability and accuracy of all the sources.
- ☐ My claims are made with appropriate hedging and boosting language.
- ☐ The essay is clearly and logically organized.

What else do you need to work on? Make further revisions to your essay if necessary.

Genre in Action: Opinion Editorial (Op-Ed)

An opinion editorial, or **op-ed**, is a newspaper column in which writers express an opinion on a topic they care about. Op-eds are generally short, around 750 words, and written for a broad audience. You should be able to find examples of op-eds on the website of your campus newspaper (or that of a local campus or any English-speaking university), usually on the Opinion page.

A. Read this op-ed from the Denver University (DU) student newspaper. The hyperlinks in the original column have been replaced with endnotes.

DU's new test-optional policy will strengthen the student body

By: Sara Loughran | April 22, 2019

①DU recently announced[1] their decision to move to a test-optional policy, under which students can choose whether or not to submit their SAT and/or ACT scores as part of their application. This will go into effect for those applying for admission for the fall of 2020, which is as soon as it could have possibly been implemented since the application deadline for the incoming class of freshmen has already passed. This new policy could give more opportunities to students who have average, or below average, test scores yet excel in other areas such as grades and extracurricular activities.

②DU cites studies[2] that show little correlation between a student's overall academic abilities and standardized test scores and states that, "high school grades are the best predictor of first-year college performance."[3] This is especially true for students with learning disabilities or those who simply aren't good test takers, because being pushed to complete a test that could determine your admission to college in just a short amount of time can be stressful and cause kids to freeze up. Furthermore, there are students who have below-average grades in high school yet score well on tests, making it possible for them to get accepted into college even if their overall academic performance does not warrant it.

③I personally wish I could have had the choice to submit my test scores when I was applying to college because they did not reflect my overall academic abilities. I was refused extra time accommodations by my school, despite having ADHD. As a result, there were a few sections where I could not finish all the questions or I simply answered quickly out of fear of not being able to finish, thus making sloppy mistakes. My scores were not bad—they were average, but my grades in school were a better indicator of how I would actually perform in college.

④It is a step in the right direction that DU has decided to go the test-optional route, and while more than 1,000 schools have become test-optional[4], many more need to take the same steps. The standardized testing system is outdated and arbitrary and can limit a good student's options for colleges if they simply aren't good test takers or have a learning disorder. Hopefully as more colleges and universities make the decision to become test-optional, others will follow suit.

Notes

[1]https://www.du.edu/news/university-denver-moves-test-optional-admission-process

[2]https://www.insidehighered.com/news/2018/04/27/large-study-finds-colleges-go-test-optional-become-more-diverse-and-maintain

[3]https://www.du.edu/news/university-denver-moves-test-optional-admission-process

[4]https://www.du.edu/news/university-denver-moves-test-optional-admission-process

B. Complete the Rhetorical Planning Wheel Analysis document from the companion website with as much information about the components as you can find from this op-ed example. If possible, look at some other op-eds for more examples of the genre.

C. You can find many guides for writing effective op-ed columns on the internet. Here is some advice:

- ☐ **Make one point.** Have one clear, central argument, and state it at the beginning or at the end of the text. You may need to provide some background, but you will not write a general introduction as in some academic papers. Get to your point quickly and make the issue very clear.
- ☐ **Be specific.** Tell readers why the issue is important to them and what specifically you want to happen or change.
- ☐ **Consider the other side.** Op-eds with counterarguments show that you are familiar with opposing arguments.

- ☐ **Keep your sentences and paragraphs fairly short**. Newspaper op-ed writers prefer concision over complexity.
- ☐ **Use effective examples**, including personal examples if they are relevant.
- ☐ **Cite your sources informally**. If you are writing for an online publication, use hyperlinks.
- ☐ If appropriate, **end with a strong call to action**. Tell the readers what they should do after reading your op-ed recommend a policy, change, or course of action.

With a partner, answer these questions:

1. How does the op-ed example or the one you read from your local newspaper follow these guidelines?
2. What other good advice about op-ed writing can you find online?

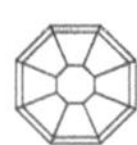

D. Plan an op-ed based on a problem that you and other students face in your classroom or institution. For example, you might discuss class size, food insecurity, concerns about violence on campus, or other current events and issues. Write your editorial for students and others on campus who will be reading the school newspaper. Answer the questions from the Rhetorical Planning Wheel.

- **Purpose:** This is the most important component of the op-ed genre. What is your purpose?
- **Context:** What does the campus context tell you about what you need to consider? For example, has the university already attempted to solve the problem you raise? If so, why isn't the problem solved? If not, why isn't the campus trying to solve the problem?
- **Audience:** Who will read your op-ed? What do you know about those who are most affected by the problem you raise and the claims that you make? Will you call them to action?
- **Writer:** What is your role as a writer? Are you an observer or a participant in the issue? Do you have any relevant personal examples or experiences?
- **Sources:** Where will collect evidence to support your argument? How do you know they are reliable? How will you demonstrate confidence in your sources in the text?

- **Language:** What register of language will you choose? How strong will your claims be? How much technical vocabulary will you use? Will you write impersonally or interactively?
- **Conventions:** What are the conventions of a newspaper op-ed? How are sources cited? What do titles look like? How are paragraphs used?

E. Use your answers to the Rhetorical Planning Wheel questions and the guidelines for writing an op-ed to plan and draft your article.

F. Peer Review: Ask one or two partners to read your op-ed. Use these questions to give peer feedback:

1. What is the issue or problem that the op-ed is raising?
2. Does the op-ed convince you that the problem is serious?
3. Does the op-ed have or need a call to action?
4. Does the op-ed writer consider other alternatives or opposing ideas?
5. Do you find the supporting ideas and sources persuasive?
6. How can the writer improve the op-ed?

G. Self-Review. Revise your op-ed using your peers' feedback. Have you done everything on this checklist?

- ☐ The op-ed has one clear, central argument.
- ☐ The op-ed ends with a call to action, if appropriate.
- ☐ The ideas, support, and examples are specific and relevant.
- ☐ The op-ed has a counterargument and rebuttal.
- ☐ I cited relevant and reliable sources.
- ☐ I used hedging and boosting language to control the strength of the claims.
- ☐ The op-ed follows appropriate conventions.

What else do you need to work on? Make further revisions to your op-ed if necessary.

References

Caulfield, M. (2019, June 19). *SIFT (The four moves)*. https://hapgood.us/2019/06/19/sift-thefour-moves/

Genova, G., Gilbert, E., Churchill, C., & Acquaire, A. (2018). Can a concussion history affect the susceptibility to the misinformation effect? *IMPULSE - The Premier Undergraduate Neuroscience Journal*. https://impulse.appstate.edu/articles/2018/can-concussion-historyaffect-susceptibility-misinformation-effect

Karimikonda, T. (2017). Tired of being tired? *JUST: The Journal of Undergraduate Science and Technology*, *31*(1). https://justjournal.org/2017/12/14/tired-of-being-tired/

Kirschenbaum, S. & Buhler, D. (2019). *Americans, especially millennials, are embracing plant-based meat products*. The Conversation. https://theconversation.com/americans-especially-millennials-are-embracing-plant-based-meat-products-124753

Loughran, S. (2019, April 22). DU's new test-optional policy will strengthen the student body. *DU Clarion*. https://duclarion.com/2019/04/dus-new-test-optional-policy-will-strengthen-the-student-body/

McNeill, K. L., & Knight, A. M. (2013). Teachers' pedagogical content knowledge of scientific argumentation: The impact of professional development on K–12 teachers. *Science Teacher Education*, *97*, 936–872. https://doi.org/10.1002/sce.21081

Racine, N. (2019). Blood, meth, and tears: The super soldiers of World War II. *History Matters: An Undergraduate Journal of Historical Research*, *16*, 7–20. https://historymatters.appstate.edu/issue/spring-2019

Schlusser, B. (2019). Progress built on a wasteland: Electronic consumerism & the dangers of e-waste. *Arak Journal*. https://www.english.udel.edu/arak-journal/10

Soukaseum, M. (2018). The price of beauty: Methacrylates in the artificial nail industry. *Arak Journal*. https://www.english.udel.edu/arak-journal/10

Streicek, M. (2019, April 24). California's recycling system is broken. *The Daily Aztec*. https://thedailyaztec.com/94424/opinion/californias-recycling-system-is-broken-2/

Vedder, R. (2011, February 17). Why students want to go to Harvard. *Chronicle of Higher Education*. http://www.chronicle.com/blogs/innovations/why-students-want-to-go-to-harvard

Wineburg, S. S. (2001). *Historical thinking and other unnatural acts: Charting the future of teaching the past*. Temple University Press.

Wingate, U. (2012). 'Argument!' helping students understand what essay writing is about. *Journal of English for Academic Purposes*, *11*(2), 145–154. https://doi.org/10.1016/j.jeap.2011.11.001

8 Respond

Goals

- ❒ Differentiate response from summary
- ❒ Write responses using three strategies (text-to-self, text-to-text, and text-to-world)
- ❒ Signal responses and concessions with appropriate language choices
- ❒ Write critiques, evaluations, reviews, and responses
- ❒ Use evaluative language effectively
- ❒ Write reflections on experiences and texts
- ❒ Pedagogical Genre: Discussion board post
- ❒ Genre in Action: Letter to the editor

What Is the Action?

You may write many different types of responses in your academic classes. These include critiques, reflections, reviews, and evaluations. In all cases, responding means engaging with a source text or educational experience by providing your thoughts, opinions, comments, connections, examples, or reactions. The source text might be a scholarly article or textbook chapter, but it could also be a movie, play, novel, website, or work of art (e.g., a book or theater review); a field trip, internship, or study abroad experience; or your own writing or performance (e.g., a reflective cover letter).

Assignments that ask you to respond may include:

- ❒ summary/response tasks
- ❒ online discussion board posts, journals, reading-response logs, and field notes
- ❒ short papers in preparation for a discussion or seminar

- ❒ reviews of books, films, plays, works of art, places, or products
- ❒ reflections on your writing, revision process, portfolio, or learning in the course
- ❒ reflections on a field trip or other experience
- ❒ evaluations or critiques of a research article

In addition, response writing can be a preparation for or part of a job interview or graduate school application, where you might be asked to reflect on your education and experiences and discuss how they prepared you for the job or program you are applying for.

Activity 8.1: What Do You Know?

How are these tasks similar and different? Which of these are you familiar with from your current or past classes? Make notes and then discuss your answers with a partner or small group.

1. reviewing a book / summarizing a book
2. critiquing an article / criticizing an article
3. arguing for a position / responding to someone else's position
4. writing a formal response paper / responding to a classmate on a course discussion board
5. responding to a reading / reflecting on a field trip

Summary and Response

While you will sometimes need to **summarize** an article or other source without giving your opinion, reaction, or ideas, in other tasks, you will also need to **respond** to your readings. There are different ways to respond, and your strategy will depend on a close reading of the assignment. Some tasks will call for a personal reaction to the ideas you read; others want you to evaluate the source (that is, discuss whether it is well written, accurate, persuasive, or effective); and others invite you to make connections to other course texts or ideas.

Activity 8.2: Analyze a Model

In Activity 4.4, you read the summary section of Julia Cooper's summary/response to an article she had read by Michaela Cullington about the effects of texting on students' formal writing (see p. 89–90). Now read the second paragraph of her article, which sets up her response.

①Although her study supports the hypothesis that texting and writing have no relationship to one another, Cullington recognizes the significance of new technology and society's evolving modes of communication. ②She writes, "The use of text messaging as a common means of communication is becoming increasingly popular; therefore, this issue should continue to be examined" (94). ③Not surprisingly, the popularity of texting has increased since the time of Cullington's article and so too has research on its effect on student writing. ④What Cullington may not have anticipated, however, are the ways in which texting itself has changed. ⑤How might innovations such as Internet access, various "apps," and software advancements have changed texting in the years since Michaela Cullington published her article in 2011?

1. **What is the purpose of Sentence 1? How do you know?**
2. **Which sentences show the writer's agreement with Cullington's original article?**
3. **Which sentences show problems, gaps, or weaknesses in Cullington's article?**
4. **Overall, do you expect the writer (Cooper) to support or challenge the conclusions of her source (Cullington)? Why? What do you expect the rest of the article to discuss?**

Cooper's response continues with her personal experience and point of view. Here is an abridged extract from her next paragraph:

People with smartphones have the assistance of spellcheck, reference apps, autocorrect, autocompletion and, most recently, voice-control. In the past, text messages were ultimately just instant, electronic versions of a brief note left for someone on his or her door. There was little time or reason for revision and little space in which to fit the message. There was no judgment of spelling and grammatical errors, nor was there confusion about improvised shorthand; senders and recipients alike recognized the restrictions of this method of communication. In short, there was a reason for writing messages in the "Post-it" style ("c u @ ur apt 2nite") ["see you at your apartment tonight"]. It was this kind of texting that evoked discontent and concern in the teachers interviewed by Cullington. Though rational for the teachers of the first texters, that fear is now largely outdated.

5. What argument in Cullington's original essay is Cooper responding to? What language does she use to introduce the idea from the source?
6. What is her response to Cullington and the writer's defense of texting? What language does she use to indicate her response?
7. How convincing do you find her response so far? What additional evidence or information would you find helpful as a reader?

Strategies for Response Writing

There are many different types of response papers. Here are some questions you can ask yourself as you prepare to write a response:

- ❐ **text-to-self response**: What do you think about the ideas in the source? Which ideas do you agree and disagree with? Why? What experiences, beliefs, or principles inform your reactions? (This type of response is not appropriate for all assignments.)
- ❐ **text-to-text response**: What else have you read about this topic? Do other writers support your source or disagree with it? Which author(s) are most convincing and why?
- ❐ **text-to-world response***:* Can you find an example that supports or challenges an idea in the source text? Depending on the assignment, your examples might come from your experience, your community, popular culture, the news, or history.

For example, in another *Young Scholars in Writing* summary/response article, Sara Smilowitz wrote a response to a case study on reader's comments to online news articles. One of her paragraphs begins with this text-to-text response:

> In her article "The Speaker Respoken: Material Rhetoric as Feminist Methodology," feminist rhetorician Vicki Burton illustrates how texts change with each re-publication and the effect that these changes have on the original author's voice. Using Burton's methodology, the reasoning behind the "disparate perceptions" surrounding the [online newspaper] comment boards becomes clearer.

She goes on to show how Burton's theoretical ideas explain the data that her source article presented. This strategy can also be used to respond to one course reading using another reading, lecture, or idea from the same or a different class.

Language Box: Signaling Responses

One of the challenges in response writing is to distinguish ideas in your source from your own comments. The choices for attributing ideas to a source were discussed in Unit 4 (p. 94). Additional phrases that may be helpful to signal your response include:

Indicate agreement	*Lee is correct to say that ....* *Lee's point about ... is widely accepted.* *This is a valid concern/idea/point/argument.*
Indicate disagreement	*This aspect of Lee's argument is hard to accept.* *However / On the other hand / Nevertheless* *On the contrary ....* *Lee fails to consider ....* *The supposed benefits / problems / dangers / etc. of .... .*
Provide an example in support	*For example/instance* *An example of X is ....* *X is especially/particularly true for ....* *X's idea about Y can be seen in ....* *X is a good example/illustration of ....*
Provide a counterexample	*However, as the following example shows/illustrates ....* *A more recent/useful/valid/relevant example can be found in ....* *However, a more important example comes from ....*
Introduce your own position	*Unfortunately / Fortunately* *In my experience ...* *As (a student athlete / an international student / a working parent), I ....* *An alternative interpretation / explanation / view / perspective is ....* *The problem / difficulty with this position / argument / view is .....* *In fact*

Note that the phrases *as I/we/you know* are not commonly used in academic writing because they make assumptions about the reader's knowledge and opinions that may be false.

Activity 8.3: Practice the Language

Read these extracts adapted from an article by Christopher Ferguson (2018), a professor of psychology. Identify the ideas he is responding to, his own responses, and the language that signals his position.

1. Much of the discussion is framed around fighting "addiction" to technology. But to me, that resembles a moral panic, giving voice to scary claims based on weak data.
2. Some people have claimed that technology use activates the same pleasure centers of the brain as cocaine, heroin or methamphetamine. That's vaguely true, but brain responses to pleasurable experiences are not reserved only for unhealthy things.
3. Comparisons between technology addictions and substance abuse are also often based on brain imaging studies, which themselves have at times proven unreliable at documenting what their authors claim.
4. In June 2018, the World Health Organization added "gaming disorder" to its International Compendium of Diseases. But it's a very controversial decision.
5. One recent paper claimed to link screen use to teen depression and suicide (Twenge et al., 2017). However, another scholar with access to the same data revealed the effect was no larger than the link between eating potatoes and suicide (Gonazales, 2018). This is a problem: Scholars sometimes make scary claims based on tiny data that are often statistical blips, not real effects.

Activity 8.4: Analyze the Language

The writer in Activity 8.3 is a professor and an expert in his field. Therefore, he has authority to state strong positions. As a student writer, you will sometimes have the authority to state your position confidently if you have enough background knowledge. However, you will also often have express your positions with a lower degree of confidence and authority.

What language choices does Ferguson use in the text in Activity 8.3 to signal his response? Make a list of phrases that show high confidence and another list of phrases that show less confidence. Add other phrases from the Signaling Responses Language Box that you think show stronger and weaker positions. Discuss your answers in a small group. In what assignments and situations would you choose the stronger or weaker language?

Language Box: Concession

A **concession** is a sophisticated writing move in which you recognize another person's idea but then encourage the reader to agree with your position instead. Concessions are usually formed with the subordinating conjunctions *although, even though, though,* or *while.* The idea that you do not agree with is usually expressed in the dependent (subordinate) clause, with your position in the independent (main) clause. The dependent clause is often at the start of the sentence so that the emphasis is placed on the writer's actual argument at the end of the sentence. For example:

- *Even though teens spend less face-to-face time together,* they interact more in other ways. [The writer acknowledges the fact that teenagers spend less time together but emphasizes the more important point that they are interacting more if we include online interactions.]
- *Although the World Health Organization (WHO) now recognizes "gaming disorder,"* some psychologists are skeptical that digital addiction is a valid term. [The writer is aware of WHO's decision, but highlights psychologists who disagree with it.]

You can also express concession with the preposition *despite*, but be careful to follow it with a noun phrase not a clause.

- INCORRECT: *Despite video games are addictive,* they rarely lead users to commit violence.
- CORRECT: *Despite the addictiveness of video games,* they rarely lead users to commit violence.

You can show stronger or weaker commitment to the concession and claim by adding adverbs and other hedging or boosting phrases:

- While *some* social-media users *may* have more online friends, they *in fact* report more feelings of loneliness. [The hedging words *some* and *may* indicate that the writer does not believe most social media of users actually do have more online friends; the boosting phrase *in fact* focuses the reader on the idea of loneliness.]

In some tasks, a concession sentence might serve as the focus, or thesis statement, for an argumentative paper. It might also signal the shift from the summary to the response actions.

Activity 8.5: Practice the Language

Use the sentences to write concessions by adding your own ideas and examples. The sentences provided could be the concession (the idea you do not fully agree with) or your own position. The first one has been done for you as an example.

1. Social media spread information more quickly than mainstream media.

   Despite the number of 24-hour cable news channels, social media spread information more quickly than mainstream media.

3. Online interaction replaces some face-to-face interactions.
4. Certain social networks are useful for job hunting.
5. Employees who use social media at work are less productive.
6. Some teachers have found creative uses for social media in their classes.

WRITING TASK 8.1: Writing a Response

Write a response to Ferguson's (2018) position in Activity 8.2 (or find his complete article online). You may choose to agree with Ferguson, disagree with him, or agree with some but not all of his statements.

A. Here are some statistics and experts' quotations you might use in a text-to-text response. Select the information you are interested in using in your response.
   1. "Talking about internet addiction starts from the premise that the technology is intrinsically bad and therefore needs to be rationed. In reality technology is neither good nor bad, but simply a means to an end" (Mauthner, 2015). *Natasha Mauthner is a professor at the University of Aberdeen Business School in Scotland and Associate Director of the Centre for Research on Families and Relationships.*
   2. "After studying two large, nationally representative surveys, we found that although the amount of time teens spent with their friends face to face has declined since the 1970s, the drop accelerated after 2010–just as smartphones use started to grow. Just as the drop in face-to-face time accelerated after 2010, teens' feelings of loneliness shot upward" (Twenge, 2019). *Jean Twenge is a professor of psychology at San Diego State University.*

3. "Overall, 24% of teens who report being constantly online say they meet with their friends in person outside of school every day or almost every day. That is nearly identical to the 23% of less-frequently online teens who say they see their friends almost daily. And when it comes to online interaction with their friends, 69% of teens who are online constantly say they talk to their friends online every day or almost every day, compared with 52% of teens who visit the internet less frequently" (Jiang, 2018). *Jingjing Jiang is a staff writer for the Pew Research Center, which conducted this survey.*

4. Digital Detox is a company in California that offers retreats (short vacations), camps, and workshops in which participants are not allowed to use any digital technology. They claim that the experience "can help reduce anxiety, stress, depression, tech dependency, fatigue, and information overload." *Digital Detox is a leader in research, training, and programming that questions the role of technology in modern life.*

B. Consider your own experiences and background knowledge on the topic, or conduct your own online research to find examples you can use in your response. Take notes on the useful information you find.

Review the Online Source Use Appendix for guidance on finding and evaluating online information using the SIFT strategies (Caulfield, 2019).

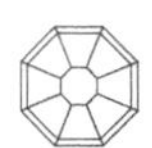

C. Before you write, consider these components of the Rhetorical Planning Wheel:

1. What is your role? Are you writing as an expert, a student, or a user of technology?
2. What is the purpose of your response? Overall, are you going to agree with Ferguson, disagree with him, or both?
3. Are you going to write text-to-self, text-to-text, or text-to-world responses?
4. What sources and evidence are you going to use?
5. How are you going to signal your response? Are you going to make strong or tentative responses? Are you going to make any concessions?

D. Draft one or more paragraphs of response using the advice in this unit and the examples in Activities 8.2 and 8.3 as models.

E. Peer Review. Share your response with one or two partners. Use these questions to provide feedback:

1. Is each paragraph a text-to-self, text-to-text, or text-to-world response?
2. Does each paragraph identify the idea that the writer is responding to?
3. Does the writer clearly signal where their response begins?
4. Is the response reasonable and persuasive to you as a reader?
5. How could the writer improve the response?

F. Self-Review. Revise your response using your peers' feedback. Have you done everything on this checklist?

- ☐ I clearly showed where I was summarizing or responding to Ferguson.
- ☐ I used appropriate support from Part A plus other experiences or research.
- ☐ I checked that any online sources I found were reliable and accurate.
- ☐ I chose language carefully to show whether I was making a stronger or weaker response.
- ☐ I use concession language to indicate alternative viewpoints, if appropriate.

What else do you need to work on? Make further revisions to your response if necessary.

Critique and Evaluation

In academic writing, **critique** is not the same as **criticism**. Critique is a form of response in which you evaluate the strengths and weaknesses of a text or idea. A good critique is fair (you do not make unreasonable criticism), balanced (you look for both good and bad aspects), and specific (you use examples, evidence, quotations, and statistics).

Writing a good critique requires you to understand the standards and conventions of the discipline. For example, to critique a quantitative research paper, you would need to understand the choices of statistical tests and the expectations for sampling and reporting in that particular field of study. However, you can also practice critique writing in less specialist genres.

Activity 8.6: Analyze Models

An everyday form of critique is a product or restaurant review. If you have read online reviews before, discuss with a partner or small group what you read and whether you found it useful. If you have written online reviews, why did you write them? Consider your answers as you read the two texts.

Text 1

I travel very often and cannot sleep AT ALL on the go (planes, trains, buses, everywhere). So out of desperation I have tried the various U-shaped pillows, leaning against my bf [boyfriend], the seat head flaps, the window, curling up in a little ball (I'm quite small so I can do this) - and nothing worked. After much research I purchased the TravelRest based on the good feedback and it made the most amount of sense: I lay on my pillow, I can lean on this product. Sold. Let me tell you, it's worth every penny. Ignore anyone who says it looks funny or that you will be embarrassed inflating it. It takes 2 breaths and though it is a bit bulky when inflated, you won't notice when you are unconsciously sleeping in bliss. You can tie it to the seat or use it like a messenger bag, it is even nice against your significant other's shoulder. It really relieves the pressure on my neck and allowed my body to relax - finally! I took 2 flights over 10 hours each that I fly regularly and the TravelRest made these trips a million times better. I now no longer fear flying in coach [economy-class seats]!

Text 2

I travel often for work and use the pillow pretty regularly. After a couple months of use, the pillow just seems to stop working. It does not stay inflated at all even on a quick 90-minute flight. I tried making sure the seal was completely tight every single time I inflated it, and still I would wake up mid-flight with a completely deflated pillow. The pillow is fantastic at first and seems like it would be perfect for those who travel less frequently and just need it for 1 or 2 long trips. It takes up no space at all and is easy to use. I just wish I could get it to last longer than a few months.

1. **For each review, identify the evaluative criteria that the writer has used. What was each reviewer looking for in the product? Was the expectation met or not?**
2. **Highlight the language that indicates positive or negative evaluation.**
3. **Go online, choose a product, restaurant, or service you are interested in, and read several more reviews. What patterns of organization, language, and evidence do you notice?**

Language Box: Evaluative Language

Most of the evaluative language you will use in a response or critique will express your attitude toward the object of the review and not just your feelings. For instance, while you could write: *I love/hate this pillow* (a statement about your *feelings*), it is probably more persuasive to write about the **attributes** of the product, such as *the pillow is soft and comfortable* or *hard and uncomfortable*.

Martin and White (2005) present these useful categories of evaluation: **impact, quality, balance, complexity,** and **valuation.** Your choice of categories and vocabulary will depend greatly on the object of your response: a new phone might be *advanced* (complexity) with *a tough screen* (quality), whereas a new restaurant might be *inviting* (impact) with *a varied menu* (balance). Some examples of adjectives you could use to express the five categories of evaluation are provided in the chart.

CATEGORY	QUESTION	POSITIVE	NEGATIVE
Impact	How did I react to it?	*exciting, moving, intense, remarkable, inviting*	*dull, boring, uninviting, flat*
Quality	What did I like about it?	*excellent, great, welcome, beautiful, brilliant, intelligent, thoughtful*	*bad, weak, unpleasant, disgusting, poor, flimsy*
Balance	Does it fit together?	*balanced, consistent, logical, varied*	*uneven, irregular, contradictory, inconsistent*
Complexity	Was it hard to follow or use?	*simple, clear, elegant, precise, detailed, organized*	*unclear, disorganized, confusing, simplistic*
Valuation	Was it worthwhile or good value?	*deep, creative, timely, insightful, helpful, effective, valuable, priceless, worthwhile, original, valid*	*shallow, insignificant, dated, fake, worthless, ineffective, unoriginal, flawed*

Adapted from Martin & White, 2005, p. 56.

You can turn most of these adjectives into nouns or use other parts of speech to express evaluation, too:

- The **value** of this research is its **originality**. *(valuation)*
- The weight of the car is **unevenly** distributed. *(balance)*
- I most appreciated the **elegance** of the design. *(complexity)*
- The author **has organized** the book **well**, but the conclusions **lack insight.** *(complexity / quality)*

Activity 8.7 Practice the Language

Peer review is another form of critique. Complete this written peer review of a student paper about technology using positive and negative evaluative language in the categories provided.

1. Valuation: The writer's argument about technology is _________.
2. Quality: I especially appreciated the __________.
3. Balance: However, the last paragraph is __________ because ___________.
4. Complexity: Overall, the paper is ______________
5. Impact: and ______________ .

WRITING PROJECT 8.2: Writing a Review

Reviews are a form of critique that can be written by professional or everyday customers, viewers, and users. They may be published in very formal contexts (academic journals and national newspapers) or very informal contexts (blogs, Yelp, Amazon, and other websites). For this project, you could review:

- ☐ a product you have recently purchased
- ☐ a book you have read (fiction or non-fiction)
- ☐ a movie or play you have seen
- ☐ a piece of art
- ☐ a website or educational technology tool

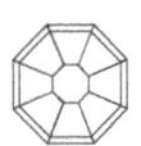

A. Look for several examples of your review genre. Two examples of product reviews appear in Activity 8.6. Other examples as well as models for other types of reviews can be found in newspapers and online. As you read the examples, answer the questions about the components of the Rhetorical Planning Wheel for your review genre.
   1. **Writer's role**: What makes the writer an expert?
   2. **Audience**: Who reads these reviews and why?

3. **Purpose**: Why are you writing this review?
4. **Context**: How much information does the audience need to know from the summary? How much previous knowledge does the audience have?
5. **Structure**: Where does the writer evaluate – e.g., the title, the opening paragraph, the description section, or the end of the review?
6. **Language**: Is the description evaluative or objective? What categories of evaluative language are appropriate? How much technical vocabulary is used?
7. **Conventions**: How do writers refer to the objects of the review and their creators? How are titles and names written? Are people referred to by their first, last, or both names?
8. **Sources**: Do writers refer to any other sources in addition to the object of the review? How are they cited?

B. Read these excerpts from the beginning of two book reviews.

Text 1 (Partington, 2019)

Side by Side, Chris Raschka's exquisite and joyous picture book ode to father-child relationships. features six diverse father-child pairs playing together, chillin' [relaxing] together, dancing together, eating together, and hanging [spending time] together under umbrellas. The text is lyrical; the watercolor illustrations by the two-time Caldecott medalist are buoyant and blissful and filled with depictions of active play and camaraderie, love and deep connection. [The Caldecott Medal is given each year to the best new picture book for children.]

Text 2 (DeBrabander, 2018)

Hugh LaFollette has offered an informative, compelling and readable contribution to the philosophical literature on America's gun debate, which, as of yet, is still relatively small. He gives an overview of three major sets of arguments for and against gun control: armchair arguments, rights-based arguments, and empirical arguments. He appraises each in turn, and ultimately points out how and where the gun rights position is wanting, and why the case for gun control is stronger. He concludes by detailing several proposals for gun control. These include some well-known (and much debated) regulations, like gun registration and background checks on gun purchases, but one idea that is rather novel and little discussed, mandatory liability insurance for gun owners.

1. Are these extracts mostly summarizing or responding to the books?
2. What evaluative language is used in both reviews? Which categories of evaluative language from the Evaluative Language Box are used?
3. How confident are the writers in their opinions? Do they seem to have the authority to make strong claims about the books?
4. How are the two reviews similar and different?
5. Look for other book reviews or examples of the type of review you are writing. What do you notice about the use of evaluative language in the summary and evaluation steps?
6. In your own review, should the summary (for a book, movie, or play) or description (for a product) section use evaluative language?

C. Table 8.1 shows the typical organization for two types of review. If you are writing a product or book review, do the patterns match your examples? If you are writing a different type of review, look at several examples and complete a similar table.

TABLE 8.1:
Typical Organization of Two Review Genres

Product Review	*Book Review*
Title of review, product name, 1–5 stars	Book title, author, publisher, pages, price
Writer's experience with the product category	Main theme, idea, or argument of the book
Description of product	Summary of the book (sometimes, summary of each chapter)
Evaluation of strengths and weaknesses	Evaluation of the book (usually positive and negative)
Recommendation	Recommendation for specific audiences

D. Draft your review. In the evaluation section, consider your degree of authority and the strength of the positions you take as you choose your evaluative language.

E. Peer Review. Share your review with one or two partners. Use these questions to give feedback:

1. Overall, is the review positive or negative? How do you know?
2. Does the writer give enough information about the product, object, or service for you to understand the review?
3. Is the evaluation fair, balanced, and specific?
4. Does the writer use evaluative language effectively?
5. What can the writer do to improve the review?

F. Self-Review. Revise your review using your peers' feedback. Have you done everything on this checklist?

- ☐ My review has all the components I identified in Part D.
- ☐ My review includes both description or summary and evaluation.
- ☐ I chose an appropriate degree of strength in my evaluative language.
- ☐ I wrote about several different attributes in my review (i.e., valuation, quality, balance, impact, and complexity; see chart in the Evaluative Language Box).

What else do you need to work on? Make further revisions to your op-ed if necessary.

Reflection

A reflection is a type of text-to-self response. Reflections may invite you to think about your writing or learning processes or reflect on an experience such as a field trip, internship, or guest speaker. The purpose of a reflection is often to encourage you to transfer your experience from one task to another. For example, if you reflect on your last writing assignment, you may discover ways to overcome similar challenges or reproduce your success in the next assignment. However, papers called *reflections* vary widely, so it is especially important to read the assignment carefully and understand the purpose, context, audience, and your role.

Activity 8.8: Understanding Reflection Assignments

These reflection assignments have been used in university courses:

- ☐ Write a one-page reflection on your experience at the botanical garden we visited, based on these questions: How does the garden resemble other gardens we have studied? How does it differ? What is something you learned that you did not know before? Did you enjoy visiting the garden? Why or why not? [Landscape Architecture]
- ☐ Please watch at least five short recorded videos of recent alumni talking about their time on campus and their current jobs. Reflect on what you have learned from these alumni, what questions you have, and what actions you plan to take to get the most out of your four years at the university? [Business]
- ☐ Write a cover letter for your writing portfolio in which you discuss your strengths and weaknesses as a writer, the feedback you received during the semester, and the course learning outcomes that you have (not) met. [English/Composition]
- ☐ The journal is a space for you to investigate your own thoughts, reactions, and feelings on particular art ideas and art works. I'm asking you to make connections between what you are learning and what you have already experienced [Art History; from Melzer, 2009]

Read the assignments and discuss the questions.

1. All these assignments require you to reflect by responding to an experience. What is the experience in each assignment?
2. What is the purpose of each assignment?
3. As a writer, how would your approach to these assignments be different?
4. What types of information, evidence, and sources are appropriate to each assignment?

Language Box: Verb Tenses to Describe Experiences

In most academic writing, you only need a limited number of verb tenses. However, when you are reflecting on your own experiences, you might choose from a wider range:

- present simple to describe something that is always true about you: *I **enjoy** art museums; I **believe** that I **am** a good writer.*
- present progressive to describe something that is changing or that you are just starting to think about: *I **am wondering** if I **am becoming** more introverted.*
- present perfect to describe an experience that you have had recently, without specifying when it happened; the present perfect also describes changes that have happened: *I **have written** three major assignments this semester; my editing skills **have improved**.*
- past simple to describe something that is finished or has a specific date or time: *I **watched** an online video about personality tests; our visit to the museum **took** place on Monday.*
- past perfect to describe something you had (not) done before another activity in the past: *I **had never studied** the theory of music before this class; I **had** only **written** essays for exams in high school.*
- *used to* (sometimes called the past habitual) to describe something that was true in the past but does not happen now; this can also show a change in your attitude or behavior: *I **used to wait** until the last minute to write my papers, but now I plan them in advance.*
- future verb forms to indicate your plan to change behaviors in the future; there is a small difference between *will* (for a decision you have just made) and *be going to* (for a decision that is the result of planning): *In the future, I **will use** the rhetorical planning wheel for all my assignments; I **am going to take** engineering classes next semester.*

The Grammar Glossary contains more information about verb tenses.

Activity 8.9: Practice the Language

Which verb tense would you choose for the verbs in parentheses in the reflection paragraph? Compare your answers with a partner. Note that more than one choice is often grammatically possible with a slightly different meaning.

In Thursday's class, we ①___________ (participate) in a group discussion about personality tests. Before I ②___________ (take) this class, I ③___________ (not experience) a lot of discussions in my classes. I ④___________ (believe) that I ⑤___________ (be) a good listener but now I ⑥___________ (begin) to doubt my listening skills. According to the survey, an active listener ⑦___________ (interact) with other group members by nodding, making eye contact, and saying things like *uhuh* and *yeah*. I ⑧___________ (done) this before, but I ⑨___________ (want) to start using these techniques now. In our next group discussion, I ⑩___________ (make) a conscious effort to be a more active listener.

Pedagogical Genre: Discussion Board Reflection

Many university and college courses require students to write posts on an online discussion board or forum. These posts may be graded, they might be included in a participation grade, or they might be used to develop ideas for discussions or other written assignments. Discussion board posts can be difficult to plan rhetorically because the audience includes both your classmates and the instructor, so although you do not usually need to write in a very formal style, you also have to make your writing appropriate for an academic setting. Clearly, a discussion board post will be very different from a post on social media, but it is also different from a formal class assignment.

A. Choose one of these contexts and write a reflection for a real or imagined online course discussion board.

1. Write a reflection on a recent class or group discussion. Briefly summarize the discussion and then reflect on your and your classmates' participation. You might answer some of these questions: Were you satisfied with the discussion? Did you feel able to participate as much as you wanted? How could you and your classmates engage in better discussions in the future?

2. Think about your last writing assignment. Write a reflection on your writing process: How did you plan, write, revise, and edit your paper? Are you satisfied with the results? Is there anything you would change about your writing process in the future?

3. Go online and find a personality test or a career self-assessment test. Take the test, and write a reflection: Do you agree with the results? Did you find the test useful? Did you think the questions were well written? How could you use the results?

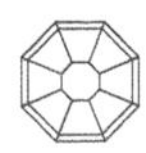

B. Consider these components of the Rhetorical Planning Wheel before you write.

1. **Purpose**: What is the purpose of this assignment? What are expected to demonstrate?

2. **Context**: Will other students reply to your post? How will that affect your writing?

3. **Evidence**: What is one specific example from your experience to support each point or observation in your reflection?

4. **Language**: In what ways can your writing be informal? In what ways should it be formal?

5. **Conventions**: How do writers use titles, paragraphs, and formatting (e.g. bold, italics, links) in discussion board posts?

C. Draft your reflection. Write about more than one aspect of the experience in a register and format appropriate for a discussion board.

D. Peer Review: Share your response with one or two partners. Give feedback to your peers by replying to their post. Use these questions to guide your response:

1. Have you had similar experiences?
2. What is your reaction to the experiences the writer described?
3. What questions do you have for the writer?

E. Self-Review. Revise your reflection using your peers' feedback. Have you done everything on this checklist?

- ☐ My reflection describes several different aspects of the experience.
- ☐ Each element, point, or observation is supported by a specific example from my experience.
- ☐ I used appropriate verb tenses to describe my experience.
- ☐ The register is appropriate for an online discussion board.

What else do you need to work on? Make further revisions to your reflection if necessary.

Genre in Action: Letter to the Editor

A letter to the editor is a genre in which readers of a newspaper or magazine respond with support for or criticism of an article they have read. Many letters try to raise awareness about a particular issue, problem, or situation that the writer is passionate about.

A. Read these two letters to editors of different newspapers. As you read, think about whether the writer is agreeing or disagreeing with the article they read.

Letter 1: (Pittsburgh Tribune-Review, a local newspaper in Pennsylvania; Jan 4, 2020)

Regarding Toni Crisci's op-ed "Every Bottle Back aims to keep empties out of waterways" (Dec. 7, 2019): The Every Bottle Back initiative may be critical for keeping our environment clean and safe for people as well as protecting wildlife habitats. The Pennsylvania Beverage Association is to be commended for promoting the development of a "circular economy" for plastic bottles in the Pittsburgh area.

While it will be critical to invest monies to educate consumers, reinforce recycling infrastructure and modernize technology, high consumer participation will be at least in part due to reliable access to home recycling services and/or drop-off locations. This may be more easily accomplished in populated areas where a critical mass of participation may be more easily achieved.

It remains to be seen how the Every Bottle Back initiative will be rolled out in surrounding, more rural areas. Alternative strategies or incentives may be required to encourage participation and promote geographical inclusivity.

Perhaps there should be a tax (e.g., 10 to 20 cents) on the plastic bottles, which would be partially refunded upon bottle collection; however, the remainder of the tax monies would be used to maintain local collection sites in more rural areas.

Walter H. Sharlow Jr.
Butler, Pennsylvania

Letter 2: (Duke Chronicle, student newspaper, July 16, 2018; web links in the original article have been replaced by endnotes)

Last week, Duke Dining announced[1] that it would ban disposable plastics, replacing [them] with plant-based alternatives.

Unfortunately, while the plastic ban is a step in the right direction, the reality is not as green as it sounds. Plant-based plastics break down only in commercial composting facilities,[2] so their biodegradable benefits occur only if properly disposed of in compost bins. However, the vast majority of Duke's buildings lack composting, meaning that most of those disposable products will end up in landfills where they will likely not break down.

Additionally, plant plastics are not marine degradable,[3] so they still contribute to pollution in oceans and waterways. North Carolina is home to a significant population of sea turtles and marine mammals, all of whom will still be vulnerable to waste accumulation in their habitats even with plant-based plastics.

Finally, plant plastics are not recyclable, and they can contaminate recycling streams[4] if tossed in a recycling bin—an easy mistake to make, since many of them sport the label of '#7 plastics.' Replacing one disposable material with another won't solve expanding landfills or garbage in the ocean.

The real solution is to reduce our consumption of single-use materials so that we can stop waste accumulation, instead of just shuffling around what we do with our trash. Reusable bottles, bags, silverware, and straws are easy to access. Switching to reusable products is just a change in habit, not a disruption in lifestyle.

Duke must also offer the composting infrastructure necessary to accommodate these new plant-based materials, and Duke students need to know how to properly dispose of them.

Plant alternatives won't be enough without broader infrastructure and behavioral improvements.

Claire Wang is a Trinity College of Arts & Sciences senior.

Notes

[1]http://www.dukechronicle.com/article/2018/07/duke-dining-bans-disposable-plastic-in-all-eateries

[2]https://www.ecoproducts.com/faqs-composting_and_recycling.html

[3]https://www.ecoproducts.com/faqs-composting_and_recycling.html

[4]http://www.biomasspackaging.com/the-pros-and-cons-of-polylactic-acid-pla-bioplastic-the-corn-plastics/

Which moves do you find in each letter? With a partner or small group, highlight the language choices in the letters that indicate each move.

1. Refer to a news event
2. Refer to a previous article in the same newspaper
3. Evaluate the article positively or negatively
4. Make claims that support the article
5. Make claims that criticize the article
6. Use sources as support for claims
7. Make a recommendation or call to action

B. Plan your letter to the editor.

1. Read a student, local, or national news site or magazine (most are available on online). Identify an article, op-ed, or editorial that you agree with, partially agree with, or strongly disagree with.

2. Collect supporting details for your claims if necessary.

Review the Online Source Use Appendix for guidance on finding and evaluating internet sources.

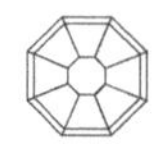

3. Consider these components of the Rhetorical Planning Wheel:

   a. **Purpose**: What do you want to achieve with your letter? What is your call to action?

   b. **Context**: Why are you writing this letter now? What events inspire your letter?

   c. **Audience**: Who are the readers of this newspaper? What do they probably already know or believe? How can they take action?

   d. **Language**: Given the purpose, audience, and context, what register of language is appropriate? How strong should your call to action be?

   e. **Conventions**: Is there a word limit for letters to this newspaper? Do letters have long or short paragraphs? How do writers refer to previous articles? Do they use web links or citations?

C. Write a draft letter to the editor. Select the most appropriate moves from Part A using your analysis of the rhetorical situation in Part B. Use evaluative language to show whether and why you agree or disagree with the original article.

D. Peer Review: Share your letter with one or two partners. Use these questions to give feedback:

1. Do you understand the context of the letter?

2. Does the writer give clear reasons for agreeing or disagreeing with an article, op-ed, or editorial in the newspaper?

3. Are the claims and supporting details persuasive?

4. Does the letter persuade you to take action?

5. How could the writer improve the letter?

E. Self-Review. Revise your letter using your peers' feedback. Have you done everything on this checklist?

- ☐ My letter has a clear focus and purpose.
- ☐ I use evaluative language to show my opinion about a previous article.
- ☐ I use effective claims and supporting details.
- ☐ I followed the conventions for a letter to the editor of this newspaper.

What else do you need to work on? Make further revisions to your letter if necessary.

References

Caulfield, M. (2019, June 19). *SIFT (The four moves).* https://hapgood.us/2019/06/19/sift-thefour-moves/

Cooper, J. (2014). A response to Michaela Cullington. *Young Scholars in Writing, 11,* 91–93.

DeBrabander, F. (2018). In defense of gun control. *Notre Dame Philosophical Reviews.* https://ndpr.nd.edu/reviews/in-defense-of-gun-contro/

Ferguson, C. J. (2018). *Debunking the 6 biggest myths about "technology addiction."* The Conversation. http://theconversation.com/debunking-the-6-biggest-myths-about-technology-addiction-95850

Jiang, J. (2018, November 28). *Many teens say they're constantly online – but they're no less likely to socialize with their friends offline.* Pew Research Center. https://www.pewresearch.org/fact-tank/2018/11/28/teens-who-are-constantly-online-are-just-as-likely-to-socialize-with-their-friends-offline/

Martin, J., & White, P. (2005). *The language of evaluation: Appraisal in English.* Palgrave Macmillan.

Mauthner, N. (2015). *We don't need digital detox, but there is a need to rethink our relationship with technology.* The Conversation. http://theconversation.com/we-dont-need-digital-detox-butthere-is-a-need-to-rethink-our-relationship-with-technology-40346

Melzer, D. (2009). Writing assignments across the curriculum: A national study of college writing. *College Composition and Communication, 61*(2), 240–261.

Partington, R. (2019, March 20). *Side by side: A celebration of dads.* Richie's Picks. http://richiespicks.pbworks.com/w/page/132635778/SIDE%20BY%20SIDE%3A%20A%20CELEBRATION%20OF%20DADS

Sharlow, W.H. (2020, January 4). Letter to the editor: Managing the plastic bottle crisis. *Pittsburgh Tribune-Review.* https://triblive.com/opinion/letter-to-the-editor-managing-the-plastic-bottle-crisis/

Smilowitz, S. (2016). A response to Olivia Weitz. *Young Scholars in Writing, 13,* 141–143.

Twenge, J. (2019). *Teens have less face time with their friends – and are lonelier than ever.* The Conversation. http://theconversation.com/teens-have-less-face-time-with-their-friends-and-arelonelier-than-ever-113240

Wang, C. (2018, July 16). Letter: Duke's plastic ban isn't as green as it sounds. *The Chronicle.* https://www.dukechronicle.com/article/2018/07/duke-bans-disposable-plastic-but-that-does-notfix-the-problem-claire-wang

9 Analyze

Goals

- ❐ Understand disciplinary frameworks and how they are used
- ❐ Apply a disciplinary framework (rhetorical appeals) to analyze written and visual texts
- ❐ Reorganize and synthesize information in an analysis
- ❐ Use nominalization to organize an analysis
- ❐ Pedagogical Genre: Visual analysis
- ❐ Genre in Action: Ad analysis

What Is the Action?

Analysis is a very broad term in academic writing that you will often see in university assignments and grading rubrics. Although it may have different meanings in some disciplines, the definition of analysis we use here is "reorganizing information from your sources in an original way according to a disciplinary framework" (Humphrey & Economou, 2015). The three key components of this definition are:

1. Analysis is based on sources.
2. You need to reorganize information from those sources.
3. The way you reorganize information depends on the disciplinary framework.

A disciplinary framework is a way of looking at the world through the eyes of a particular theory or academic discipline (Pessoa & Mitchell, 2019). This unit offers practice applying a disciplinary framework from the field of **rhetoric** to analyze texts and images. Rhetoric is the study of persuasion—that is, the components of an effective argument. You will also be able to apply the principles of analysis to frameworks from other disciplines you are studying.

Analysis is not the same as explanation or summary, both of which require you to display knowledge. It is also different from argument because you do not need to persuade your reader that a claim is valid. However, analysis is sometimes used as part of an argument. An analysis can also be a form of synthesis because you will usually draw on multiple sources in your writing.

You will use analysis in:

- ❐ case studies (especially in business, nursing and the health professions, and information studies)
- ❐ reports (in engineering, business, and other applied disciplines)
- ❐ academic assignments in many disciplines in the humanities and social sciences, including papers, in-class essays, and tests
- ❐ some library-based research papers and literature reviews

Activity 9.1: What Do You Know?

The extracts are taken from a Canadian case study on food waste (Nance et al., n.d.). Citations have been omitted. Is each extract an *explanation, analysis,* or *argument*? How do you know? Discuss your answers with a partner or small group.

1. Food loss is defined as the edible food that is lost throughout production, postharvest, and processing, whereas food waste refers to edible food lost at the end of the food chain due to behaviour of retailers and consumers. Fruits and vegetables have a higher wastage rate than any other food products, with roughly 40–50% of global production lost every year.

2. The modern food supply chain consists of three principal actors—consumers, markets, and farmers—who all contribute to food waste at various levels. Consumers are responsible for 28 percent of the fruit and vegetable waste, which represents the majority of edible produce that goes to waste among the supply chain. Consumers are the main force that drives demand; therefore, they expect supermarkets and farmers to provide a plentiful amount of produce that adhere to specific aesthetic requirements.

3. Remedial action is required throughout the food supply chain. While the participation of all actors in reducing the source of food waste is critical, alternative disposal methods should be utilized to avoid the environmental, economic, and social costs caused by food loss and waste.

Disciplinary Frameworks

Analysis is sometimes defined as breaking down a text into smaller pieces. You can discuss those pieces through a disciplinary framework (Pessoa & Mitchell, 2019). These frameworks include:

- ❒ feasibility (business)
- ❒ innovation (information systems)
- ❒ user experience (design)
- ❒ forms of capital (sociology)

This unit introduces a framework from the study of rhetoric that is commonly used in writing studies, English, and composition but is also relevant to marketing, psychology, and other fields. One of the most influential rhetorical frameworks has been developed from the work of the ancient Greek philosopher, Aristotle. According to Aristotle, there are four primary ways to convince an audience, known as the **rhetorical appeals,** which are commonly referred to by their original Greek names:

- ❒ ***ethos*, the appeal to authority:** What is the writer's authority on the topic? What have experts said about this topic? What does the research say? Who supports this argument and why?
- ❒ ***pathos*, the appeal to emotion:** How does the argument make the reader feel? How does it attract the reader's sympathy? Does the writer use anger, joy, frustration, fear, or sadness to support the claims?
- ❒ ***logos*, the appeal to logic:** What evidence does the writer provide? Is the evidence appropriate for the discipline, audience, and topic? How do the evidence and examples support the claims? What are the cause-effect relationships? How does the writer use contrast or comparison to support the argument and reject counterarguments?
- ❒ ***kairos*, the appeal to urgency or timeliness:** Why is the topic important now? What will happen if the argument is (not) accepted soon? How does the writer use current events as support?

As with all writing, the choice and success of the appeals in a text (including a visual or online text) depend on the writer's understanding of certain components of the Rhetorical Planning Wheel:

- ❒ Who is the audience? What are their beliefs, values, and expectations?
- ❒ What is your role and authority as a writer?
- ❒ What is the context? When and where will the argument be read?

For example, appeals to emotion are very effective in fundraising campaigns but are not as effective in most academic writing, where appeals to logic and authority are most persuasive. Op-ed writers, meanwhile, often appeal to timeliness because they are responding to current events.

Activity 9.2: Identifying the Framework

The first stage in an analysis involves identifying categories from the framework in the text you are analyzing. We use the framework of the four rhetorical appeals as an example of analysis in this unit.

Read the three texts, which all make arguments about women's participation in STEM (science, technology, engineering, and mathematics). Text 3 includes visual elements as well as words. As you read, think about which of the four rhetorical appeals the writers are using and how they use those appeals to persuade you.

Text 1: Extract from an undergraduate student's research paper in psychology

> The results measuring both male and female participation in [an undergraduate mathematics] class in terms of asking a question, voluntarily answering, and answering when called upon, found that men are more involved and vocal in the classroom. In addition, it appears that female students felt more comfortable asking the instructor questions privately before or after class in a more personal and intimate environment, thus avoiding the vulnerability associated with speaking in front of the entire class.

In conclusion, these observations suggest that women are participating less than men in the mathematics classroom and receiving less encouragement from their instructor. Therefore, it is important that instructors create a comfortable classroom environment, free of sexist attitudes. Montgomery and Barrett (1997) made several suggestions for instructors to encourage women to raise their confidence in their mathematics skills including acknowledging women's individual achievements and encouraging them to apply for workshops, internships and graduate school in their field. Female guest speakers also serve as role models for women and demonstrate female success in male-dominated fields (Montgomery and Barrett, 1997). In addition, if females are hesitant to participate in class, instructors should request answers from specific quiet tables with a mixture of males and females. In the observation study, the classroom observer found that this instructor technique was effective and helped the female students.

Text 2: From the "About" page of the U.S. Ad Council's "She Can STEM" campaign

STEM stands for Science, Technology, Engineering and Mathematics. Studies show that children with an understanding of these disciplines are better prepared for a lifetime of problem-solving and innovation.

We need more girls to feel confident stepping up and taking an interest in STEM. With girls in STEM, we can keep the world pushing forward.

Girls can't be what they can't see, which is why having female role models in STEM impacts their desire to stick with it. Our campaign gives visibility to women currently dominating the world of STEM so girls see they have a future in it too.

She can STEM. So can you.

Text 3: A social media advertisement from the "She Can STEM" campaign

FIGURE 9.1:
Ad Council Advertisement

Use the document on the companion website to help you complete Activity 9.2.

1. How would you complete the chart in the online document with examples from the texts of each of the four rhetorical appeals: ethos (authority), logos (logic), pathos (emotion), and kairos (timeliness)? The first row has been done for you as an example.

	TEXT 1 (RESEARCH PAPER)	TEXT 2 (ABOUT PAGE)	TEXT 3 (AD)
Ethos (authority)	*Citations to other research* *Reference to the author's own research*	*Reference to "studies"*	*Quoting a successful research scientist* *Referring to a well-known company*

2. What differences in language choices do you notice between Texts 1 and 2? How are they related to the rhetorical appeals that the texts make? Look in particular at the use of hedging (making a claim weaker or less confident), boosting (making a claim stronger or more confident), pronouns, verb forms, and sentence structure.

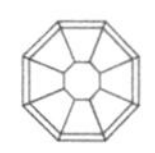

3. Identify the writer's role, audience, and purpose for each text. How does this information help you explain the choices of rhetorical appeal that you have noticed?

4. Which of these sentences are good examples of analysis of the STEM texts? For each sentence, discuss your answer in a group, and give reasons.
   a. According to Aristotle, there are four types of rhetorical appeal.
   b. I was impressed by the STEM advertisement.
   c. In Text 1, the writer cites previous research.
   d. The writers of the About Us page appeal to the readers' emotions by using *we* and referring to the positive idea of progress.
   e. The letters S-T-E-M are prominent in the ad because the term is often used in education today, which means the ad successfully employs *kairos* and is likely to attract attention.
   f. The research paper uses logic to make an argument.

Rhetorical Analysis

This unit is taking a common disciplinary framework (Aristotle's four appeals) as an example of the action of analysis. Next, you will use your understanding of this framework to write a **rhetorical analysis**, a pedagogical genre in which you are asked to consider how an argument works. This involves applying a rhetorical framework such as the four appeals to go beyond **describing** the text and start **analyzing** it in a structured way.

Activity 9.3: Analyze a Model

Read the opening of a rhetorical analysis of the "She Can STEM" website and ad from Activity 9.2.

①"She Can STEM" is an Ad Council campaign designed to encourage girls aged 11-15 to study science, technology, engineering, and mathematics (STEM) and consider future careers in those fields. The campaign consists of a website, TV and internet ads, and a social media campaign featuring women who hold senior positions in science and technology. The goal is to show girls "female role models" in industry so that they can "see they have a future in it too." The campaign was launched in 2018 and has proved to be popular. In its first two years, it attracted over 20,000 followers on both Instagram and YouTube, and the hashtag #shecanstem was used in almost 15,000 social media posts.

②The campaign appeals most clearly to its target audience by invoking the authority of women who have been successful in STEM fields. For instance, one print ad features Maya Gupta, a research scientist at Google. The photograph of Ms. Gupta—a young, fashionable woman of color—dominates the page, challenging the stereotypical image of a scientist as a white, middle-aged man dressed in a lab coat. The choice of this photograph suggests that if "she can [be successful in] STEM," then so can the reader. The website attributes the success of women like Ms. Gupta to their education in science, technology, engineering, and math, which the writers support with a reference to a research study, another form of authority. Although the details of the research are not provided, for many casual readers, the existence of research support makes the ad credible.

③The website claims that women are not only present in the "world of STEM," but they are also "changing" it. The support for this claim consists of a further appeal to the ethos of the women featured in the ads. They all work for high-profile companies and have job titles that indicate senior, influential, or technical positions such as "structural analysis engineer" or "chief technology officer." The ads clearly show that women have been successful in STEM fields by reaching high levels in the most well-known firms in the industry, such as Google. The individuals chosen as the faces of the campaign therefore present highly effective role models and authoritative examples of the potential impact of STEM education on girls.

Discuss the questions with a partner or small group.

1. **Is the first paragraph mostly descriptive or analytical? How do you know?**
2. **Which one of the four rhetorical appeals do Paragraphs 2 and 3 discuss? Identify the language that signals this to the reader.**
3. **What evidence from the ads and website does the writer use as examples of the appeal?**
4. **Which verb tenses are used in each paragraph? Why?**

Language Box: Verbs in Analytical Writing

It is important to go beyond description in analytical writing. One way to show this is by choosing your verbs and verb tenses carefully.

- You can use a range of **verb tenses** in a description, including the present simple (to describe the object of your analysis), the past simple (to present its history or background), and the present perfect (to show how it has developed or changed). However, most analysis is written only in the present simple tense. See the Grammar Glossary for more information on verb tenses.
  - The campaign *was launched* in 2018 and *has proved* to be popular. [Description]
  - This appeal to ethos *is* credible. [Analysis]
- Verbs that introduce **categories** are useful since analysis often involves breaking down a large concept into categories from a disciplinary framework. Examples include *be, classify, include, consist of, comprise,* and *there is/are*.
  - **There are** logical and emotional appeals in this ad.
  - Rhetorical appeals can **be classified** into three categories.
- Verbs that express **cause and effect** allow you to explain how the categories from the framework impact your analysis. Examples include *make, result from/in, lead to, cause, attribute to*.
  - The use of vibrant colors **makes** the ad stand out.
  - The rhetorical effect of the argument **results from** the writer's emotional choices.
- Verbs that give an **interpretation** are important because you often need to analyze the meaning of the elements you identify in your analysis. Examples include *mean, show, indicate, suggest, present imply*. Note that *present* cannot be followed by a *that* clause.
  - There are few citations in the book, **meaning** that readers cannot check the validity of the claims.
  - The slogan "She can STEM" is a logical appeal because it **implies** "and so can you."

Activity 9.4: Practice the Language

Read the next paragraph of the rhetorical analysis in Activity 9.3. Which verbs from the Analytical Writing Language Box would you use to complete the gaps? Choose from the list, using the most appropriate tense and form for the verbs.

be (is/are)	*indicate*	*make*
result	*show*	*suggest*

④Although pathos unsurprisingly plays a role in both texts, there ❶________ an interesting difference in use of emotional appeals between the ad and the website. On the web page, the target of the campaign are referred to as "girls," which ❷________ that it is really aimed at parents and teachers. However, the text of the ad is written as commands: "Don't just solve the problem, write the code," ❸________that it is directly at the girls themselves. Despite this difference, both texts invite the reader to imagine a future in which more girls study STEM disciplines. The strength of this vision ❹________ from the use of verbs such as *need* and *can't* as well as emotive phrases such as "pushing the world forward." The happy expression on Ms. Gupta's face ❺________ this emotional message stronger.

Reorganizing and Synthesizing Information

One of the key skills in analytical writing is reorganizing information to fit the categories of the disciplinary framework. For example, in a literary analysis of a book, you might bring together several examples of a character's behavior from the beginning and end of the book in a single paragraph. This is similar to the action of synthesis because you have to draw on multiple sources, or different sections of a single source, to organize your analysis. To do this, you have to decide which information from your text(s) fits into each category in your framework. For example, in Activities 9.3 and 9.4, the writer chose examples from both "She Can STEM" texts to support paragraphs about the first two appeals in the rhetorical framework.

WRITING TASK 9.1: Analysis through Synthesis

A. Read these statistics from the National Girls Collaborative Project, which will help you to determine whether the "She Can STEM" campaign appeals to *kairos*, or urgency, in the U.S. context (National Girls Collaborative, 2018):

- ☐ At the secondary school level, there is no difference between boys and girls in their participation in math and science courses or in their scores on standardized tests.
- ☐ Boys are much more likely to take advanced high school courses in engineering.
- ☐ Women are underrepresented in undergraduate computer science (18%), engineering (20%), physical sciences (39%), and mathematics degrees (43%).
- ☐ Women make up only 28% of the science and engineering workforce.
- ☐ There have been increases in the numbers of women in all racial and ethnic groups in science and engineering jobs; however, overall, African Americans and Hispanics remain underrepresented in these fields.

In addition, the American Association of University Women claims that "workforce projections for 2024 confirm that the top 10 fastest-growing occupations requiring at least a bachelor's degree will need significant science or math training" (AAUW, n.d.). To increase the number of women in STEM fields, the AAUW has several recommendations, including:

- ☐ "Cultivate girls' achievement by exposing them to female role models in STEM and encouraging high school girls to take calculus, physics, chemistry, computer science, and engineering classes."

B. Write a paragraph to continue the rhetorical analysis of the "She Can STEM" campaign by reorganizing the information in Part A. Here are suggested opening sentence, outline, and concluding sentence for Paragraph 5 of the analysis:

⑤The "She Can STEM" campaign has been launched at a time when there is a growing realization of the gender gap in science and technology.

a. Evidence of the STEM gender gap in secondary schools and universities

b. Effects of the gender gap on women, and women of color in particular

c. Recommendation for addressing the gender gap and its connection to "She Can STEM"

Therefore, the campaign is timely because it addresses a serious equity issue that is part of current discussions in education.

Language Box: Nominalization

A useful cohesive technique in analysis is writing the elements of the framework as nouns, even if they refer to actions (usually verbs) or qualities (usually adjectives). This is known as **nominalization**. The nouns can then be used in the sentences that introduce them, often as subjects. For example:

- The author *appeals* to emotions → The **appeal** to positive emotions can be seen in ....
- The argument is persuasive because it is *timely*. → The **timeliness** of the argument means that ....

This technique works for frameworks in other disciplines, too:

- **Competition** leads to ....
- The **evolution** of the fruit fly is explained by ....
- Disruptive **innovation** occurs when ....
- The first aspect of user experience is **simplicity**.

The chart shows five ways to form a noun from a different part of speech (Caplan, 2019, p. 127). Check a dictionary to find out whether a word exists before selecting it, however, since the reformulation does not always create an acceptable word.

Use the noun as a verb.	Sometimes there is a change of spelling.	*appeal, choice, impact, influence*
Use the *-ing* form of the verb as a noun.	This is sometimes called a *gerund*.	*writing, teaching, learning*
Add a suffix to the verb to form a noun.	The suffix may be *-ment, -ation, -ion,* or *-ance.*	*competition, measurement, globalization*
Add a suffix to an adjective to form a noun.	The suffix may be *-ness* or *-ity.*	*timeliness, simplicity*
Add a suffix to a concrete noun to form an abstract noun.	The suffix may be *-ship, -hood,* or *-ism.*	*adulthood, ownership, capitalism*

Activity 9.5: Practice the Language

Read the sentences that introduce different disciplinary frameworks. Write one sentence to introduce each aspect of the framework. These sentences might be used as the first sentences of the paragraphs (much like topic sentences). Use nominalization techniques from the chart to help you. The first sentence has been completed for you as an example.

1. Products and services that offer an excellent user experience are simple, elegant, and easy to use.

   The first aspect of user experience is simplicity.

   Another aspect is ____________.

   ______________ is the final characteristic of an excellent user experience.

2. There are two main types of experiment in biology. Some experiments are conducted in test tubes in a laboratory, while others involve human subjects.

3. In this analysis, we will consider whether the company is competitive, profitable, and sustainable.

WRITING TASK 9.2: Argument Analysis

Choose an op-ed (opinion editorial) column from a local or campus news site. See page 193 for example of an op-ed. Plan and write a rhetorical analysis of the op-ed writer's argument in answer to this question: What rhetorical appeals does the writer use to make the argument?

A. Find examples of the four appeals (ethos, logos, pathos, and kairos) in your op-ed. This will help you reorganize information from the op-ed into the categories of the rhetorical framework.

B. Overall, do you find the argument in the op-ed effective, based on your analysis of the appeals? Why, or why not? Conduct additional online research if you want to check the information or determine the timeliness of the argument.

Review the Online Source Use Appendix for a guide to evaluating the reliability of online sources using the SIFT strategies (Caulfield, 2019).

C. Plan your rhetorical analysis. Consider these questions:
   - ☐ Which appeal is dominant? Do you want to start or end your analysis with it?
   - ☐ In what order will you discuss the other appeals?
   - ☐ How many paragraphs will you need for each appeal?
   - ☐ How will you reorganize information from the op-ed article and your (optional) additional research into your analysis?

D. Draft your rhetorical analysis, using the example paragraphs in Activities 9.3 and 9.4 to help you.

E. Peer Review. Share the draft of your analysis with one or two partners. Use these questions to give feedback:
   1. Does the writer discuss the four rhetorical appeals with examples from the op-ed?
   2. Which appeal dominates? Was this a good choice? Why or why not?
   3. Does the order of the appeals make sense to you?
   4. Does the writer use nominalization to create cohesion?
   5. What else can the writer do to improve the analysis?

F. Self-Review. Revise your rhetorical analysis using your peers' feedback. Have you done everything on this checklist?
   - ☐ I gave specific examples of the appeals that I discussed in my analysis.
   - ☐ I started my analysis with the most dominant appeal.
   - ☐ I reorganized information from the article (and other sources) to fit the rhetorical framework.
   - ☐ I checked the information using online sources that I evaluated using the SIFT strategies.
   - ☐ I chose verbs and verb tenses carefully to show that I was analyzing and not describing the op-ed.

What else do you need to work on? Make further revisions to your rhetorical analysis if necessary.

Pedagogical Genre: Visual Analysis

Arguments are not only found in writing: images can make arguments, too, as revealed in Activity 9.2. Images can also inspire emotions, communicate ideas, and tell the viewer something about the world. A visual analysis is a class assignment you might encounter in a composition or art history class that helps you understand how images work rhetorically. The assignment is also an opportunity to practice the action of analysis, which you can then apply to other disciplines.

In a **visual analysis**, you consider different elements of a photograph, cartoon, image, or other form of graphic and consider the effects they have on the viewer. As with any analysis, you need to start by choosing your disciplinary framework or lens. You can organize a visual analysis using the rhetorical framework (the four appeals) or a framework from the study of art and design. Some of the questions you might ask are listed in Figure 9.2. You do not need to ask every question about every image you analyze. For each of the questions, you should follow up by asking yourself, "What effect does this choice have on the image and the viewer?"

FIGURE 9.2:
Disciplinary Frameworks for Visual Analysis

Disciplinary Framework: Rhetoric	
Ethos	▪ Who produced the image? When? What was the context? ▪ What do we know about the artist? ▪ Do we know why the artist produced this image? ▪ Where was the image displayed?
Logos	▪ What is in the image? ▪ What do the colors, framing, and composition tell the viewer? ▪ What is the style of the image (formal, informal, snapshot, portrait, etc.)? ▪ Is the image vertical (portrait) or horizontal (landscape)? ▪ Is the image authentic or modified? ▪ Did the image occur spontaneously (candid) or was it planned (staged)? ▪ What do you think is the purpose of the image? Is it making an argument? How?
Pathos	▪ What stands out to you in the image? Why? ▪ Who was the intended audience? Are you part of that audience? ▪ What emotions does the image generate? How? ▪ Would different audiences react with different emotions to the image? Why? ▪ Do you think the image is beautiful? Is it supposed to be?

Disciplinary Framework: Art and Design Example	
Line	▪ How does the design of the image lead your eye from one area to another? ▪ What is dominant in the foreground and what is in background? ▪ What is the perspective? ▪ Are the parts of the image in balance? What contrasts do you see?
Value	▪ How does the artist use light and dark? ▪ How does the artist use contrast (changes between light and dark)? ▪ What is emphasized in the image? ▪ What patterns can you see?
Shapes and Forms	▪ What shapes (two-dimensional) and forms (three-dimensional) can you see in the image? ▪ Are the shapes found in nature (organic) or drawn on purpose (geometric, e.g., circles, triangles, and squares)? ▪ What are the dimensions (sizes) of the shapes and forms? ▪ How do the shapes interact with each other? ▪ What is the scale? Are the shapes, people, and objects the same size as in real life?
Space	▪ What is the space around the objects, people, shapes, and forms? ▪ Is there empty space? How is it used? ▪ Are the elements of the image in proportion, that is do the different elements fit together?
Color and Texture	▪ What colors are used? ▪ Are the colors natural or artificial, expected or surprising? ▪ What are the surfaces like - rough, smooth, soft, or hard? ▪ Do the colors and textures create unity (everything is in harmony) or tension (elements do not seem to fit)?

A. Choose an image to analyze. Your teacher may give you specific directions to find an image based on a current project. Or you may be able to choose one of these suggestions:

1. Use Google Images to search for an image on a topic you are interested in.
2. Choose an image from a newspaper, magazine, or website that illustrates an important current event.
3. Find an interesting example of public art or graffiti in your local area.
4. Take a photograph from an unusual perspective or a photograph that illustrates some aspect of your daily life.
5. Choose two different images that are connected by the same theme, one of which is a photograph you take yourself.

B. Choose a framework: the rhetorical framework, the art framework, or a different, but appropriate, disciplinary framework. Use the framework to organize your notes on your image.

C. Draft your analysis.

D. Peer Review. Share your analysis with one or more partners. Use these questions to give peer feedback:

   1. Does the writer use a framework and provide supporting evidence from the visual for their analysis?
   2. Does the writer analyze the image in addition to describing it?
   3. Is the analysis clearly and logically organized?
   4. How can the writer improve the analysis?

E. Self-Review. Revise your visual analysis using your peers' feedback. Have you done everything on this checklist?

   - ☐ The analysis is introduced and connected with references to the framework, including nominalization where appropriate.
   - ☐ Each component of the framework is supported by evidence from the visual.
   - ☐ The categories in the framework are discussed in a clear and logical order.
   - ☐ I chose verbs and verb tenses carefully to analyze examples and evidence from the image.

What else do you need to work on? Make further revisions to your visual analysis if necessary.

Genre in Action: Ad Analysis

Advertisements are everywhere—on TV, on the radio, on the internet, on social media, and in newspapers and magazines. Companies spend large amounts of money on advertising campaigns, which means they must feel there is some benefit to them. But why do ads work? An ad analysis is an opportunity to look at an advertisement from any medium and ask if and why it is effective for the target market. Ad analyses are found in publications aimed at marketing professionals, such as *AdWeek* and *Marketing Dive* as well as some popular newspapers and magazines. You might also be assigned an ad analysis in a marketing or business class.

Read this published analysis of an ad by the candy company Sweetarts (Adams, 2019). Note that "Gen (Generation) Z" generally refers to the generation of people born between 1997–2012.

> ①A candy brand trying to court younger consumers is nothing new, but Sweetarts is leaning into widely held perceptions about the Gen Z cohort, such as their favoring of diversity-minded marketing, to create a more tailored approach to "Be Both." The ads themselves make vague nods to the types of political causes more brands are embracing—with phrases like "Fight for Change" and "Pro this/anti that" flashing on the screen—while avoiding potentially controversial topics around diversity to instead focus on a positive message.
>
> *[a link to the video of the ad is embedded in the actual ad]*
>
> ②The demand for brands to better reflect the more complex identities of Gen Z in their advertising has become oft-repeated across the industry, especially as the broader pressure for more purposeful marketing grows. For candy companies, in particular, the need to win over the next generation of customers could be greater since sales in the segment have slid in recent years.

③"Be Both" marks the second major campaign launched by a Ferrara brand this month that plays into colorful, animated creation to increase consumer appeal. The darkly humorous ads also got an assist from the London-based animation shop Blinkink and content creators Becky Sloan and Joseph Pelling, who have developed a cult following for their surreal YouTube videos.

A. Identify the functions of these sections of the text:
   1. Sentences 1–2
   2. Sentences 3–4
   3. Sentences 5–6

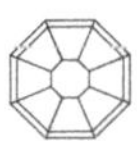

B. Look at the Marketing Dive website to help you answer the questions about additional components of the Rhetorical Planning Wheel.
   1. What is the role of the writer?
   2. Who do you think reads this type of text?
   3. What is the overall purpose of the text?
   4. What types of evidence, examples, and sources are used?
   5. What are some of the conventions of these articles (e.g. look at the videos and references to ad agencies)?

C. To expand your ad analysis, use the framework developed by MBA faculty at Northwestern University. The original is called ADPLAN if you want to research it further. A simplified version is provided in Table 9.1.

TABLE 9.1:
The ADPLAN Framework

Component	*Questions You Can Ask*
Attention	Does the ad get people to pay attention? How?
Difference	Is the ad different from ads for similar products?
Message	What message does the ad use to appeal to its target audience? What is the benefit to buying this product or using this service?
Linking	Does the ad create a strong link between the brand and the creative message? Would you and your friends remember that the ad was for this particular product? Are viewers likely to talk about the ad online or with friends?
Reputation	Does the ad fit the image and reputation of the brand?

Source: Adapted from Tim Calkins and Derek Rucker's ADPLAN framework (Kellog School of Management, 2021).

1. Which aspects of the ADPLAN framework does the analysis in Part A discuss?
2. Which categories of the framework do the following short analyses discuss?
   a. The ad stood out for its emotional tone; this helped it break through the clutter. The benefit was very apparent, both the benefit that the adaptive controller helps kids and the bigger benefit that Microsoft uses technology to make the world a better place.
   b. Expensify ran an engaging and effective spot. The ad featured the classic expensive music video and the attentive, annoying character from the finance department. The benefit was clear: Expensify makes it easy to keep track of your receipts and deal with your expense reports.
   c. The ad celebrated the role of journalists and facts and recognized some of the journalists that have been killed in recent years.
   d. The ad was striking and distinctive. The news source wisely stayed away from politics.
   e. The spot embraced the idea of women's empowerment and connected it back to their technology and approach.

D. Plan and draft your analysis using the example above, other ad analysis articles, and the most relevant components of the ADPLAN framework.

E. Peer Review. Share your ad analysis with one or more partners. Use these questions to give peer feedback:

1. Does the writer use enough categories from the ADPLAN framework (see Table 9.2) and provide supporting evidence from the ad for their analysis?
2. Does the writer analyze the ad in addition to describing it?
3. Is the ad analysis clearly and logically organized?
4. How can the writer improve the ad analysis?

F. Self-Review. Revise your ad analysis using your peers' feedback. Have you done everything on this checklist?

- ☐ The analysis is introduced and connected with references to the framework, including nominalization where appropriate.
- ☐ Each component of the ADPLAN framework is supported by evidence from the visual.
- ☐ The categories are discussed in a clear and logical order.
- ☐ I chose verbs and verb tenses carefully to analyze examples and evidence from the ad.

What else do you need to work on? Make further revisions to your ad analysis if necessary.

References

Ad Council (2019). *She can STEM*. Retrieved August 23, 2019 from https://shecanstem.com/about/

American Association of University Women. (n.d.). *AAUW issues: Science, technology, engineering, and mathematics (STEM) education*. https://ww3.aauw.org/what-we-do/public-policy/aauw-issues/stem-education/

Adams, X. (2019, April 24). *Sweetarts looks to win over Gen Z with diversity-driven "Be Both" campaign*. MarketingDive. https://www.marketingdive.com/news/sweetarts-looks-to-win-over-gen-z-with-diversity-driven-be-both-campaign/553356/

Caplan, N. A. (2019). *Grammar choices for graduate and professional writers* (2nd ed). University of Michigan Press.

Caulfield, M. (2019, June 19). *SIFT (The four moves)*. https://hapgood.us/2019/06/19/sift-thefour-moves/

Humphrey, S. L., & Economou, D. (2015). Peeling the onion–A textual model of critical analysis. *Journal of English for Academic Purposes, 17*, 37–50. https://doi.org/10.1016/j.jeap.2015.01.004

Kellog School of Management at Northwestern University (2021). *SuperBowl ad review*. https://www.kellogg.northwestern.edu/news-events/super-bowl.aspx

Nance, E., Vadnais, A., Hicks, C., & Lawson, T. (n.d.). *Insistence on cosmetically perfect fruits & vegetables*. University of British Columbia Open Case Studies. https://cases.open.ubc.ca/insistence-on-cosmetically-perfect-fruits-vegetables/

National Girls Collaborative Project. (n.d.). *Statistics*. https://ngcproject.org/statistics

Pessoa, S., & Mitchell, T. D. (2019). Preparing students to write in the disciplines. In N. A. Caplan & A. M. Johns (Eds.), *Changing practices for the L2 writing classroom: Moving beyond the five-paragraph essay* (pp. 150–177). University of Michigan Press.

PART 3:
INTEGRATING ACTIONS

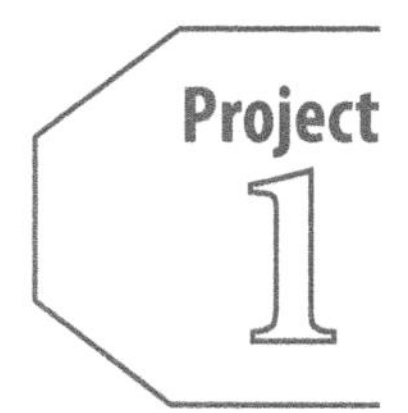

Transforming Texts

Goals

- ❒ Read and analyze texts about bilingualism from different genres
- ❒ Prepare a blurb for a book, based on an author's preface
- ❒ Write a summary and response to a blog entry
- ❒ Conduct an interview with a bilingual/multilingual person
- ❒ Shift perspective between direct and indirect speech
- ❒ Write a magazine profile based on your interview

Project Overview

What does it mean to be bilingual? What are the benefits of bilingualism? Are there any disadvantages? How do bilinguals experience life in their different languages? In this project, you are going to explore these questions by reading texts in different genres. Each writing task asks you transform or reuse the answers to these questions in new ways. You will learn that how content is organized and discussed in a text depends on its genre and where and how it is situated, as well as the writer(s) and the audience(s) involved. During this project, you will be writing three texts in different genres as you explore what can happen to information, text structures, language use, and other components of the Rhetorical Planning Wheel in different contexts.

In this project you will use many actions including **summarizing, responding, arguing, and explaining.**

Step 1: Analyze a Preface to an Academic Book

A **preface** is a short text at the beginning of a book that, along with other texts like an introduction, typically presents the volume's key themes and ideas. A preface may serve other purposes, such as acknowledging those who helped with the book or discussing what motivated the author to write it. The author of Text 1, Professor Ellen Bialystok, is one of the world's best-known researchers into bilingualism, the topic of this project. As you read her preface, think about how she prepares her audience for the book that follows, *Bilingualism in Development: Language, Literacy, and Cognition* (2001).

Text 1

❶Parents often ask me for advice about exposing their children to two languages in the home. Typically, one of the parents speaks some language other than English and they are concerned that their linguistic decisions will have consequences for the child's development. The requests come in many forms (although e-mail has become the channel of choice) and from people with obviously different levels of background knowledge, education, and experience. The motivation for their questions is usually the same—will the child learn English, and will the experience of learning two languages lead to either cognitive or linguistic confusion?

❷These questions are interesting because of the assumptions they reveal about the folk wisdom of childhood bilingualism. First, people intuitively believe that language learning is a fragile enterprise and can be easily disrupted. Second, they assume that languages interact, and that learning one language has implications for learning another. Finally, they expect that what happens with language can impact on the rest of cognition.

❸All of these assumptions are empirical questions and all of them entail theoretical controversies. Moreover, they are questions for which controlled investigation is difficult, if not impossible. Ironically, it is bilingual children who also provide the most promising forum for their examination and a means of potentially resolving the theoretical disputes. What happens to children's developing knowledge of language if they are learning two languages at the same time? How do children sort out the words and meanings from the two systems and incorporate them into thought? The questions resonate to pervasive issues in the philosophy of mind, such as the relation between language and thought and the viability of an autonomous language center in the brain.

❹The research and ideas in this book examine the language and cognitive development of bilingual children. The discussion explores these three assumptions, demonstrating how the study of bilingual children can clarify these basic controversies. The outcomes of that inquiry have implications both for practical concerns regarding the development of bilingual children and for theoretical debates that frame our study of development. My primary interest in bilingual children, therefore, is for the story they can tell us about human cognition and development.

With a partner or group, answer the questions.

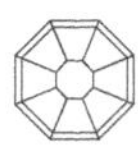

1. Why did Bialystok conduct this research and write this book? What are her motivations?
2. What are the three assumptions about language that Bialystok will address in her book?
3. Who are the participants (subjects) in her studies?
4. Who are the audiences for the book? How do you know?
5. How would you describe the register of this preface (see Unit 2)? What does the register indicate about the book's audience(s)?

Step 2: Analyze the Book Blurb

A **blurb** is a short text that generally appears on the back cover of a book or in online advertising. Texts in this genre are purposefully positive because their job is to sell the book to people who pick it up in a bookstore or look it up online. Blurbs can be written in many different ways. However, they share one central purpose: to persuade people to buy a book.

Read these three blurbs from books about bilingualism. As you read, think about how the blurbs are similar and different.

Text 2a

Whether in family life, social interactions, or business negotiations, half the people in the world speak more than one language every day. Yet many myths persist about bilingualism and bilinguals. In a lively and entertaining book, an international authority on bilingualism explores the many facets of life with two or more languages. (Written to promote *Bilingual: Life and Reality* by Francois Grosjean and published by Harvard University Press in 2010.)

Text 2b

This book covers research topics in bilingual education, language policies, language contact, identity of bilingual speakers, early bilingualism, heritage languages, and more, and provides an overview of current theory, research and practice in the field of bilingualism. Each chapter is written by a specialist in the field. Part I focuses on the numerous and heterogeneous relations between languages as well as the implications arising from bilingual speech processing. In Part II, a series of contextualized studies on bilingual classrooms are presented, with diverse research designs applied in different educational settings being a key feature of these studies. Part III bridges theory and practice by offering an insight into mono- and multilingual school settings showcasing examples of educational institutions where bilingualism successfully soared and depicts the needs related to language education. (Written to promote *Current Research in Bilingualism and Bilingual Education*, edited by Romanowski & Jedynak and published by Springer in 2018.)

Text 2c

In this accessible guide to bilingualism in the family and the classroom, Colin Baker delivers a realistic a picture of the joys and difficulties of raising bilingual children. The Q&A format of this book makes it the natural choice for the busy parent or teacher who needs an easy reference guide to the most frequently asked questions. This revised edition includes more information on bilingualism in the digital age and incorporates the latest research in areas such as neonatal language experience, multilingualism, language mixing and the effect that siblings have on family language choice. (Written to promote *A Parents' and Teachers' Guide to Bilingualism, 4th edition*, by Colin Baker and published by Multilingual Matters in 2014.)

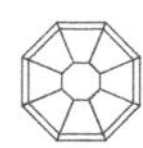

Discuss the questions with a partner about the three book blurbs.

1. What do these book blurbs have in common? That is, what are the "family resemblances" the texts in this genre share?
2. What are the blurbs' secondary purposes, beyond persuading readers to buy the book?
3. Who are the audiences for each of these books? How do you know?
4. How are the blurbs different? What do you think might be the reasons for these differences?
5. Do you notice any language features that the blurbs have in common? Look, for example, at the verb tenses, prepositional phrases, and the use of the word *this*.

Step 3: Write a Book Blurb

A. Re-read Bialystok's preface (Text 1), focusing on her own motivations for writing and her research. Use your answers to the discussion questions and the sample blurbs in Step 2 to write a blurb of 100 to 250 words designed to sell Bialystok's book, particularly to parents who are raising bilingual children.

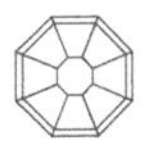

B. Before you write, consider these questions from the Rhetorical Planning Wheel:

1. **Audience(s):** Who are the audience(s) for this book? Why would they be interested?
2. **Purpose(s):** What are the purpose(s) for writing this book blurb? You are trying to sell it, but are there other purposes, as well?
3. **Conventions:** What are the "family resemblances" among the book blurbs?
4. **Structure:** How will you organize your blurb? What information will you include and in what order?
5. **Language:** What register will you choose? For example, will you ask questions or describe the book? Will you refer to the audience as *you*? Will you use the author's name? Will you write in an academic or everyday style?

C. Peer Review. Share your draft blurb with one or two partners. Read your peers' blurbs as if you were looking at the book online or in a bookstore. Use these questions to give peer feedback:

1. Would the blurb convince you to buy the book if you were part of its intended audience? Why, or why not?
2. Does the draft share the family resemblances with the example book blurbs? Which ones?
3. Which the language choices in the blurb help sell the book?
4. How could the writer make the blurb more persuasive?
5. What could the writer do, in general, to improve the blurb?

D. Self-Review: Revise your blurb using your peers' feedback. Have you done everything on this checklist?

- ☐ My blurb clearly introduces the main ideas and motivations of the book.
- ☐ My blurb is appropriate for the intended audience(s) for the book.
- ☐ I have used some of the conventions and common language features of the genre.
- ☐ My blurb is the right length (100-250 words).

What else do you need to work on? Make further revisions to your blurb if necessary.

Step 4: Analyze an Expert Commentary

Read this expert commentary published on the website *The Conversation*. The author is a lecturer in linguistics at Cambridge University in England. Note that the original article included many links to research and other sources, which are not shown here. As you read, think about your reactions to the ideas in the article.

Speaking in tongues: The many benefits of bilingualism

Teresa Parodi, November 4, 2015

❶We live in a world of great linguistic diversity. More than half of the world's population grows up with more than one language, and we all know families where bilingualism or multilingualism are the norm because the parents speak different languages or because the family uses a language different from that of the community around them.

❷How difficult is it for a child to grow up in such an environment? And what are bilingual children capable of? Well, they are capable of quite a lot, even at a very young age. They can understand and produce expressions in more than one language, they know who to address in which language, and they are able to switch very fast from one language to the other.

Noses for grammar

❸Clearly we are talking here of a range of different skills: social, linguistic and cognitive. Social skills are the most known: bilingual children are able to interact with speakers of (at least) two languages and thus have direct access to two different cultures.

❹But they also have linguistic skills, some very obvious, such as understanding and using words and expressions in different languages. A less obvious aspect is that bilingual children have a raised awareness for how language "works." For example, bilinguals are better than monolinguals of the same age at pinpointing that the sentence "apples growed on trees" is bad, and "apples grow on noses" is fine but doesn't make sense.

❺Less known are the cognitive skills developed by bilinguals, an issue of great interest for research at the moment, as seen, for example, in work by Ellen Bialystok and colleagues. Probably due to the practice of switching languages, bilinguals are very good at taking different perspectives, dealing with conflicting cues, and ignoring irrelevant information. These skills can be applied to domains other than language, making them an added value of bilingualism.

Is it worth it?

❻What if one of the languages is not a "useful" one because, for example, it does not have many speakers (for example, Cornish, a language spoken in Cornwall in South-West England)? Is it worth exposing the child to it? The linguistic, social, and cognitive advantages mentioned above hold, independently of the specific languages. Any combination of languages has the same effect.

❼A common worry is that trying to speak two (or more) languages could be too strenuous for the child. But there is no need for concern: learning to speak is more similar to learning to walk than it is to learning a school subject. Learning to speak is genetically programmed. The brain is certainly able to cope with more than one language, as research and experience show.

❽There could be a practical problem, though, in providing enough exposure to the languages. The stress is then on the parents to ensure the opportunity to interact with speakers of the languages in question. Bilingualism is not genetic: having parents who speak different language does not guarantee a bilingual child.

Code-switching is cool

❾Another frequent worry is that of the child learning two half languages, short of the "proper" version of either of them. One may, for example, hear bilinguals – children and adults – using words or expressions from two or more of the languages in their linguistic repertoire in a single sentence or text, a phenomenon known as *code-switching.*

❿Often people assume that the main reason for doing this is a lack of sufficient proficiency in one of the languages, such that the speaker cannot continue in the language they started in. They also often assume that the choice of the words from one language or the other is random. Far from it! Code-switching is common among bilinguals and, contrary to popular belief, it follows grammatical rules.

⓬Additionally, if asked for clarification, bilinguals know if they have spoken too quietly or used the wrong language, and they only switch in the latter case. Both bilingual children and adults have a range of reasons to code-switch. Code-switching can be cool!

⓭All typically developing children will learn one language. To learn more than one they need the opportunity and the motivation. Growing up with more than one language is an asset well worth the investment.

Discuss the questions about this text with a partner or small group.

1. What are the benefits of bilingualism, according to this commentary?
2. Do you agree or disagree with any of the author's points?
3. Can you think of any other advantages of bilingualism or any other challenges for bilinguals?

4. *The Conversation* publishes "commentary and analysis" written by researchers and edited by journalists. Who do think is the audience for these articles? How do you know?

5. Does the article relate to current events, your friends, your family, or your own language use?

Step 5: Write a Response to the Commentary

Prepare to write a response to the commentary for your own blog. Since your readers may not have read the original article, you should start by summarizing Parodi's text. Therefore, you will be writing a summary and response, a common academic assignment.

1. Review the Summary and Response section in Unit 8, including the Signaling Responses Language Box (see page 203) and Activities 8.3, 8.4, and 8.5.

2. Draft a blog post for other students in which you summarize Text 3 and respond to comments that the writer of the text makes about bilingualism, based on your own experiences with language learning or use. Conduct additional research if necessary.

   Review the Online Source Use Appendix for guidance on finding and evaluating online and library database sources.

3. Peer Review: Share your draft blog post with one or two partners. Use these questions to give peer feedback:
   1. Is the summary of the commentary accurate and complete? Why or why not?
   2. Does the writer respond to specific ideas from the original text?
   3. Are you convinced by the writer's points? Why or why not?
   4. Is the writer using language recommended in the Language Boxes in Unit 8? What language use is particularly good?
   5. How else could the writer improve the blog post?

Step 6: Prepare to Write a Magazine Profile

Researchers like Bialystok (Text 1) note that they cannot generalize about language use or the benefits of speaking several languages because the populations studied in the research vary considerably. In addition, as one researcher points out: "Many studies compare monolingual and bilingual people who vary in more ways than the number of languages they speak, including their nationality, educational level, socioeconomic background, immigrant status, and cultural traits" (Yong, 2016). A study of a single individual and their experiences with language can, instead, reveal the complexity of language use in different contexts.

In this task, you will interview a multilingual person and write a magazine profile that focuses on how this person uses two or more languages in different ways.

1. Find a bilingual or multilingual person in your writing class, your college or university, your family, or among your friends who, in your view, would be an interesting subject for a magazine profile. What makes your subject choice appropriate? Because you are interested in bilingualism, the answers should relate to the home and school experiences of your subject and their use of one or more languages in their life or work.

2. With others in the class, create a series of questions about the interviewee's bilingualism that will form the basis of your profile. For example:
    - What language(s) did your family speak at home when you were a child?
    - What language(s) did you use or learn in school? Did those languages change as you grew up?
    - Did you grow up in a bilingual or multilingual community?
    - Did you learn your additional languages in school or elsewhere? When and why?
    - Has your use of one or more of your languages changed during your life? What were the key events that affected your bilingualism (or multilingualism)?
    - How and where do you use your languages today? Is one of your languages predominant in your academic life and another in your home life or with your friends, for example?

- ☐ Which of your skills is dominant in each of your languages (speaking, listening, reading, or writing)? Why?
- ☐ How do you feel about the languages you speak? What is your attitude toward each of these languages? Have these attitudes changed over time?
- ☐ What are the advantages or disadvantages of being bilingual?

What other questions might you write for the interview? Add these to your list.

Step 7: Analyze a Magazine Profile

Read this example of a magazine profile about Sabrina, a trilingual adult from Algeria, a country in North Africa. As you read, think about how Sabrina's use of languages has changed during her life.

Profile: Three Languages, One Complex Identity

❶After ordering her expresso in colloquial Algerian Arabic from a local coffee shop, Sabrina greets her colleagues on campus in French and begins to prepare her university lecture in that language. But because she is well-aware of her students' interest in English, she considers how she can pepper her lecture with anecdotes about her experiences in the United States. Following her lecture, she lunches with colleagues in French and Arabic, then answers an overseas phone call in English and prepares for the English Conversation Club meeting that she runs in the late afternoon. On the street following the meeting, she hails a cab in Algerian colloquial Arabic and converses with the driver as he returns her to her home, where she is greeted by her family in French.

❷Sabrina Lamia Halli, the trilingual, code-switching subject of this profile, was a recipient of a prestigious Fulbright grant from 2016-2018, when she studied petroleum geology in English at the University of Oklahoma. Before her U.S. stay, she worked, using both French and Arabic, as a geologist in the Algerian desert for several years for an oil and gas company. She now serves as an instructor at the University of Boumerdès, where academic French is the medium of instruction but her English is much-admired, particularly by her students. Here is her story.

"I first loved French—and then English."

❸For religious and nationalistic reasons, Arabic and Amazigh (also known as Berber) are the official languages of Algeria. However, Sabrina's parents, grandparents, and great-grandparents were educated and fluent in French. They were also progressive, unconditionally encouraging women to be educated. In fact, her great-grandfather, a famous communicator and mediator, sent his girls to school and insisted upon their bilingualism (French and Arabic) and intellectual growth. Her grandmother married a law student from the French-dominant university in Algeria, and their children and grandchildren were raised with an understanding of the importance of independence, cognitive development, and speaking, reading, and writing academic French. English did not play a role in Sabrina's education (except for two hours of class per week) or in her home, for "my family thought that studying English might interfere with my French learning."

❹Sabrina notes that she has "loved French for as long as I can remember." Her mother always read her a night-time story in that language, and since the house was filled with books in French, she worked hard to improve her academic understanding of the language, studying dictionaries and biology textbooks. As a result, her French became somewhat antiquated. Her classmates wondered at her language use: "I can remember that my fellow students asked why I spoke the French of the 14th century." But she also spoke the French of the cafés, where the men in her family invited her to participate in discussions on a broad range of issues.

❺Now she loves English, too, happily reporting that "my first exposure to that language was through music." With a scarcity of English books available in Algeria during the 1970s and 1980s, "music lyrics were the most viable option for me." Her cousins, who lived in Switzerland, sent CDs with English lyrics printed on a sheet inside, and she developed a system for studying them.

> "First, I listened and got the general idea of the topics; then I listened again to jot down the lyrics; and finally, I listened to pick up the difficult words, which I then looked up in the dictionary. Whenever I found time to spare, I rehearsed my new words from the lyrics. I was so fascinated by English that I dreamed of interviewing Lady Diana! When I started my first job, at a call center (all in English), I enrolled in a language school in order to continue my improvement."

❻Sabrina's K–12 education was in a mix of French and increasingly, classical Arabic. But she occasionally experienced English at university since a group of students from the science club were conducting field-related research in the U.S. model, so they were improving their language skills by conversing in English on campus.

"My English was valued—and challenged."

❼Sabrina's proficiency in French facilitated an understanding of complex topics in the field and helped her gain the respect of her university instructors, who had studied exclusively in French. But her English was also valued. Due to her continued interest in that language, when she began work, "the managers would ask me to translate documents from English to French and to host visiting native English speakers when they came to inspect our work."

❽However, she was in for some surprises! After winning a Fulbright scholarship and settling into her university in Oklahoma, she found that she had trouble understanding local people because they "talked fast with an accent and swallowed their words." But she was determined to improve her comprehension, so during her two years in the United States, she didn't look for French-speaking or Arabic-speaking people with whom to communicate but moved out of her comfort zone to speak English with Americans. She urged her American friends to "talk as they are used to," since she saw it as her responsibility to bring her English level up to theirs. She worked on her English reading proficiency by visiting the library, where "I took out many books and read the American newspapers."

"I am now more proficient in English."

❾Having returned to her native country, Sabrina uses colloquial Arabic for her grocery shopping or when she speaks to people for whom Arabic is the dominant language. French is used predominantly with family and close friends and at the university. She teaches in French, but she "elaborates" her lectures by explaining topics in English and has initiated an English Conversation Club to assist students in improving their fluency.

❿Before living in the United States for two years, her reading, writing, speaking and listening skills were well developed in academic and spoken French. Her English skills were also good "except for listening, which depended upon the speaker and the context." After her U.S. stay, the language situation changed: "I am now more proficient in English in terms of all the skills and find myself looking for words or double-checking spelling when writing in French." However, she knows that more work on English can, and should, be done. Arabic, which is supposedly her mother tongue, comes in third in terms of proficiency: "I rarely had good grades in school Arabic classes, and although I can get along in colloquial Arabic, I do not feel comfortable with academic Arabic and have trouble understanding it," she says, quite sadly.

"Being bilingual is certainly an advantage!"

⓫Sabrina points out that being bilingual in French and English "definitely carved my path to success both in my career and academia," but she also knows that some Algerians believe that because these two languages are dominant in her speech, she is "showing off" by switching to one of them whenever she can.

⓬Sabrina was born in the 1960s to an educated family that treasured French. She notes that "these days, much is changing in Algeria." For example, in elementary and secondary schools, both modern standard Arabic and Amazigh are used for instruction, and students can choose to take English or French as their foreign language. In universities, which continue with instruction in French, there is an increasing interest in the use of English because of its dominance throughout the world.

⓭Despite concerted efforts in recent decades to Arabize education, commerce, and politics, French or French and Arabic code-switching dominate the speech of much of the educated population. As can be seen, Sabrina's language-use story, like that of her country, is a complicated one.

Discuss the questions with a partner or small group.

1. Why do you think Sabrina is an interesting subject for a magazine profile?
2. What are Sabrina's languages? When and where does she use each language and with whom?
3. Does the writer of this profile use first- (*I*), second- (*you*), or third(*she*)-person pronouns, and in which parts of the text?
4. When and why are Sabrina's actual words included in quotations?
5. Do you think the writer used all the information that Sabrina provided in her interview or a selection? What may have motivated the writer's choices?
6. How does the last paragraph connect to the ideas in the first paragraph?
7. Does the profile writer express any opinions of her own in the text? Does she have a point of view?
8. What's the writer's "angle"? That is, what perspective does Sabrina's story bring to our understanding of bilingualism?

Step 8: Conduct Your Interview and Plan Your Profile

1. Revise your questions (Step 6), if necessary, based on your analysis of the profile in Step 7.
2. Conduct your interview. Record the interview so that you can concentrate on the interviewee, not your notes.
3. Listen to your recording. List some good quotes in the speaker's exact words that you can use in your profile.
4. What does the interviewee tell you that gives you an angle or perspective? How can you use this in your profile?

5. Read Sabrina's profile again and identify these moves in the article:
    - Begin with the lead: An interesting anecdote that introduces your perspective or theme.
    - Introduce the interviewee.
    - Discuss the interviewee's early language experiences.
    - Bring in some important points or ideas about these experiences.
    - Discuss the next stage of the interviewee's life, particularly as it relates to language use or learning experiences.
    - Bring in an important idea or change at this stage.
    - Explain the interviewee's current experiences with languages.
    - Conclude with a final thought, related to the lead or to the interviewee's comments about being bi- or multilingual.
6. Plan your magazine profile using a similar structure.

Use the document on the companion website to plan your profile.

Language Box: Shifting Perspective Between Direct and Indirect Speech

When you interview your profile subject, that person will describe their experiences from their perspective. However, when you transform the interview into a magazine profile, you are writing from your perspective by reorganizing the information and perhaps adding an angle to make the article more compelling to your readers. This shift in perspective requires you to make a number of language choices.

First, your profile will contain a mixture of paraphrase, summary, and direct quotation. This may mean shifting the perspective of your text in other ways, including:

- changing colloquial (spoken) language to a more written register
- expanding contractions to full words

- combining clauses using subordinating conjunctions rather than coordinating conjunctions or lots of short sentences
- adding sentence connectors
- removing interactive features of spoken language (e.g., questions, or phrases such as *you know*).

Read the examples in the chart of quotations from an interview that have been rewritten for a profile article:

DIRECT QUOTATION	PARAPHRASE, SUMMARY, OR REPORTED SPEECH
My mom and dad came here from South Korea before I was born.	She was born after her parents immigrated to the United States from South Korea.
I'm studying in English, but I dream in Korean.	Today, although she lives her academic life in in English, she still dreams in Korean.
You know how sometimes you can't remember the right word even though you know it? That happens to me now in Korean.	Sometimes she cannot recall a word she used to know in Korean.
I'm gonna go to medical school.	She pointed out that she was going to go to medical school.
I want to help other people.	She said she wanted to help other people.

Another way that you will shift perspective is in the use of pronouns. As noted in Unit 2, the choice of pronouns in a piece of writing depends on many factors, including the genre, context, and role of the writer. The profile assignment poses special challenges. In your interview, the interviewee will answer in the first person (*I* or *we*) for the most part, but your profile task requires you to use the third person (*he, she,* or *they,* depending on the pronoun the interviewee asks you to use). Therefore, you need to transform much of the interview from the first person to the third person.

Step 9: Practice the Language

Read these extracts of an interview with Leketi Makalela, who grew up in a small village in northern South Africa, one of nine children. He is now Professor of Languages at the University of Witwatersrand in Johannesburg. Leketi refers to *apartheid*, the policy of racial segregation in South Africa from the 1940s until the 1990s. As you read, think about how you would need to change the perspective and organization in a profile article.

INTERVIEWER: *Please tell me something about the role languages played in your family and school when you were a child.*

LEKETI: I didn't start school until late because my mother couldn't pay the school fees for all her kids. I was nine when I really seriously started and by then apartheid was almost over, so I studied in English. But the classes were very big—sometimes 100 kids—and we had maybe five books for a class. So whenever I found something in English, like part of a newspaper or a science book, I would read it eagerly. I also had classes in Sepedi, my home language, from Grades 1 through 4, but there were hardly any books for that language, so we did a lot of copying from dictation. At home, I spoke Sepedi with my family, and I tried to teach my younger brothers and sisters English. Outside, I worked for some farmers from the time I was nine so I could pay my school fees and buy some shoes and they forced me to speak Afrikaans with them. With the other workers, I spoke Sepedi, Tshivenda, isiXhosa, or isiZulu, depending on their languages. I sang in church choirs in any languages that they were singing in. Lots of church services were in two or more languages.

INTERVIEWER: *What languages do you use now for speaking, reading, and writing?*

In reading and writing, there is a clear answer: I use English for academic matters and Sepedi for social and community events because English dominates in academic life now in South Africa. Even though I write in English all the time, my thought processes and ways of writing are still influenced by my other languages. Speaking is much more complicated. All my friends and many people on the street are multilingual and we use several languages fluidly. There is no clear-cut case for use. The degree of use differs from context to context and this means that I have to be sensitive to each situation and adjust accordingly. My wife and I both speak Sepedi, but mostly we speak English with our children who have lots of games and entertainment online in that language.

INTERVIEWER: *What are the advantages or disadvantages of being bilingual?*

Of course, in this country, being multilingual is an advantage. It gives you knowledge that you would not get in just one language and helps with social relationships. The disadvantage is that the schooling system favors one language—and other language forms are not valued. This country has eleven official languages in schools, but English really dominates—and that's alienating for lots of kids.

Select five direct quotations of one or more sentences from Leketi's interview. Rewrite them as a paraphrase, summary, or reported speech for a profile article using the techniques from the Shifting Perspectives Language Box.

For example:

- "I didn't start school until late because my mother couldn't pay the school fees for all her kids. I was nine when I really seriously started... ."
- Paraphrase: Since Leketi's mother could not afford school tuition for all her children, he started attending school regularly when he was nine years old.

Step 10: Write and Revise Your Profile

1. Write a draft of your profile in about 700 to 800 words, using your outline, interview notes, and the Shifting Perspectives Language Box.
2. Peer Review: Ask one or two partners to read your profile. Use these questions to give peer feedback:
    1. Does the profile have an interesting lead with a clear perspective on bilingualism?
    2. Does the profile introduce the interviewee well? Do you think the readers will know enough about the interviewee to be interested in reading the profile?
    3. Are the early language experiences of the interviewee clear and interesting?
    4. Does the profile show how the interviewee developed as a language user?
    5. Are other stages in life well explained, including the interviewee's current uses and attitudes towards languages?

   6. Does the writer conclude by connecting to the lead or discussing the advantages or disadvantages of bi- or multilingualism?
   7. What else could the writer do to improve the profile?

3. Self-Review: Revise your profile using your peers' feedback. Have you done everything on this checklist?
   - ☐ The profile is complete, interesting, and detailed.
   - ☐ The profile includes a lead, introduction of the interviewee, and final thought.
   - ☐ I paraphrased, quoted, and/or reported the interviewee's speech, shifting perspective as needed.
   - ☐ The profile is written in the correct length and format.

   What else do you need to work on? Make further revisions to your profile if necessary.

4. Publish the final version of your profile online or in a class or university magazine if possible.

Step 11: Reflection

What did you learn about transforming content into different genres from this unit? How might you apply what you learned to other assignments or writing experiences?

References

Bialystok, E. (2001). *Bilingualism in development: Language, literacy, and cognition*. Cambridge University Press.

Parodi, T. (2105). *Speaking in tongues: The many benefits of bilingualism*. The Conversation. https://theconversation.com/speaking-in-tongues-the-many-benefits-of-bilingualism-49842

Yong, E. (2016, February 10). The bitter fight over the benefits of bilingualism. *The Atlantic*. https://www.theatlantic.com/science/archive/2016/02/the-battle-over-bilingualism/462114/

Problem-Solution Inquiry

Goals

- ❒ Explain a specific problem, its root causes, and possible solutions
- ❒ Evaluate and respond to solutions
- ❒ Use signaling language in problem-solution writing
- ❒ Research, plan, and outline an inquiry project
- ❒ Summarize and synthesize sources to support the project
- ❒ Write a problem-solution report with a reflective cover letter
- ❒ Present your problem in a public genre

Project Overview

Many types of academic writing involve investigating problems and potential solutions. In this project, you will research and write about a problem in a community you know well or in an academic discipline you are studying. This is mostly a **library research paper** because your sources will be published articles, websites, books, and perhaps videos. You will report your findings in both a pedagogical and a public genre.

Problem-solution is a very common form of organization in many other genres, including op-ed columns, case studies, engineering project reports, proposals, and business plans (Carter, 2007). It is a useful way to approach a research paper or inquiry project since much research aims to find and evaluate solutions to important problems. As an example, we are going to work through a problem-solution project on nutrition. You might write your project on this topic or a different topic, depending on your instructor's assignment.

You will use these actions in the project: **summary, synthesis, explanation, and response.**

Step 1: Choosing a Problem

There are two ways to start your inquiry project. One way is to start with a problem in your community:

1. What are the communities that you belong to (e.g., home communities, school communities, clubs, sports, social groups, religious communities, etc.)?
2. What are some of the problems you see or read about in these communities? The problems may be complex or somewhat simple but should be ones that you feel are difficult or frustrating to solve.
3. Focus on one specific issue or problem that is an obstacle, frustration, or complication for you or other members of the community.
4. Identify the root causes. Why does this problem exist? Where does it come from?
5. Set a clear goal. What is one specific change or improvement you could make? Consider physical changes to the environment (new buildings, new facilities, renovations, etc.) as well as new resources and changes in behavior. Solutions that are practical and limited are usually easier to achieve than goals that are very broad.
6. What are some tactics you can use to address the problem?
7. Consider whether you can find all the information you need from library or online sources or whether you need to conduct your own original research.

Another way is to consider your coursework:

1. Consider the topics you have studied in this (or other) classes.
2. What questions, problems, or issues have been raised that you cannot fully resolve?
3. Tell a classmate why you are interested in these questions or write about them in a journal or on a class discussion board.
4. Narrow your focus to one specific issue or problem that you would like to investigate further.

5. Identify the root causes. Why does this problem exist? Where does it come from?
6. What would a solution to the problem or an answer to the question look like? Where would it be found?
7. Consider whether you can find all the information you need from sources or whether you need to conduct your own original research.

Step 2: What Do You Know?

Look back at your notes from Step 1 and complete a K-N-L table (Johns, 2009). In the first column, write everything that you already **know** about the problem. In the second column, write what you **need** to know to solve the problem. After you have done some research, you can come back and complete the third column: what have you **learned?**

For example, here is the start of a K-N-L chart on the topic of unhealthy eating. The writer is brainstorming, so these questions could lead to several different papers after the writer has focused the problem.

K(NOW): WHAT IS YOUR CURRENT KNOWLEDGE OF YOUR PROBLEM?	N(EED TO KNOW): WHAT QUESTIONS DO YOU NEED TO ANSWER IN ORDER TO SOLVE THE PROBLEM?	(L)EARNED: WHAT INFORMATION HAVE YOU FOUND TO ANSWER YOUR QUESTIONS, AND WHAT SOURCES DID YOU USE?
Increase in obesity Lots of fast food restaurants on or near campus Salt, sugar, fat cause health problems Some areas are "food deserts" Healthy food is expensive	Does public policy change consumer behavior? Why is bad food cheaper than good food? Who runs university dining halls? Where are "food deserts," why do they occur, and how could they be fixed?	

Step 3: Focusing the Problem

Before you plan and write your paper, it is very important to make sure your problem is focused. You cannot write effectively if your topic is much too broad (a set of problems with multiple causes). For example, "the effects of unhealthy eating habits on the U.S. population" is a problem that too broad for this assignment. There are many different types of unhealthy eating habits, many causes of those behaviors, and different solutions depending on the segment of the U.S. population. You might narrow down this topic in several ways until you can state the focused problem as a specific question.

Example 1

Unhealthy eating habits → high quantities of sugar and fat in the diet
U.S. population → cities with high rates of obesity and health problems → Philadelphia
Focus problem: How can Philadelphia reduce health problems caused by consuming too much sugar and fat?

Example 2

Unhealthy eating habits → cost of eating healthy food
U.S. population → university students → my campus
Focus problem: Why is healthy food more expensive than unhealthy food on my campus?

To solve a problem, you have to explain the **root causes**, the situations or phenomena that most impact the problem. For example, the root causes of poor nutrition include poverty, geography, education, and the marketing of unhealthy food. Focus your problem and determine its root causes:

1. Review your K-N-L chart (Step 2). Choose one or more specific questions from the N column, or ask a new specific question. Start reading about the problem or discussing it with members of the affected community.
2. Identify one or more root causes of the problem. If any of the causes is itself a problem, ask yourself whether it is, in fact, the focus problem you should be studying.
3. What is the population of people affected by the problem? Is it too large to write about effectively? If so, narrow your target.
4. Identify two or more solutions from your own ideas, your reading, and your interviewees.

Step 4: Analyze Problem-Solution Organization

Academic and public writing is often concerned with identifying and solving problems. The most common and logical way to structure a problem-solution inquiry is shown in Figure P2.1.

The first steps do not vary very much in problem-solution writing:

1. First, you usually need to explain the **situation** and provide some background so that the reader can understand the problem and recognize its importance. For example, in their online article about self-regulation of children's meals by restaurants, Moran and Roberto (2017) start by explaining the situation: "Chain restaurants are not known for serving up healthy kids' meals."
2. After giving details about the food that is served and a program that was designed to improve the nutritional quality of children's menus, they state the **problem**: "Despite the promises, kids' plates still look much the same."
3. They then go on to explain the **causes** of the problems and the reasons that the program, called Kids LiveWell, has not improved children's meals at restaurants.

FIGURE P2.1:
Problem-Solution Organization

Stage	Action(s)	Questions You Can Ask
Situation	Explain and summarize	What is the context for the problem?
Problem	Explain (definition, process, etc.)	What is the problem, why is it a problem, and for whom?
Causes	Explain (cause-effect)	Where does the problem come from? What are its causes and contributing factors?
Solution(s)	Summarize and synthesize	How can the problem be solved? What solutions have been attempted?
Evaluation(s)	Respond	Does each solution seem to solve the problem? Why, or why not? Which solution do you recommend, and why?

It is in the solution and evaluation stages of the text that you have more choices in organizing your text.

Read two versions of the solution and evaluation stages of an inquiry project into the problem of unhealthy children's meals at U.S. restaurants (Figure P2.2). Then, answer the questions.

FIGURE P2.2:
Two Approaches to Organizing Solutions and Evaluations

Text A

❶The National Restaurant Association launched its Kids LiveWell program in 2011, and it initially turned out to be popular with over 42,000 locations (Moran & Roberto, 2017). Restaurants that participated in the program were required to offer at least one healthy child's meal. The program's website lists nutritious choices such as "steak, broccoli, and apple juice" and salads as side dishes instead of fries (National Restaurant Association, n.d.). However, researchers found that the program overall did not make a meaningful difference in the nutritional value of the children's meals offered at participating restaurants (Moran et al., 2017). Therefore, this kind of voluntary self-regulation is an ineffective solution.

❷A more promising solution is to impose a tax on unhealthy foods such as sodas. This approach has been successfully implemented in Mexico, where a 1 peso per liter tax resulted in a 7.6% decrease in the purchase of sugary drinks and a 2.1% increase in sales of healthier drinks (Colchero et al., 2017). However, a similar but very controversial tax that started in Philadelphia in 2017 (1.5 cents per ounce) may have had the unintended negative consequence of forcing supermarkets in low-income neighborhoods to close (McCrystal, 2019). While public policy may have a role to play in improving children's diets, it does not appear to be effective without cooperation from the food and beverage industries.

Text B

❶The restaurant industry's solution to the problem of unhealthy children's meals has been to develop a program that encourages members to add a healthy choice to kids menus. Kids LiveWell was launched in 2011 and quickly grew to cover over 42,000 restaurants (Moran & Roberto, 2017). The program's website lists nutritious choices such as "steak, broccoli, and apple juice" and salads as side dishes instead of fries (National Restaurant Association, n.d.).

❷An alternative to this kind of voluntary self-regulation is government action through taxes. For example, in Mexico, a 1 peso per liter tax was imposed on the sale of sugary drinks (Colchero et al., 2017). Meanwhile in Philadelphia, after a long debate, a soda tax of 1.5 cents per ounce took effect in January 2017, despite heavy opposition from the beverage industry (McCrystal, 2019).

❸Neither program has been completely successful. Although Kids LiveWell did increase the number of healthy options on restaurant menus, it had little overall effect on the nutritional value of children's menus (Moran et al., 2017). Soda taxes have been somewhat more effective at decreasing unhealthy choices. In Mexico, sales of sugary drinks dropped 7.6%, while sales of healthier drinks increased by 2.1% (Colchero et al., 2017). However, Philadelphia's tax may have had the unintended negative consequence of forcing supermarkets in low-income neighborhoods to close (McCrystal, 2019). Therefore, it seems that governments will need to work with the food and beverage industries on new collaborative solutions.

1. How are the solutions and evaluations organized in Texts A and B? For example, in Text A, the first paragraph contains Solution 1 and Evaluation 1. What about the other paragraphs?
2. Highlight the words and phrases that the author uses to connect the paragraphs.
3. Is there any evaluative language in the description of the solutions, or are they presented neutrally (see Unit 8: Respond)? Identify language choices that help you answer this question.
4. How confident is the author in the evaluations of the two solutions? Identify the language choices that help you answer this question.
5. Does the writer mainly summarize or synthesize sources in these texts? How do you know? What is the function of the citations?

As an extension activity, either (a) write a paragraph to be included before the texts explaining the *situation* and *problem* of unhealthy food choices for children or (b) write a final paragraph to conclude the paper with an alternative solution.

Language Box: Comparing Solutions

If you have identified more than one solution, your evaluation will probably synthesize, drawing comparisons between them. Here are some of the language choices for comparisons:

1. **Comparative adjectives** (one solution is better or worse):
   - *a better solution, a more practical answer,*
   - *a less successful response*
   - *Taxes are less effective than self-regulation.*
2. **Equatives** (the solutions are the same or similar in some way):
   - *Self-regulation is as effective as government policies.*
   - *Advertising is not as effective as taxation in changing consumers' behaviors.*
   - *The Canadian solution has the same drawbacks as the European solution.*

3. *Both, neither, all, none* (to say something about both, all, or none of the solutions):

   - *Neither program has been successful.*
   - *Both programs are equally successful.*
   - *Both self-regulation and taxation are promising solutions.*
   - *All (of) the solutions are expensive.*
   - *None of the solutions will be easy to implement.*

Be aware of these common errors with comparative structures:

- Use *-er* with most short adjectives (*smaller, cheaper, easier*) but *more* with most adjectives of two or more syllables (*more practical, more expensive, more promising*). Do not mix the two forms (~~more~~ *cheaper*).
- Use *than* (not *then* or *as*) with comparatives:
  - Taxes are less effective ~~as~~ / ~~then~~ / than self-regulation.
- Use *as ... as* or *the same ... as* to show that two solutions are equivalent.
  - The Canadian solution is *as promising as* the European solution.
  - TV advertisements do not spread *as quickly as* internet memes.
  - Radio reaches almost ~~as~~ *the same audience as* newspaper advertisements.
- If you use *neither/nor* or *either/or* in the subject of a sentence, the verb agrees with the second noun:
  - Neither self-regulation nor increased *taxes are* effective.
  - Neither increased taxes nor *self-regulation is* effective.
- *None* as a pronoun is singular in formal writing (*none of the solutions is cheap*).

Step 5: Practice the Language

Choose the best words from the parentheses to complete the sentences.

1. A more (efficient / cheaper) solution for universities would be to decrease the number of food vendors.
2. This solution faces (as / the) same objections as a mandatory meal plan.
3. The second solution is (less / as) expensive than a new dining hall.
4. Both proposals (is / are) difficult to implement, but neither (is/are) certain to succeed.
5. A soda tax would affect more people (than / as) a fast-food tax.
6. The new menu is almost (as / the) popular as the old one.

Step 6: Plan Your Problem-Solution Project

So far, you have identified a problem, its causes, and the situation or community in which it occurs. At this point, you need to analyze the prompt or instructions from your teacher for the inquiry project. Here is an example of a prompt for a problem-solution inquiry project.

> Identify a problem in one of your communities and research more than one possible solution. Evaluate the solutions and make a recommendation for one or more actions that could contribute to solving the problem. Write a clear, organized, and detailed problem-solution paper of approximately 5 pages (typed and double-spaced) using a minimum of four reliable sources. Use the current APA style to document your sources, and write for an educated, non-expert audience of your instructor and classmates.

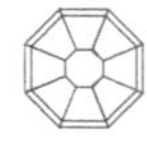

Start planning your problem-solution inquiry paper by answering questions about components of the Rhetorical Planning Wheel based on your initial research and analysis of the prompt. You will need to revise your answers as you work on your project.

1. **Audience**: Who is your real or imagined audience for this paper? Are you only writing for your instructor or do you need to consider possible audiences such as your peers, administrators, or public officials? Do you expect them to be aware of the problem? Why?

2. **Purpose and Writer's Role**: What is the purpose of your paper and your role as a writer? Are you going to support a particular solution or present the pros and cons of different solutions?
3. **Context**: What is your paper responding to? What is happening in your community or discipline?
4. **Sources**: What type of sources are expected? Do you need to use library resources? Are internet sources acceptable?

Step 7: Research Your Topic

Your research for this paper will consist of reading and synthesizing articles, ideas, arguments, research, and data. As with any use of sources, you should make sure that all the information you find is accurate, relevant, and reliable. However, you might also collect your own original data with interviews or surveys to make your writing more relevant to your particular community or situation.

Review the Online Source Use Appendix for guidance on finding and evaluating sources.

Which of these sources of information might be useful for your chosen project? Discuss your choices with a partner or small group.

1. Reading journal articles from the library database
2. Conducting a survey or questionnaire
3. Using textbooks to explain a theory or framework
4. Conducting an experiment in a lab or elsewhere
5. Collecting and analyzing websites, news reports, or student writing
6. Watching online videos or TED talks
7. Finding newspaper or magazine articles that propose solutions to the problem
8. Interviewing members of a community about the problem or possible solutions
9. Using a published opinion poll or survey to support your solution

You may need library sources that help you:

- ❐ explain the problem
- ❐ identify root causes of the problem
- ❐ report useful statistics
- ❐ propose solutions
- ❐ evaluate solutions (that is, respond to solutions that would be effective or not effective)

Use this procedure to identify sources and take notes.

1. List several possible search terms you can use to find more information. Think about synonyms (words with similar meanings), place names that are relevant to your topic, specific terminology, and groups of people who are affected by the problem and/or its solution.
2. Use the internet and library databases to identify sources that explain the problem, offer solutions, and evaluate or respond to those solutions. As you search, write down new search terms that can help you in your research.
3. Look carefully at who wrote and published each source. For example, if you are researching a soda tax, you will find articles written by members of the beverage industry criticizing it and articles written by public-health officials defending it. You may be able to use the sources, but you need to be aware of their opinions and positions.
4. Complete a chart with information about your sources. Two examples are provided.

CITATION	STAGE(S) OF MY PROJECT	MAIN IDEAS	WRITERS' IDENTITY
Moran et al. (2017)	Solution, evaluation	Self-regulation has little or no positive effect on children's meals	Researchers, no known connection to industry
Okamoto (2019)	Problem, cause, solution, evaluation	Problems of obesity, benefits of soda tax	Doctor in an area with high obesity

5. On the basis of your research, revise your Rhetorical Planning Wheel notes (Step 6) and continue to focus your problem and solutions.

Step 8: Organize Your Paper

Before you draft your paper, try using one of these techniques to organize the information in your project.

1. Use a piece of paper or index card for each section of your paper (e.g,. situation, problem, cause, solution, evaluation), and list everything you want to include in that section. Use numbers or arrows to organize the information.
2. Write each relevant fact, statistics, or finding from your research on a notecard. Sort the papers or cards into stacks according to the section of the paper where you will use them.
3. Color-code your information (in a computer document, on different colored cards or paper, or with highlighters) by topic, section, or purpose (e.g. claims, supporting data, definitions).
4. Write a formal outline for this paper before you start writing. A formal outline shows different levels of information, as in Figure P2.3.

Add citations to the relevant parts of your outline to help you integrate your sources when you write.

FIGURE P2.3:
Extract from a Formal Outline

II. Problem: Healthy food is more expensive than unhealthy choices

A. Cause 1—high cost of healthy food

1. Statistics about cost of fruit and vegetables

Etc. ...

B. Cause 2—low cost of fast food

Etc.

Language Box: Signaling Problems and Solutions

It is important to use signaling phrases to help the reader follow your organization as you explain the problems, solutions, and evaluations.

Problem	*However, ...* *Despite this progress / improvement / proposal ...* *Although / While / Even though ...* *A potential/serious/major/social/financial problem* *face a problem/challenge/dilemma/threat* *... pose a problem/threat/challenge/danger/difficulty/ obstacle* *A problem has arisen/emerged with ...*
Cause	*This problem/condition/situation/disease/harm/risk is caused by ...* *There are two root causes ...* *The roots of this situation lie in ...* *Another reason why ... is ...*
Solution	*One way to address this problem/situation is ...* *Experts have suggested/offered/proposed three solutions ...* *In order to address/resolve this problem ...*

Step 9: Practice the Language

Read the extracts from the problem-solution inquiry project in Step 4 on unhealthy food targeted at children in U.S. restaurants. Decide whether each extract is from the problem, cause, or solution section. What signaling language could you use to complete the sentences?

1. Public-health researchers have ____________. Either the restaurant industry needs to regulate itself, or the government should develop rules and guidelines that discourage restaurants from serving unhealthy children's meals.

2. ____________some of the largest chain restaurants publicly promise healthier children's meals, the actual content of the food on their menus has changed very little.

3. Another ____________ is the use of "tie-ins" to movies, where popular characters and films are attached to sugary drinks and fatty foods.

4. ____________ the amount of money that is at stake in children's meals. According to U.S. government data, 36% of children and teenagers eat fast-food on any particular day (Herrick et al., 2018).

5. ____________ the problem of children automatically choosing sodas and fries with a kids' meal, restaurants could make the "default" option milk and fruit slices.

6. ____________ kids' meals have not become any healthier is that some restaurants have simply substituted soda for other sugary drinks, such as fruit juices and flavored milk (Moran & Roberto, 2017).

Step 10: Write and Revise

1. Draft your inquiry project.
2. Peer Review. Share your draft with one or two partners. Use these questions to give feedback:
    1. What is the specific issue or problem the writer addresses?
    2. Does the writer explain the problem and its causes clearly?
    3. Does the writer use sources effectively in the paper?
    4. Does the writer provide and respond to at least two solutions?
    5. How could the writer improve the paper?
3. Self-Review: Revise your paper using your peers' feedback. Have you done everything on this checklist?
    - ☐ The paper has all the required parts: situation, problem, causes, solutions, and evaluation.
    - ☐ The parts of the paper are clearly and correctly signaled.
    - ☐ I compared more than one solution and responded with a recommendation, proposal, or call for more research.
    - ☐ I followed all the requirements in the assignment, including format and referencing conventions.

What else do you need to work on? Make further revisions to your paper if necessary.

Step 11: Reflective Cover Letter

When professional writers submit a manuscript to their editors, they write a cover letter to introduce the piece. In your cover letter, you will introduce your paper to your instructor and reflect on the process of writing it. Write a letter, not an essay or a list of questions and answers! You could answer some or all of these questions.

1. How did your paper develop as you planned, wrote, and revised it?
2. What do you see as the strengths and weaknesses of your paper?
3. What did you learn from completing this inquiry project?

Step 12: Public Presentation

Before or after you write your final paper, consider how you could present the information outside your class context. If you are proposing a solution or a change in policy or behavior, what would be the best venue to share it? Who is your audience? How are they affected by the problem? Do they have the power to make the solutions happen? What will they find persuasive? Some suggestions are listed, but you may have other ideas that are more relevant to your situation and topic.

1. Write an op-ed column for your local or campus newspaper.
2. Write a blog post or FAQ (frequently asked questions) page for a website.
3. Write a letter to an official with the power to make decisions or changes.
4. Draft a petition and ask classmates or other people affected to sign it.
5. Give a presentation or record an online video.
6. Design a poster or public service advertisement.

References

Carter, M. (2007). Ways of knowing, doing, and writing in the disciplines. *College Composition and Communication, 58*(3), 385–418.

Colchero, M. A., Rivero-Dommarco, J. Popkin, B. M., & Ng, S. W. (2017). In Mexico, evidence of sustained consumer response two years after implementing a sugar-sweetened beverage tax. *Health Affairs, 36*, 564–571. https://doi.org/10.1377/hlthaff.2016.123

Johns, A. M. (2009). *AVID college readiness: Working with sources.* AVID Center.

Herrick, K., Fryar, C., & Ahluwalia, N. (2018). Percentage of youths aged 2–19 years consuming any fast food on a given day, by race and Hispanic origin. *Morbidity & Mortality Weekly Report, 67*(40). http://dx.doi.org/10.15585/mmwr.mm6740a8

National Restaurant Association. (n.d.) *Kids LiveWell.* http://www.kidslivewell.com/

McCrystal, L. (2019, Apr 29). *A timeline of Philadelphia's soda tax.* Philly.com. https://www.philly.com/news/timeline-philadelphias-soda-tax-20190429.html

Moran, A., & Roberto, C. (2017). *Restaurants pledged to make kids' meals healthier—but the data show not much has changed.* The Conversation. https://theconversation.com/restaurants-pledged-tomake-kids-meals-healthier-but-the-data-show-not-much-has-changed-71761

Moran, A., Block, J.P., Goshev, S.G., Bleich, S.N., & Roberto, C.A. (2017). Trends in nutrient content of children's menu items in U.S. chain restaurants. *American Journal of Preventive Medicine, 52*, 284–291. DOI: https://doi.org/10.1016/j.amepre.2016.11.007

Okamoto, E. (2019, April 9). *The Philadelphia soda tax, while regressive, saves lives of those most at risk.* Philly Voice. https://www.phillyvoice.com/philadelphia-soda-tax-regressive-saves-lives-most-at-risk/

Project 3 Research Paper

Goals

- ❒ Understand the major sections of an IMRaD (Introduction, Methods, Results, and Discussion) research paper
- ❒ Analyze IMRaD research papers from your discipline or a class you are taking
- ❒ Compare your analysis with a research paper in the field of public health
- ❒ Collect data and write a short research paper relating to health and nutrition or on a topic selected by your instructor

Project Overview

The **IMRaD or IMRD** (Introduction, Methodology, Results, and Discussion) research paper has become the most common genre for publishing research in the sciences, engineering, and many social sciences. IMRaD papers are typically published in academic journals, which are periodical publications for the scholarly community (researchers, professors, and some advanced students). One purpose of these journals is for writers to share new advances, experiments, or ideas in their field. Academic journals often focus on very specific sub-disciplines, or research areas within a larger academic field. For example, IEEE—a large academic association in engineering—publishes journals including *Computational Intelligence and AI in Games, Biomedical Engineering,* and *NanoBioscience.* Each discipline, and sometimes each journal, has its own style guide with its required reference and citation system, such as APA (psychology and social sciences), MLA (English and humanities), or AMA (medicine).

Because the IMRaD structure is so common, students at both the undergraduate and graduate levels often write IMRaD research papers both to report on their own original research and to learn the conventions of writing for future publication in their majors. A common assignment in undergraduate science courses is the **lab report**, which follows some of the conventions of an IMRaD research paper.

There is considerable variation in structure, content, and argumentation among research papers in academic disciplines (e.g., biology) and sub-disciplines (e.g., biochemistry). As a result, there is no single, rigid set of structural rules for writing these research papers because effective texts always depend on context and the other components of the Rhetorical Planning Wheel. However, there are similarities among most IMRaD research papers, as well. Table P3.1 shows the major headings of a typical IMRaD research paper, the purpose of each section, and the actions writers take when writing these sections.

Course assignments usually require you to follow a particular style guide for references and citations, and this is typically stated in the syllabus or assignment directions. Read the Online Source Use Appendix for more help with citation, references, and style guides.

TABLE P3.1:
The Structure and Actions of a Typical IMRaD Research Paper

Section	*Purposes*	*Typical Actions*
Abstract	Brief summary of all sections of the paper	summarize
Introduction (I)	Explains the purposes of the paper, moving from a general discussion of the topic to the particular question, issue, or hypothesis being investigated	explain, synthesize, argue
Methods (M)	Describes what the researchers did, what materials they used or which populations participated, and the procedures (e.g., interviews, surveys, experiments) that were conducted	explain
Results (R)	Reports the results of the research by organizing and presenting the data, often with the help of figures and tables	report data
Discussion (D)	Interprets the meaning of the results, referring back to the research questions in the Introduction and previous research to make hedged claims about the results. Sometimes mentions study limitations and/or suggests future research based on the results.	interpret data, analyze, argue, explain, summarize

Source: Adapted from various portions of Swales & Feak, 2012. Used with permission.

In this project, you will analyze IMRaD research papers in a discipline you are studying or interested in, investigating each of the major sections. You will compare your analysis to a short research paper dealing with public health. Finally, you will collect data and write a short research paper in the area of health and nutrition or on another topic assigned by your instructor.

Step 1: Identify and Discuss an IMRaD paper

Journals are academic publications that include original research papers, review articles, and sometimes book reviews, letters, and responses. An important difference between journals and news sources or magazines is that research papers in high-quality journals are **peer-reviewed** before they are published. This means that the papers are read by several experts who recommend to the editors whether the paper should be accepted, rejected, or revised. This process should ensure that the research is well designed, accurate, useful, and current.

Find a peer-reviewed journal article online or from a library database that reports on research in your major, the discipline of a class you are taking, or an academic area you are interested in. Look for an article that has similar headings (IMRaD) to those in Table P3.1. Answer the questions about your article, and compare them with a classmate's article from another discipline.

1. What is the title of the journal in which this article is published?
2. What is the title of the research article you selected? What does the title tell you about the research reported on? Does the title suggest any of the findings or conclusions of the research, for example?
3. Does your research article example have headings that mark the four sections IMRaD? If not, what are the headings?
4. What are the first sentences in each of the sections? What are the purposes of these initial sentences which introduce the section?
5. What else do you notice about this article? For example:
    a. Are there multiple authors? Do they work in different countries?
    b. Are visuals included (e.g., tables, graphs, maps, diagrams)? In which section are the visuals found? What do the visuals show readers?
    c. Is there a synthesis of previous research (also called a literature review)? If so, where does it appear? How long is it? How many different sources does it include?
    d. How are outside sources cited? Where are the sources listed (e.g., a references or works cited page)?

Step 2: Analyze an IMRaD Research Paper

You are going to read a research paper (Singh et al., 2016) that was published by the U.S. Centers for Disease Control and Prevention in a weekly online publication "of timely, reliable, authoritative, accurate, objective, and useful public health information and recommendations." It is written for doctors, nurses, researchers, and public health practitioners. The abstract has been omitted, the table of data simplified, and the article edited for length. Note that this publication follows the International Committee of Medical Journal Editors (ICMJE) style guide. Citations appear as numbers in the text in italics (*1*), and the references are at the end.

Before you read, answer the questions in Step 1. Then, read the text carefully and discuss the questions that follow.

Exposure to Electronic Cigarette Advertising Among Middle School and High School Students

Morbidity and Mortality Report Weekly

January 8, 2016 / 64(52); 1403–8

Tushar Singh, MD, PhD[1]; Kristy Marynak, MPP; René A. Arrazola, MPH; Shanna Cox, MSPH; Italia V. Rolle, PhD; Brian A. King, PhD

Introduction

Electronic cigarettes (e-cigarettes) are battery-powered devices capable of delivering nicotine and other additives (e.g., flavorings) to the user in an aerosol form. E-cigarette use has increased considerably among U.S. youths in recent years. During 2011–2014, past-30-day e-cigarette use increased from 0.6% to 3.9% among middle school students and from 1.5% to 13.4% among high school students; in 2014, e-cigarettes became the most commonly used tobacco product among middle school and high school students (*1*). Youth use of tobacco in any form (combustible, noncombustible, or electronic) is unsafe (*2, 3*). E-cigarettes typically deliver nicotine derived from tobacco, which is highly addictive, might harm brain development, and could lead to sustained tobacco product use among youths (*2*). In April 2014, the Food and Drug Administration (FDA) issued a proposed rule to deem all products made or derived from tobacco subject to FDA jurisdiction (*4*).

In the United States, e-cigarette sales have increased rapidly since entering the U.S. marketplace in 2007, reaching an estimated $2.5 billion in sales in 2014 (*5, 6*). Corresponding increases have occurred in e-cigarette advertising expenditures, which increased from $6.4 million in 2011 to an estimated $115 million in 2014 (*7, 8*). Tobacco product advertising is causally related to tobacco product initiation among youths (*9*). Many of the themes used in conventional tobacco product advertising, including independence, rebellion, and sexual attractiveness, also are used to advertise e-cigarettes (*9, 10*). Moreover, almost all tobacco use begins before age 18 years, during which time there is great vulnerability to social influences, such as youth-oriented advertisements and youth-generated social media posts (*9*). This report assesses exposure to e-cigarette advertisements among U.S. middle school and high school students.

Methods

Data from the 2014 National Youth Tobacco Survey (NYTS) were analyzed to assess exposure to e-cigarette advertisements from four sources: retail stores (convenience stores, supermarkets, or gas stations); Internet; TV and movies; and newspapers and magazines. NYTS is a cross-sectional, school-based, self-administered, pencil-and-paper questionnaire administered to U.S. middle school (grades 6–8) and high school (grades 9–12) students. A three-stage cluster sampling procedure was used to generate a nationally representative sample of U.S. students who attend public and private schools in grades 6–12. In 2014, 207 of 258 selected schools (80.2%) participated, yielding a sample of 22,007 participants (91.4%) among 24,084 eligible students; the overall response rate was 73.3%.

Sources of exposure to e-cigarette advertisements were assessed by participants' responses to the following four questions: (1) Internet: "When you are using the Internet, how often do you see advertisements or promotions for electronic cigarettes or e-cigarettes?" (2) Newspapers and magazines: "When you read newspapers or magazines, how often do you see advertisements or promotions for electronic cigarettes or e-cigarettes?" (3) Retail stores: "When you go to a convenience store, supermarket, or gas station, how often do you see advertisements or promotions for electronic cigarettes or e-cigarettes?" (4) TV and movies: "When you watch TV or go to the movies, how often do you see advertisements or promotions for electronic cigarettes or e-cigarettes?" For each question, respondents could select the following options: they do not use the specific source (e.g., "I do not read newspapers or magazines"), "never," "rarely," "sometimes," "most of the time," or "always." Respondents who said they saw promotions or advertisements "sometimes," "most of the time," or "always" were considered to have been exposed to advertisements from the source; those who selected "never" or "rarely" were considered not exposed. Respondents who did not use a source were also classified as not exposed. Population estimates of exposure for each source were assessed. The number of exposure sources was summed for each student and reported as the proportion who were exposed to one, two, three, or four sources.

Results

All students. Overall, 68.9% of participants (an estimated 18.3 million students) were exposed to e-cigarette advertisements from one or more source (Figure 1). Retail stores were the most frequently reported exposure source (54.8% of respondents, or an estimated 14.4 million students), followed by the Internet (39.8%, 10.5 million), TV and movies (36.5%, 9.6 million), and newspapers and magazines (30.4%, 8.0 million) (see Table 1). Exposure to e-cigarette advertisements on the Internet and in newspapers and magazines was reported more frequently by females than males. Exposure was higher among students in higher grade levels for all sources. Overall, 22.1% of participants (5.8 million students) reported exposure to e-cigarette advertising from one source, 17.2% (4.5 million) from two sources, 14.1% (3.7 million) from three sources, and 15.4% (4.1 million) from four sources, as seen in Figure 1.

Middle school students. Among middle school students, 66.4% (7.7 million) were exposed to e-cigarette advertisements from at least one source (Figure 1). Retail stores were the most frequently reported source of exposure (52.8% of respondents, or an estimated 6.0 million middle school students), followed by the Internet (35.8%, 4.1 million), TV and movies (34.1%, 3.9 million), and newspapers and magazines (25.0%, 2.8 million) (Table 1). Exposure to e-cigarette advertisements on the Internet was higher among female than male middle school students. A single source of exposure was reported by 23.4% of participants (2.7 million middle school students); two sources by 17.4% (2.0 million), three sources by 13.7% (1.5 million), and four sources by 11.9% (1.3 million) (Figure 1).

FIGURE 1:
Proportion of U.S. Students Exposed to E-Cigarette Advertisements, by School Type and Number of Exposure Eources

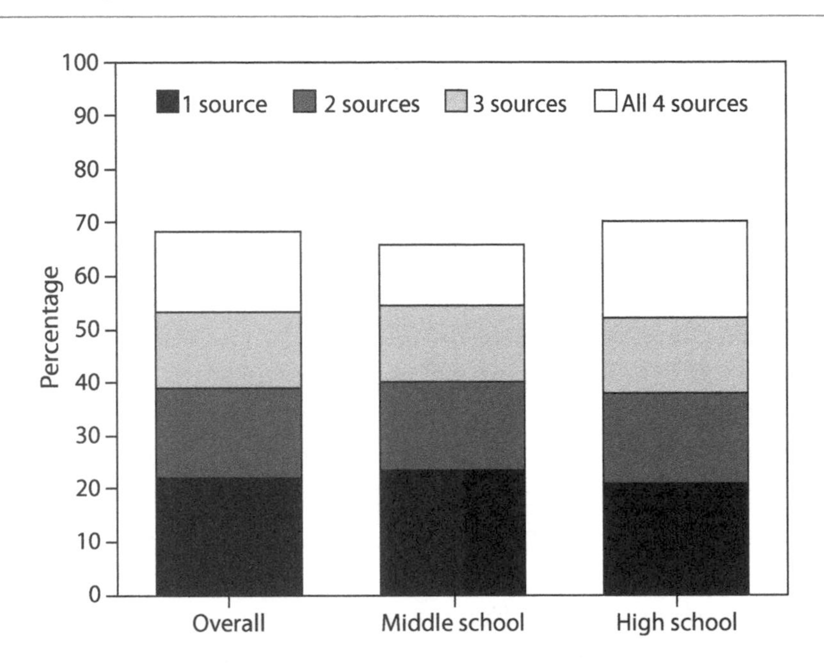

TABLE 1:
E-cigarette Advertisement Exposure among U.S. Middle School and High School Students, by Sources of Exposure

Source	*Retail Stores*		*Internet*		*TV and Movies*		*Newspapers and Magazines*	
	%	population	%	population	%	population	%	Population
Total	54.8	14.4	39.8	10.5	36.5	9.6	30.4	8.0
Female	54.9	7.2	41.1	5.4	36.4	4.7	32.1	4.2
Male	54.6	7.1	38.5	5.0	36.7	4.8	28.7	3.7
Middle School	52.8	6.0	35.8	4.1	34.1	3.9	25.0	2.8
High School	56.3	8.3	42.9	6.3	38.4	5.6	34.6	5.1

Notes. Population estimates are in millions, rounded down to the nearest 0.1 million. Middle school consists of Grades 6–8; high school is Grades 9–12.

High school students. Among high school students, 70.9% of respondents (an estimated 10.5 million high school students) reported exposure to e-cigarette advertisements from at least one source (Figure 1). Similar to middle school students, more than half of reported e-cigarette advertising exposures (56.3%, 8.3 million) occurred in retail stores, followed by the Internet (42.9%, 6.3 million), TV and movies (38.4%, 5.6 million), and newspapers and magazines (34.6%, 5.1 million) (Table 1). One source of exposure was reported by 21.1% of participants (3.1 million high school students), two sources by 17.0% (2.5 million), three sources by 14.5% (2.1 million), and four sources by 18.2% (2.7 million) (Figure 1).

Conclusions and Comments

In 2014, nearly seven in 10 (18.3 million) U.S. middle school and high school students were exposed to e-cigarette advertisements from at least one source, and approximately 15%, or 4.1 million students, were exposed to e-cigarette advertisements from all four sources. Approximately half were exposed to e-cigarette advertisements in retail stores, whereas approximately one in three were exposed on the Internet, on TV or at the movies, or while reading newspapers or magazines. Although there were slight variations by sex and race/ethnicity,* the magnitude of exposure was consistent across groups. Implementation of comprehensive efforts to reduce youth exposure to e-cigarette advertising and promotion is critical to reduce e-cigarette experimentation and use among youths.

Retail store exposure to e-cigarette advertising in this study (54.8%) was lower than levels of exposure to conventional cigarette and other tobacco product advertising reported in the NYTS in 2014 (80.6%), but comparable to exposure on the Internet (39.8% versus 46.8%, respectively) and in newspapers and magazines (30.4% versus 34.3%, respectively) (*11*). Advertising for conventional tobacco products, such as cigarettes, has been shown to prompt experimentation as well as increase and maintain tobacco product use among youths (*9*). Similarly, according to a recent randomized controlled study, adolescents who were exposed to e-cigarette advertisements on TV were 54% more likely to say they would try an e-cigarette soon, and 43% more likely to say they would try an e-cigarette within the next year, compared with adolescents who were not exposed to e-cigarette advertisements (*12*). The study also determined that youths exposed to e-cigarette advertisements

** The data and discussion of race/ethnicity have been omitted here for space, but the analysis did not find meaningful differences based on the race or ethnicity of the students.*

were more likely to agree that e-cigarettes can be used in places where smoking is not allowed (*12*). This is consistent with findings that certain e-cigarette marketers are using advertising tactics similar to those used in the past to market conventional cigarettes, including youth-oriented themes, and promoting e-cigarette use as an alternative in places where smoking is not allowed (*2, 9, 10*). An analysis of 57 online e-cigarette vendors determined that 70.2% of vendors used more than one social network service to market e-cigarettes (*13*). Moreover, 61.4% of vendors only required users to click a pop-up or dialog box to self-verify age, and 35.1% of vendors had no detectable age verification process. This unrestricted marketing of e-cigarettes, coupled with rising use of these products among youths (*1*), has the potential to compromise decades of progress in preventing tobacco use and promoting a tobacco-free lifestyle among youths (*2, 9*).

Research supports the importance of a multifaceted approach to youth tobacco prevention involving multiple levels of government (*2, 9, 14*). Local, state, and federal efforts to reduce youth access to the settings where tobacco products, including e-cigarettes, are sold could reduce youth e-cigarette initiation and consumption, as well as advertising exposure. Potential strategies include requiring that tobacco products, including e-cigarettes, be sold only in facilities that never admit youths; limiting tobacco outlet density or proximity to schools; and requiring that e-cigarette purchases be made only through face-to-face transactions. Adding e-cigarettes and other tobacco products to the list of current tobacco products prohibited from being sent through U.S. mail and requiring age verification for online sales at purchase and delivery could also prevent sales to youths. In addition, potential strategies at the federal or state level include regulation of e-cigarette advertising in media, Internet, and retail settings that are demonstrated to appeal to youths or are viewed by a substantial number of youths. The evidence base for restricting advertisements for conventional tobacco products indicates that these interventions would be expected to contribute to reductions in e-cigarette advertisement exposure and use among youths as well (*2, 9*).

To effectively implement these strategies, there is a need for fully funded and sustained comprehensive state tobacco control programs that address all forms of tobacco use, including e-cigarettes (*14*). These programs are critical to support the implementation and maintenance of proven population-based interventions to reduce tobacco use among youths, including tobacco price increases, comprehensive smoke-free laws, and high impact mass media campaigns (*14*). Additionally, parents, caregivers, and health care providers can talk to children about the dangers of tobacco use, encourage or set limits on media use, and teach children critical media viewing skills to increase their resistance to pro-tobacco messages (*15*).

These findings are subject to at least two limitations. First, advertising exposure was self-reported and is subject to recall bias. Second, exposure to e-cigarette advertisements might have been underestimated, as survey questions asked only about exposure from four sources and did not assess exposure from other potential sources such as sporting events, radio, or billboards.

This report highlights youth exposure to e-cigarette advertisements, which might be contributing to increasing youth experimentation with and use of e-cigarettes in recent years. Multiple approaches are warranted to reduce youth e-cigarette use and exposure to e-cigarette advertisements, including efforts to reduce youth access to the settings where tobacco products, including e-cigarettes, are sold, and regulation of youth-oriented e-cigarette marketing. The implementation of these approaches, in coordination with fully funded and sustained comprehensive state tobacco control programs, has the potential to reduce all forms of tobacco use among youths, including e-cigarette use.

References

1. Arrazola RA, Singh T, Corey CG, et al. Tobacco use among middle and high school students—United States, 2011–2014. MMWR Morb Mortal Wkly Rep 2015;64:381–5.
2. US Department of Health and Human Services. The health consequences of smoking—50 years of progress. Atlanta, GA: US Department of Health and Human Services, CDC; 2014. Available at http://www.cdc.gov/tobacco/data_statistics/sgr/50th-anniversary/index.htm.
3. England LJ, Bunnell RE, Pechacek TF, Tong VT, McAfee TA. Nicotine and the developing human: a neglected element in the electronic cigarette debate. Am J Prev Med 2015;49:286–93.
4. Food and Drug Administration. Deeming tobacco products to be subject to the Federal Food, Drug, and Cosmetic Act, as amended by the Family Smoking Prevention and Tobacco Control Act; regulations on the sale and distribution of tobacco products and required warning statements for tobacco products. Federal Register 2014;79:1-67. Available at https://www.gpo.gov/fdsys/pkg/FR-2014-04-25/pdf/2014-09491.pdf.
5. Herzog B, Gerberi J, Scott A. Tobacco—Nielsen c-store data—e-cig $ sales decline moderates. Charlotte, NC: Wells Fargo Securities; 2014. Available at http://www.c-storecanada.com/attachments/article/153/Nielsen%20C-Stores%20-%20Tobacco.pdf.
6. Herzog B, Gerberi J, Scott A. Tobacco talk: vapors/tanks driving next wave of e-vapor growth. Charlotte, NC: Wells Fargo Securities; 2014. Available at http://www.vaporworldexpo.com/PDFs/Tobacco_Talk_Vapors_Tanks_%20March%202014.pdf.

7. Kim AE, Arnold KY, Makarenko O. E-cigarette advertising expenditures in the US, 2011–2012. Am J Prev Med 2014;46:409–12.

8. Truth Initiative. Vaporized: majority of youth exposed to e-cigarette advertising. Washington, DC: Truth Initiative; 2015. Available at http://truthinitiative.org/research/vaporized-majority-youth-exposed-e-cigarette-advertising.

9. US Department of Health and Human Services. Preventing tobacco use among youth and young adults: a report of the Surgeon General. Atlanta, GA: US Department of Health and Human Services, CDC; 2012. Available at http://www.cdc.gov/tobacco/data_statistics/sgr/2012/index.htm.

10. Legacy for Health. Vaporized: e-cigarettes, advertising, and youth. Washington, DC: Truth Initiative; 2014. Available at http://truthinitiative.org/sites/default/files/LEG-Vaporized-E-cig_Report-May2014.pdf.

11. CDC. National Youth Tobacco Survey; 2014. Atlanta, GA: US Department of Health and Human Services, CDC; 2014. Available at http://www.cdc.gov/tobacco/data_statistics/surveys/nyts/.

12. Farrelly MC, Duke JC, Crankshaw EC, et al. A randomized trial of the effect of e-cigarette TV advertisements on intentions to use e-cigarettes. Am J Prev Med 2015;49:686–93.

13. Mackey TK, Miner A, Cuomo RE. Exploring the e-cigarette e-commerce marketplace: identifying Internet e-cigarette marketing characteristics and regulatory gaps. Drug Alcohol Depend 2015;156:97–103.

14. CDC. Best practices for comprehensive tobacco control programs, 2014. Atlanta, GA: US Department of Health and Human Services, CDC; 2014. Available at http://www.cdc.gov/tobacco/stateandcommunity/best_practices/index.htm.

15. American Academy of Pediatrics. Committee on Public Education. Media education. Pediatrics 1999;104:341–3.

A document to help you complete the activities in Step 2 is available on the companion website.

1. Identify the organization of this research paper, using the chart on the companion website to help you. For each heading (Introduction, Methods, Results, Conclusion and Comments), decide the purpose and main point of the section.
2. How is this research paper similar to and different from the paper you analyzed in Step 1? Use the questions in Step 1 to help you.

Step 3: Analyze the Introduction

The general purpose of the introduction in a research paper is to "create space" for the authors' research to be reported. This involves the actions of **explaining** the topic (and often defining key terms and pointing out its importance) and **synthesizing** previous research to **argue for** the purpose of the study. Swales (1990) discovered that many research papers follow a pattern of organization he called "creating a research space," or CARS. According to Swales, the traditional research paper introduction follows three **moves**, or steps: establishing the topic, identifying a gap in the research, and filling that gap.

A document to help you complete the activities in Step 3 is available on the companion website.

1. Re-read the introduction to the research paper on e-cigarettes in Step 2 (Singh et al., 2016). Where do you find these three moves? What phrases indicate each move?
   a. Establish what the article is about and why this research is important, including reviewing previous research.
   b. Identify the gap in the previous research or the need for this study.
   c. Show how this paper will fill the gap.
2. Look again at the Introduction to the research paper you found in your discipline (Step 1). Can you find these three moves? What phrases identify the moves in your paper?
3. Research into the Introduction section has found considerable variation in the third move. Which of the following actions do you see in Singh et al. and in your paper?
   a. stating the purpose of the research
   b. asking specific research questions
   c. presenting hypotheses (guesses about the results of the research)
   d. listing the main findings of their study at the end of the introduction
   e. something else (what is it?)

active voice! Therefore, while there is no good reason to avoid the passive voice, it should be used carefully.

In the Methods section, many writers use the passive voice to emphasize the participants, procedures, and analysis rather than the actions of the researchers. However, some style guides, editors, and professors prefer the active voice, especially when the identity and role of the researchers is important for the methodology. For example, if the research involves interviews, it can be essential to know who conducted the interviews and how the identity and approaches of the interviewer may affect the results.

Step 5: Analyze the Results Section

The main purpose of the Results section is to **report** the most significant or interesting data from the research. This section often includes figures and tables with detailed data as well as a written report of the most important findings. The structure of the results section varies considerably depending on the type of research. Table P3.2 describes some common patterns.

TABLE P3.2:
Structures of Results Sections

Structure	*Description*
Research questions	If the Introduction included research questions, the Results section may report the relevant results for each question in turn, starting by repeating the question.
Hypotheses	If the Introduction included hypotheses, the Results section might report the data that support or contradict each hypothesis in turn, starting by restating the hypotheses.
Groups of participants	If the Methods of the study involved different groups of participants, the Results might start with a summary of the data for the complete sample and then report data on specific sub-groups.
Multiple experiments	Some scientific research papers report on more than one study or experiment. Their Results sections might be organized as Experiment 1, Experiment 2, etc.
Themes	Qualitative research results are often organized into themes, or common ideas that the researcher found in the data.

Look again at the results section of the article you found in Step 1 and the Singh et al. article in Step 2. Answer the questions.

1. What is the structure of each Results section?
2. How does the structure reflect the Introduction or Methods section of the paper?
3. Do the writers use figures and tables? How does the text make reference to the figures and tables (e.g., *see Figure 1*, or *Figure 1 shows that*, or *as shown in Figure 1*)?
4. For quantitative research papers: How much data do the writers include in the text of the results section? Do they report all the statistics or just selected data points? For qualitative research papers: how many examples of each theme do the writers include? Do they also use tables to summarize the data?
5. What do you notice about these language features in both Results sections?
   a. What verb tenses do the writers use to report the results of their research?
   b. What phrases are used to refer to the tables and figures?
   c. Do the writers compare data? What language do they use for the comparisons?

Step 6: Analyze the Discussion Section

The main purpose of the Discussion (or, sometimes, Conclusion) section is to **interpret** the results, often beginning with a summary of the research project and then interpreting what the results mean. In traditional IMRaD papers, this is a key difference between the Results and Discussion sections: writers **report** data in the Results but **interpret** them in the Discussion. Researchers may also compare the results with the work of other researchers to show how their results confirm or contradict previous findings. They often also **analyze** the findings using established or developing theories and **argue** for the importance of their work and its implications for research, theory, and application.

In many fields, near the end of the Discussion section comes a paragraph or more on the **limitations** of the study. Here the writer **explains** any reasons why readers should be careful interpreting the results or applying them to other contexts. There may also be a separate conclusion summarizing the main ideas of the paper and **arguing** for the implications for research and/or practice.

A document to help you complete the activities in Step 6 is available on the companion website.

1. Re-read the Results section in the research paper on e-cigarettes in Step 2 (Singh et al., 2016). Which of these moves do you find? What phrases indicate each move?
   a. Summary of the project and method
   b. Comparison with previous research
   c. Analysis of the findings using established theories or frameworks
   d. Argument for the implications of the research project
   e. Explanation of limitations
   f. Conclusion or summary of the main finding
2. Look again at the Methods section in the research paper you found in Step 1. Can you find these moves? Are there any additional moves?
3. How does each research paper end? What are the purposes of the last paragraph(s) of the paper?
4. What do you notice about these language features in both Discussion sections?
   a. Do the writers use hedging language to show uncertainty about the data or to make less confident predictions and recommendations? Identify some examples.
   b. Do the writers use boosting language to show confidence about the data, predictions, or recommendations? Identify some examples.
   c. Do the writers use personal pronouns or passive voice in interpreting the data (see Active and Passive Voice Language Box, pp. 303–304)?
   d. Do the writers cite other research in the discussion? What language do they use to argue that their research agrees or disagrees with previous findings?
5. You have now completed your analysis of two research papers. Before moving on to your own research in Step 7, reflect on your work in Steps 1–6. What have you learned about research papers in general or research papers in your discipline?

Step 7: Draft a Research Question

A research question is a question that you try to answer by collecting and analyzing data. ***A good research question is specific, focused, and practical.*** This means that you are able to collect the data to answer the question. It is also **based on previous research**, either extending it or filling a gap in existing knowledge, which is why there is always some sort of literature review in an IMRaD research paper.

Here are a few draft research questions. Which of these are good choices for a research project into health and nutrition for undergraduate students?

1. Are college cafeteria meals healthy?
2. Are students eating enough protein?
3. Does my diet meet experts' recommendations for healthy eating?
4. Why do some students at this university skip meals?
5. How does food insecurity affect those students who suffer from it?
6. How does my college approach issues of nutrition?
7. Are college cafeteria meals healthier than restaurant food?
8. What are the effects of nutritional choices upon students' attitudes toward their education?

Choose three of these research questions that need revision. How could you improve them by making them more specific and focused? Or, draft one or more research questions for your current research project. Use the Language Box on page 308 to check your questions are grammatically correct.

Language Box: Writing Research Questions

There are two forms of questions in English:

1. **Yes/No questions** are formed by inverting (reversing) the subject and the verb. If you cannot invert the main verb, use *do/does/did* as the auxiliary verb in the question form. For example:

   - Cafeteria meals **are** healthy.
     Are cafeteria meals healthy?
   - Students **make** healthy meal choices.
     Do students **make** healthy meal choices?
   - Cafeteria menus **have improved** since 1990.
     Have cafeteria menus **improved** since 1990?
   - University dining halls offered less variety in the past.
     Did university dining halls **offer** less variety in the past?

Yes/no questions can be answered simply with *yes* or *no*. However, you may also find through your research that the answer is *sometimes*, and then you would discuss when the answer is yes, when it is no, and when the answer is unclear.

2. ***Wh-* questions** also require inverting the subject and verb, using *do/does/did* if necessary. These questions start with a question word that indicates the unknown element (X). For example:

   - The causes of poor nutrition among college students are X.
     What *are* the causes of poor nutrition among college students?
   - X chooses healthy options in the cafeteria.
     Who *chooses* healthy options in the cafeteria?
   - College students skip meals because X.
     Why *do* college students skip meals?
   - Food standards changes in the last 20 years in X ways.
     How *did* food standards *change* in the last 20 years?

The form of the question needs to match the type of research you are conducting. For example, if you want to know *who* chooses healthy options, you must be able to collect demographic data about your respondents. If you are asking if cafeteria meals are healthy, you need to have some standard of healthy food to compare the cafeteria food against, not just customers' opinions.

Step 8: Conduct a Review of the Literature

You now need to know what other people have said about your topic. As you saw in Step 3, researchers always put their work in the context of other studies and theories, which they synthesize in the Introduction or a separate Literature Review section.

Refer to the Online Source Use Appendix for more help with finding and citing academic sources.

1. What are possible keywords and synonyms you can use to search for sources for your current research project? Who or what is affected by your research? You might use these groups as keywords in your searches (e.g., college students, international students, food banks, dining services, public health, public policy, etc.).

2. What types of sources are appropriate for this project? Are you expected to use only peer-reviewed journal articles? Can you also use trade publications (that is, magazines produced for particular groups of professionals such as school nutritionists or economists)? What about news sources and magazines? Can you cite sources that express strong opinions (e.g., editorials or op-ed columns) or only research articles? Can you cite press releases or summaries of research (e.g., www.futurity.org), or do you need to refer only to the original research papers? You will need to read the assignment directions carefully or ask your instructor for clarification.

3. Where will you look for your sources? Consult a librarian if possible to discuss the resources available to you. Check your sources are reliable using the SIFT technique in the Online Source Use Appendix (Caulfield, 2019).

4. Make a chart or spreadsheet to take notes on the useful ideas from the sources you are reading. Be sure to save all the useful sources and write down the information you need for referencing. Your chart might look like the one provided on the companion website, but the headings will depend on your topic and the type of sources you are reading. For example, if you are reading research papers from journals, you might use these headings: author(s), year of publication, type of research, study population, and main results.

A chart for Step 8 can be found on the companion website.

5. List your research question(s). You can introduce them with a sentence like:
   - *This paper answers the following research question(s):*
   - *In this paper, I address this/these research questions(s):*
   - *This study attempted to answer one/two/three research question(s).*
   - *The (two/three) research questions that guided this study is/are:*

Step 11: Collect and Report Data

As your original research for this project, you will use interviews, a questionnaire, or a survey. To plan your data collection, answer the questions:

1. Who are you going to interview or give your survey to? Why did you choose these people? How many responses do you need?
2. **Closed questions** have a limited range of answers, such as yes/no. **Open questions** allow respondents to speak or write freely (e.g., What do you think about ...?). Make a list of possible questions you could ask. For example:
   - *Did you buy a meal plan this semester?* (closed)
   - *How many times per week do you eat fast food?* (closed)
   - *What do you like about the food options on your campus?* (open)
3. Questions that have a scale of responses (e.g., strongly agree-agree-disagree-strongly disagree) are called **Likert-type scales**. The most important decision is between an odd and even number of responses. With an odd number, you can have a neutral option (e.g., neither agree nor disagree); with an even number, respondents are forced to give positive or negative responses. Which approach is best for your survey? Make a list of possible questions and scales. For example:
   - *Do you ever skip meals to save money?* (Often-sometimes-rarely-never)
   - *Do you agree with the following statement* (strongly agree-agree-neither agree nor disagree-disagree-strongly disagree)? *Restaurant menus should present nutritional information.*
4. Sometimes respondents have ideas that you did not expect in your planning. Therefore, you could end your survey or interview by asking, "Is there anything else about this topic you would like to tell me?" Are you going to include this question?
5. What demographic (personal) information do you need to collect about your respondents (e.g., age, gender, occupation, year at school, major, country of origin, languages spoken, etc.)? Only ask for information you may need for your analysis! Will your survey be anonymous, or will you ask respondents for their name? Why?

After you have collected your data, complete these planning tasks.

- ☐ Make figures and tables to represent the most important quantitative (numerical) data.
- ☐ Make a list of useful quotes from your interviews or open-ended survey questions that you can use in your paper.

Step 12: Write Up Your Research

Use the example IMRaD papers you read to finish your research paper with these sections:

1. **Methods**: Explain the survey or interview you used. Describe your participants (How did you find them? How many people responded?). Summarize the demographic information you collected about them in a short paragraph and perhaps a table (e.g., age, major, year in school, etc.).
2. **Results**: Report the data you collected. Use tables and graphs to summarize the results. Organize your results around the research questions you asked in the introduction of the main sections of your survey or interview.
3. **Discussion:** Interpret the data. What did you learn from your research? What are the implications for students and/or your school? What changes would you like to see as a result of your research?
4. **References:** Take the references from your annotated bibliography, and write a list of the sources you used in alphabetical order (for APA style) or the correct order for your reference style. You must include all the references you cited in your paper. Do not list a source if you did not cite it.

Use the Online Source Use Appendix for more help with citation, references, and style guides.

Step 13: Revise and Edit

1. Peer Review: Ask one or two partners to read your research paper. Use these questions to give peer feedback:

    a. What did the writer study, and what did the research find?

    b. Does the Introduction explain why the topic is important, synthesize relevant literature, show a gap in previous research, and state the research question(s) or purpose of the paper?

    c. Can you understand exactly what the researcher did from reading the Methods section? What other details would you like to know?

    d. What is the pattern of organization in the Results section? Is it clearly organized?

    e. Is the Discussion an effective interpretation of the data? What other questions do you have about the results?

    f. What else could the writer do to improve the research paper?

2. Revise your research paper using your peer's feedback.

3. The last step before you finish your research paper is writing the abstract. An **abstract** is a short summary of your paper. Published research and some student assignments require abstracts. When readers search library databases or browse academic journals, they often read the abstract first to decide whether they want to read the rest of the paper. Abstracts are usually written as a paragraph of about 75–150 words, but the length varies by discipline and context. A simple structure for an abstract is shown in the chart. Note that each answer will be approximately one sentence.

What is the topic and what do we already know?	E-cigarette advertising is associated with e-cigarette use among youth.
What is the gap your research fills?	However, it is not clear how many young people are exposed to e-cigarette advertising and at what age.
What did you do?	Data from the National Youth Tobacco Youth Survey were analyzed.
Who responded to your survey or interview?	A nationally representative sample of U.S. students in Grades 6–12 were asked how often they saw advertisements for e-cigarettes in different media.
What did you find?	Almost 80% of school-aged children see advertisements for e-cigarettes. Exposure was highest for retail stores, followed by the Internet, television, and newspapers and magazines.
What does your research mean?	E-cigarette advertising should be restricted to reduce the number of young people who use e-cigarettes. In particular, youth access to tobacco products in retail settings needs to be controlled, and tobacco education campaigns should be targeted at middle- and high-school students.

D. Self-Review: Have you done everything on this checklist?

- ☐ My research paper has all the required sections: Title, Abstract, Introduction, Methods, Results, Discussion, References.
- ☐ I have used appropriate verb tenses throughout the text.
- ☐ I have used hedging and boosting language that is appropriate the strength of my claims.
- ☐ I have cited all the sources in the reference list, and all sources cited in the text are listed in the references.
- ☐ I have formatted the paper correctly according to the required style guide.

Step 14: Reflection

How is the IMRaD research paper similar to or different from research papers you have written in the past? In what ways was this project useful for your future studies? How will you apply what you learned to work in other classes or assigned research?

References

Caplan, N. A. (2019). *Grammar choices for graduate and professional writers* (2nd ed). University of Michigan Press.

Caulfield, M. (2019, June 19). *SIFT (The four moves).* https://hapgood.us/2019/06/19/sift-thefour-moves/

Singh, R., Marynak, K., Arrazola, R.A., Cox, S., Rolle, I.V., & King, B.A. (2016, January 8). Exposure to electronic cigarette advertising among middle school and high school students. *Mortality and Morbidity Report Weekly, 64*(52), 1403-1408. https://www.cdc.gov/mmwr/preview/mmwrhtml/mm6452a3.htm

Swales, J. M. (1990). *Genre analysis: English in academic and research settings.* Cambridge University Press.

Swales, J. M., & Feak, C. B. (2012). *Academic writing for graduate students: Essential tasks and skills* (3rd ed.). University of Michigan Press.

Personal Statement

Goals

- ❒ Understand the importance of the writer's role in the personal statement
- ❒ Analyze the audience, purpose, and structure of different personal statements
- ❒ Revise an unsuccessful personal statement
- ❒ Plan and write an effective personal statement for a job, scholarship, or university application

Project Overview

Throughout this textbook, the term *genre* has been used to identify a category of texts that generally have the same purpose(s) and share some features, called "family resemblances" (Swales, 1990, p. 49). In some cases, texts in a given genre only share one or two components of the Rhetorical Planning Wheel. This project introduces one of those genres, the **personal statement**, sometimes called "application essay." You will write a personal statement when you apply for admission to a college or university or when you apply for a grant, scholarship, or internship. Some job applications may also require a personal statement.

Personal statements share and highlight these rhetorical features:

> **Purpose:** For you, the writer, to **promote yourself** to reach a specific goal.
>
> **Writer's role**: To convince your audience that **you** should be selected.

Because personal statement prompts are designed for specific contexts, such as an internship or acceptance to a particular university, there is considerable variety among them. For example, there are detailed prompts with questions about the writer's character and academic or professional goals and interests. Here is one of this type from a medical school that requires 3 to 4 pages in a response.

> Answer these questions: Why am I interested in the field I have chosen? What am I looking for in the university program? What are my professional goals? What are my major accomplishments? What outside interests do I have?

Other prompts are very general, such as: *In 200 words, tell us about yourself.* Whatever the case, you, the writer, are highlighted, and success of your text depends on how well you demonstrate your motivations, qualifications, and characteristics.

In this project, you will use these actions: **respond, summarize**, and **explain.**

Step 1: What Makes a Good Candidate?

Read these prompts for personal statements in university and scholarship applications. What kinds of applicants are these institutions looking for?

a. Describe the world you come from, for example, your family, community or school, and tell us how your world has shaped by your dreams and goals. (Undergraduate application, University of California).

b. Describe a leadership experience in which you made a difference in your campus or community. (Udall Undergraduate Scholarship)

c. What challenges, if any, did you face in your decision to study or intern abroad? (Boren Scholarship)

d. What are your professional aspirations? How will your educational plans help you to meet your goals? (Colorado College Graduate School)

e. Describe something you have observed or experienced which has had a significant impression on you. (Fulbright Award)

1. With a partner, list the important characteristics of successful applicants responding to any two of these prompts.
2. Discuss your lists with a small group or the class.

Step 2: Analyze a Prompt

Read this prompt, designed by the University of California (2017) for the Personal Statement in the Common Application for undergraduate admission:

> Describe the world you come from—for example, your family, community or school—and tell us how your world has shaped your dreams and aspirations.

This prompt is asking two questions. What are the questions, and how would you answer them?

Step 3: Analyze Personal Statements for University Admission

Examine two responses to the prompt you analyzed in Step 2. Remember that the writer is the highlighted component of the personal statement. Read each response and pay special attention to who the writers are—that is, how the writers construct themselves in these texts.

Text 1

❶"What a rich, feminist essay!" A scribbled note by my history teacher in 10th grade affected me in ways that no other comments from my other teachers, most of which focused on minor issues like my terrible spelling, had done. Though I didn't know what Miss Boyd meant by "rich," and I certainly didn't know what she meant by "feminist," as soon as I had deciphered her handwriting, I understood that she was impressed by my text.

❷In her history class, where I was struggling to maintain a "B" average, I had selected for my long paper (10 pages; 40% of the grade) the 12th-century story of Pierre Abelard, the famous teacher and monk, and his secret marriage to Eloise, his young student. It is a tragic story, resulting in the birth of a child and the almost immediate separation of the lovers: Abelard to a monastery and Eloise to a convent from which she wrote poignant letters of love as she yearned for forgetfulness. Totally absorbed in the story, I wrote for the first time with commitment to the topic as well as sorrow for the two lovers, and for the first time, one of my teachers was impressed with both my research and my writing style.

❸This event was central to me. I felt that I had been freed: to take risks in both oral and written discourse and to make scrupulous commitments to my reading and research, building upon this one comment to develop my confidence as a student and a scholar.

❹What has writing become for me, then? When given a prompt in my classes, I bury myself in the topic, and then I ask, "What problems, issues, or ideas can I put into play that are of interest to me—and might be of interest to my reader?" For example, when I was asked to write a paper on *The Scarlet Letter,* I began to explore the possibility of the innocence of Hester Prynne, and, to my surprise, I was able to use the novel to make that argument. When in my American history class, I was required to write about a group that has influenced American thought and ideologies, I selected the Shakers, a remarkable 19th Century religious group led by two women who argued for the equality of the sexes and refused to marry. My topic: "What would happen to the world if all the world became Shaker?" was taken from a tract written at the time, and it appealed to my teacher audience.

❺I have used these new writing freedoms to address audiences beyond the classroom, as well, with efforts that I have come to realize are especially challenging. For these texts, I needed to go beyond my own chance-taking to testing out the audiences I was addressing. For an opinion editorial for the school newspaper that critiqued the direction my school was taking, I consulted a number of audiences (teachers, students, parents, local citizens) to test whether they accepted or rejected my claims, but also to integrate their ideas into my own text. I wanted to appeal to as many people as possible as I addressed those who would definitely not agree with me: the school board and principal.

❻And Miss Boyd began it all with one scribbled comment at the end of my paper. It was she who, with this short note, freed me from my novice writer's inhibitions and enabled me to move on into a more sophisticated and chance-taking realm. As I improved, other teachers have commended me on my close reading, my style, and my unusual insights. However, it is Miss Boyd who must take credit for shaping this chance-taking writer.

Discuss these questions about Text 1 with a partner or small group.

1. What might the audience be looking for in the response to this prompt? What kinds of students are they probably trying to find and enroll? Look at your answers in Step 2 for suggestions.
2. Does the student writer in Text 1 meet the reader's expectations? Why or why not?
3. What is the structure of this personal statement? Continue the chart with what the writer is **doing** and **saying** in Paragraphs 4, 5, and 6:

PARAGRAPH	WHAT IS THE WRITER DOING?	WHAT IS THE WRITER SAYING?
1	**Telling** a story that sets the stage for the text.	I was delighted that my instructor complimented my assigned paper.
2	**Explaining** the background for the story.	I had not been doing very well in class, but my choice of topic and the quality of my paper impressed the instructor.
3	**Responding** to the effects of this incident upon my self-image and motivation.	The instructor's comment set me free to become a change-taking and more confident writer.

4. A personal statement needs to be coherent. That means the parts of the text fit together to create a whole. What does the writer do to make the text coherent? For example, what themes are developed in the response? How does the writer lead the reader from one idea to another?
5. Using no more than three sentences, summarize Text 1 in your own words.

Now read Text 2. Note that the SAT is a standardized test taken by many high-school seniors in the U.S.; the GRE is a standardized test required for some graduate programs.

Text 2

❶Shankar Vendatam, creator of *The Hidden Brain* hosted a podcast (June 9, 2019) in which he argued, using research, that it is not test scores like the SAT that determine an individual's success and happiness in life. Instead, it is the development of character and "grit," and of certain "soft skills" that support good choices in life. I was very pleased to hear this podcast because though my SAT and other high-stakes exam scores are about average, I believe that I have had more than average opportunities to build my character and my soft skills during my short life.

❷One constituent of character mentioned in the program is *problem-solving skills,* a set of abilities that I have developed through family tragedy and misfortune. When my mother, the sole support of our family, died suddenly when I was eighteen, it was up to me to figure out how to anchor and encourage my three younger siblings into a family unit—to keep them together and continuing their education in very difficult and emotional times. Much of this effort included careful *planning,* another of the character traits that was mentioned on the podcast. Sitting down with my siblings, I helped them to plan their activities, their education, and their social life, urging them to live almost normal lives at a time of tragedy.

❸It should be no surprise that during this period, my grades plummeted and I temporarily turned away from schooling. I wasn't anti-school; in fact, I really wanted to continue to do well. However, for more than a year after my mother died, my family became my highest priority as I helped my siblings to plan and problem-solve. It wasn't easy. My brother was tempted by drugs and disappeared for a while, and my two sisters became very emotional and had considerable problems with concentration upon their studies. So each night, I sat down with my sisters and helped them with their homework. I spoke with their teachers, hoping for compassion and flexibility from their schools. I chased down my brother and devoted hours to listening to him as he poured out his sorrow and worries.

❹In time, things got better for our family, and I was able to return, highly motivated, to my studies. I was undoubtedly *more mature* as a result of my family experiences, and my abilities to plan and problem-solve had been strengthened. In a year, I have completed my high school degree with rising grades. Now I am much more than ready for college.

❺We are told by teachers and counselors that hard times can strengthen us. Much depends upon how we respond to setbacks and whether we can grow, whether we can bounce back. I am a "bounce-back" kid. There is no question in my mind that I am a better student and have a more mature approach to life as a result of the tragedy in my family and the responsibilities I took on as a result. This doesn't mean that I will achieve better scores on high stakes examinations like the SAT or GRE. What it does mean, however, is that I am ready to take on and appreciate a college education. I am an excellent planner. I think well on my feet and have solved difficult problems. Having lived through and worked with trying experiences, I know I have the "grit" necessary to succeed.

Discuss these questions with a partner or small group.

6. Do you think the writer of Text 2 meets the reader's expectations (see Question 1)? Why or why not?
7. What is the structure of this personal statement? Identify what the writer is **doing** and **saying** in each paragraph.

Step 4: Review a Personal Statement

You have now examined two successful personal statements. What do you see as the important characteristics of a text from this genre? Your answers to this question will determine your criteria for reviewing a personal statement text. Compare your list with a partner, and then as a class, agree on approximately five criteria that you will use for the rest of this project.

Now read a personal statement by a multilingual writer (Text 3) responding to the same prompt. How well does this writer meet each of the criteria you developed?

Text 3

❶To write about only one, either my family or my community would be impossible. The two are linked together, they go hand in hand. If I choose to write about a single topic from the two, I wouldn't be capable of going into depth without bringing up the other. Both parts of these concepts that molded me are like a sentence that when separated would sound as incomplete as a fragment. The family part is my mom and the community part is the neighborhood I live in.

❷My mom's first actual paid position, that she still holds, was for an environmental organization called Environmental Health Care, currently known as Environmental Health Coalition. At first she was just a volunteer that strongly supported of the organization and their mission to make San Diego and especially Barrio Logan a cleaner and safer place; she attended walks, rallies, and community meetings. This went on for quite a while when she then was approached to be interviewed and talk about the struggles of having a son with asthma. This was what the organization was looking for since they were attempting to get rid of chemical-releasing factories near domestic areas in the neighborhood. The story really helped get the point across to the heads of corporate companies that were refusing to cooperate. This lead them to acknowledge the problem that was at hand. It also lead to a job for my mom.

❸My mom's job really had an effect on me. I was taken to meetings on the improvement of Barrio Logan. I heard a lot of reasons, complaints, and demands for action to be taken about the poor state our neighborhood was in. As I grew older and went to high school in Point Loma, I was given a different environment, a different neighborhood to compare my own to. I didn't envy any aspect of this particular part of San Diego, it just made me notice how different other places could be. Through school, friends, and pop culture, the bubble I had been living in my whole life had bursted. I learned that because of my racial background my living conditions were nothing out of the norm. I was where I was suppose to be, living in the hood.

❹Things were making sense now. I was seeing the world as it was seen by many others. Having lived in the same neighborhood my whole life, made me accustomed to every crack on the sidewalk, to every abandoned building covered in graffiti, to the occasional greeting from a homeless man on the edge of our apartments. All those things I saw as normal and even welcoming when coming back from visiting family in Mexico, were seen as unpleasant.

❺This doesn't bother me as much as I think it should. Maybe it's because it didn't hit me all at once. Maybe it's because I was fortunate to have a loving home. Maybe it's because I believe ignorance is bliss, which is why after having the blindfold lifted and getting a glimpse of what my world actually looks like, I just pulled it back down.

Step 5: Revise a Personal Statement

Review the prompt in Step 2. Then, compare and contrast Texts 1 and 2 with Text 3. In what ways could the writer of Text 3 improve their text? Imagine that you are the writer of Text 3, and use the criteria you developed in Step 4 to revise this personal statement.

Step 6: Analyze a Personal Statement for a Scholarship Application

Another situation where you might write a personal statement is when you are applying for a scholarship. Text 4 was prepared by a third-year undergraduate for the Cheng-Mo Sun Memorial Scholarship, which is open to undergraduate engineering students in the United States and abroad. This is the prompt:

> Submit an essay that will enable those making scholarship decisions to learn more about you. Write about what motivated you to choose your major or program, your future career goals, and any other information that will help reviewers make a well-informed decision.

With a partner or group, discuss these questions:

1. What applicant characteristics are the readers looking for? Are they the same as or different than the prompt for university admission (Step 2)?

2. Which of these characteristics seem to be most important for this scholarship? Why?
3. If you were responding to this prompt, what topics would you include under "any other information that will help reviewers make a well-informed decision"?

As you read Text 4, keep your answers to the questions about the readers' expectations in mind. Note that STEM stands for science, technology, engineering, and mathematics, and AI stands for Artificial Intelligence.

Text 4

❶Though I've always been very interested in science and technology, computer engineering was never a definitive career choice for me. Initially, I chose to apply for the major based on the advice of my parents and relatives—all of whom made careers in engineering and STEM-related fields—and not explicitly because of any specific enthusiasm on my part for the program. Explicitly, I was interested in what the field of computer engineering had to offer, but I had an underlying anxiety regarding my entry into [my university] and its Computer Engineering program. This combination of my own ambivalence towards the major and uncertainty in studying in a new school in a new country contributed to my failing the second semester of my freshman year.

❷This experience put my academic career in perspective, as I not only had to consider the economic and academic costs of taking those courses again and fixing my GPA respectively, but also whether I had made a mistake in entering the Computer Engineering program. Ultimately, I reflected on these notions while retaking my failed pre-major courses and acquired a newfound interest in the concepts introduced in these classes. I learned from my failed semester to both become more responsible as a student and develop new skills such as learning programming languages like C and C++ on my own that would help me succeed both academically and career-wise. In applying for the Cheng-Mo Sun Memorial Scholarship, I wanted to point out my academic failure because I believe that to improve in a discipline like engineering, the process for success is recursive; by failing early in the Computer Engineering program, I was able to recognize what type of thinking led me to failing a semester and allowed me to modify my behavior and better realize my interests within computer engineering. Those improvements are reflected in my grades: since repeating those failed classes, I have maintained a 3.74 overall GPA, and I regularly get As in all my pre-major classes.

❸I mentioned my doubt towards the Computer Engineering program earlier, but I have maintained my fervor towards computer hardware and software. Though I already have real experience with computer engineering through hobbies like PC building, I have also continued that passion for hardware and software through building and analyzing computer hierarchies and circuits as well as learning programming languages and creating a variety of software programs in side and class projects; these projects range from building simple blinking lights on a circuit board with a Raspberry Pi to creating a text-based game of the TV show Jeopardy. Those side projects are an expression of what I love about engineering, as my time in the program allowed me to apply what I learned in classes to utilize tools to create solutions to engineering problems.

❹In continuing my academic career in the Computer Engineering program, I not only want to keep learning new languages like Python or Java and keep creating more side projects to develop my proficiency with programming, but also branch out in my learning to take classes with more specified subject matter like artificial intelligence, networks, or algebraic coding theory. After graduating, I hope to enter a graduate program that allows me to learn more about specific concepts of computer science and computer engineering like data science and machine learning that will help me find a career in that field of study.

❺Because we live in an age of information, I realize fields like data science are important and necessary for large-scale data analysis and the development of artificial intelligence. I want to have a career learning about and developing tools for those purposes, as they are among the most innovative technological developments of our time. In the long-term, I envision myself working at a company that does AI research and development using data science, such as Google's AI residency program. Eventually, I want to develop tools that will help propel AI into being technologically viable on a comprehensive scale; if that occurs, practical solutions to multiple prominent management and pattern recognition problems can be provided, which can range from large-scale implementations of autonomous driving systems that can reduce motor collisions and increase the efficiency of traffic to resource management of food and other resources that can help drive down inequality, poverty, and famine. Essentially, learning about AI and data science can help me contribute to finding solutions to these global problems.

Discuss these questions with a partner or small group.

4. Does the writer of Text 4 meet the reader's expectations for the prompt (see Questions 1–3)? Why or why not?
5. What is the structure of this personal statement? Identify what the writer is **doing** and **saying** in each paragraph.
6. Do you find Text 4 to be coherent? In other words, do all the parts fit together, and does the writer lead the reader through the text?
7. Summarize Text 4 in no more than three sentences.

Step 7: Plan Your Own Personal Statement

You have read three examples of successful personal statements as well as one that required revision. Now, you are going to prepare your own personal statement for a scholarship, internship, or job or for admission to an undergraduate or graduate program.

1. Identify a grant, scholarship, university program, or another opportunity that requires a personal statement or application essay. Or use the prompt and your notes from Step 2.
2. Research the granting agency (for a scholarship), employer, university or academic department. What is its mission? Are there particular emphases, interests, or goals to which you can appeal?

3. Analyze the prompt:
   a. What might the readers who evaluate your application look for in your response to this prompt?
   b. What kinds of applicants are they trying to find and accept?
   c. What positive personal characteristics do you have that are relevant to the prompt? Share examples and don't be modest!
4. What topics will be of most interest to readers of this application? What can you write in response to these topics to strengthen your personal statement? You might ask your family, friends, and instructors because they may have insights into these topics that you do not.
5. Think about detail. In each case of a successful personal statement, the writer gives specific details so that the reader can sense the writer's experience:
   a. In Text 1, the writer selects a seemingly simple event, a comment by an instructor, for which she attributes her interest in and ability to write.
   b. In Text 2, the writer draws from a radio program on "grit" to tell his story.
   c. In Text 3, the author could have used his work for and with his activist mother as a springboard for his activism.
   d. In Text 4, the author uses specific experiences and his own confusion to explain why his grades suffered at one stage of his academic career.

   What specific details from your life stories could you use in your statement that would assist readers to understand why your personal characteristics and motivations are relevant?

6. Consider how you will organize your text. Study the text structures you have analyzed. Which structures might be successful in your application based on your understanding of the institution or granting agency and the prompt? For example, you could begin with an anecdote (a story, event, or dialogue) that leads to the most important point you want to make throughout the text, as the writers of the successful personal statements did in Texts 1, 2, and 4. What will hold your text together and help to lead the reader through your text?

Step 8: Write and Revise Your Personal Statement

1. Draft your personal statement.
2. Organize your statement. Decide what you will do and say in each paragraph.
3. Is the structure of your personal statement effective? Is there a clear action in each paragraph? Compare your structure with the structures of the successful personal statements in this chapter.
4. As the four examples revealed, an effective personal statement is coherent and can be summarized in a few sentences because it has a theme that leads the reader through the text. Write a summary of your personal statement in no more than three sentences, or ask a partner to read and summarize it for you.
5. Use your responses to Questions 2-4 to revise your personal statement.
6. Peer Review. Share your personal statement with one or more partners. With your peer reviewer, discuss the prompt to which you were responding, the institution or granting agency, and the characteristics you identified of a successful applicant. Then, your peer reviewer will use these questions to give feedback:
    1. Does the writer fully address the prompt and target the intended reader of the application?
    2. Does the personal statement present the writer as someone who meets the desired characteristics of a successful applicant?
    3. Does the personal statement start with an engaging anecdote or other information that grabs your attention?
    4. Is the first paragraph used to support the main ideas or themes in the rest of the personal statement?
    5. How could the writer improve the personal statement?
7. Self-Review: Revise your personal statement using your peers' feedback. Have you done everything on this checklist?
    - ☐ My personal statement fully addresses the prompt and is written for the specific university, institution, or granting agency.
    - ☐ My role and identity as a writer, as well as my motivations, are clear and appropriate for the application.

- ☐ The paragraphs each have a clear function and are logically organized.
- ☐ I have proofread the language of the personal statement for clarity and accuracy (see Proofreading Language Box).

What else do you need to work on? Make further revisions to your personal statement if necessary.

Language Box: Proofreading

The final step in preparing any important piece of writing is **proofreading,** which means reading it very carefully to correct any remaining problems with grammar, punctuation, word choice, and formatting. Although non-standard grammar may be acceptable in many contexts, it could reduce the impact of writing in high-stakes texts like a personal statement.

There is no one way to proofread effectively, but you may find some of these strategies useful:

- Make a list of common problems in your own writing by looking at feedback on previous assignments. Read your paper several times, looking for type of error each time.
- If you are writing on a computer, print your paper and proofread using a pencil, or try changing the font or color of the text when you proofread. It is sometimes easier to see mistakes if you make the text look unfamiliar.
- Read the paper backward. Start by reading the last sentence and then the one before it, and so on. This forces you to focus on the sentences rather than the meaning of the whole text.
- Use your computer's spelling- and grammar-check functions to help you, but remember that they are not perfect because they cannot understand your meaning.

Some common errors that all writers, and English learners in particular, should look for include (*indicates non-standard grammar):

- **Subject-verb agreement**: *this experience has had; the subject interests me; these qualities are; my school does not offer; this problem will results in.*

- **Run-on sentences (comma splices)**: **I have a lot of experience with performance, I sang in my local community choir for five years.*
- **Fragments**: **Because I wanted to help other students. *Which I thoroughly enjoyed. *For example, a summer camp in Germany.*
- **Commonly confused words**: *their / there / they're; hear/here; its/it's; effect/affect; imply/infer; lose/loose; principal/principle; then/than; who's/whose*
- **Capitalization**: Proper nouns (names of people, places, companies, brands, books, movies, schools, months, days, etc.), the pronoun *I*, and adjectives referring to countries and languages (English, Chinese, Mexican) should also be capitalized. The *internet* is no longer usually capitalized. School subjects (history, linguistics, physics) are usually not capitalized, except languages (Spanish) and titles of specific courses (e.g. Educational Psychology, Geography 101).
- **Apostrophes**: Use for possessives (*my sister's homework*) and contractions (*don't, it's, can't*) but not plurals (*buses, all As, the 1960s*) unless they are also possessive (*the laws' effects*).

Finally, check the formatting requirements of the task, such as:

- font and size
- margins and paragraph indentation
- spacing (single-spacing or double-spacing)
- lines between paragraphs
- alignment (left-justified or fully justified)
- page numbering
- length (word count, character count, or page limit?)
- heading and sub-heading styles

The standard formatting for a student paper in the APA 7th edition style is 11-point Calibri or 12-point Times New Roman, double-spaced, with 1-inch margins on all sides, left-justified, and the first line of every paragraph indented by 0.5 inches. For more details, consult your style guide, syllabus, assignment directions, instructor, or librarian.

Step 9: Reflection

What did you learn about academic writing from studying the personal statement? What strengths do you have as a person that will enable you to write effective personal statements in response to a variety of prompts?

References

Swales, J. M. (1990). *Genre analysis: English in academic and research settings.* Cambridge University Press.

Grammar Glossary

active voice: a clause in which the subject is the agent of the main verb (e.g., *we completed the experiment)*

boosting: increasing the strength of claim, for example with an adverb (e.g., clearly) or modal verb of certainty (e.g., *will)*

clause: a group of words connected by a verb; clauses can be dependent or independent

conditional clause: a dependent clause that gives the condition or situation under which the main clause is true; conditional clauses can be real (e.g., *if the policy is changed*) or unreal (e.g., *if the policy were different*)

conjunction: a word that connects two clauses into a sentence; see coordinating conjunction and subordinating conjunction

coordinating conjunction: a word that joins independent clauses to make sentences (e.g., *and, but, or, so, yet)*

dependent clause: a clause that is missing its subject (e.g., *writing a paper*) or starts with a subordinating conjunction or relative pronoun and cannot be used as a sentence in formal writing (e.g., *because it was late; that we knew*)

fragment: a dependent clause used as a sentence without connecting it to an independent clause; this is considered an error in formal writing

hedging: reducing the strength of a claim, or showing that an idea comes from a source not the writer; hedging resources include modal verbs (e.g., *may, might, can*), conditional clauses, adverbs (e.g., *perhaps, possibly*), and other word choices

independent clause: a clause with a subject, verb, and other elements that represents a complete thought and can be used as a sentence in formal writing

linking verb: a verb that gives information about what the subject *is* or *is related to* (e.g., *be, become, have, define, refer*)

modal verb: a verb that adds a meaning of certainty, possibility, necessity, or prediction to the main verb (e.g., *will, can, may, should*)

nominalization: changing a verb (or any other part of speech) into a noun (e.g., *assign* → *assignment*)

non-restrictive relative clause: a dependent clause that elaborates on the meaning of something in the main clause by adding additional information, meaning, or comments; commas separate non-restrictive relative clauses from the rest of the sentence (e.g., *this book focuses on genre, which means a category or type of text*)

noun clause: a dependent clause introduced with *that, if, whether,* or another question word; noun clauses are usually the objects of reporting verbs

part of speech—see word form

passive voice: a clause in which the subject is not the agent of the main verb (e.g., *the experiment was completed*)

past perfect: the verb tense that describes an action or state that happened before another time in the past; the past perfect is formed by *had* plus the past participle (e.g., *had written, had claimed, had become)*

past simple: the verb tense that indicates an action or state that happened and was completed in the past (e.g., *wrote, claimed, became*)

phrase connector: a preposition that shows a logical connection between ideas (e.g., *during, because of, due to, in the process of)*

present perfect: the verb tense that connects a time in the past to the present, such as showing an action that *has happened* or a state that *has occurred*; the present perfect is formed by the verb *have* plus the past participle (e.g., *has written, have claimed, has become)*

present progressive: the verb tense that shows an action that *is happening* at the present time; the present progressive is formed by the verb *be* plus the *-ing* form of the verb (e.g., *is writing, are claiming, is becoming)*

present simple: the verb tense that indicates a fact or a verb that is always true; the present simple is the base form of the verb (e.g., *write, claim, become*) with an *-(e)s* in the third-person singular (e.g., *writes, claims, becomes*)

quantifier: an element of the noun phrase that specifies the quantity of the main noun (e.g., *much, many, few, some*)

reduced relative clause: a relative clause from which the relative pronoun has been omitted; the verb is usually also changed (e.g., *the paper assigned by the professor is due on Tuesday*)

relative clause (or adjective clause): a dependent clause in which a relative pronoun (e.g., *that, which, who*) takes the place of a subject, object, or object of a preposition

reporting verb: a verb that reports the words, thoughts, or ideas of another person or source (e.g., *say, believe, claim)*

restrictive relative clause: a relative clause that identifies or defines a noun; restrictive relative clauses do not use commas (e.g., *I agree with the article that I read*)

run-on sentence (also called a **comma splice**): two independent clauses joined by a comma and no conjunction; this is considered an error in formal writing

sentence connector (or **transition phrase** or **conjunctive adverb**): a word or phrase that shows the relationship between ideas in two separate sentences (e.g., *however, then, also, on the other hand, next, first)*

subject-verb agreement: a feature of some tenses, where the verb changes to agree with the subject (e.g., *he/she/it shows; they are*)

subordinating conjunction: a word that joins an independent clause with a dependent clause (e.g., *because, when, while, although, after)*

verb tense: the meanings of time (past or present) and aspect (simple, progressive, or perfect) that can be marked on a verb

word form: the part of speech that allows the word to fit the rest of the sentence (e.g., noun, verb, adjective, adverb)